WHY
THE POO

ORGANIZING THE TWENTY-FIRST CENTURY RESISTANCE

EDITED BY
MICHAEL TRUSCELLO
AND AJAMU NANGWAYA

AK
PRESS

Why Don't the Poor Rise Up?: Organizing the Twenty-First Century Resistance

© 2017, copyright rests with the individual authors, as noted

This edition © 2017 AK Press (Chico, Oakland, Edinburgh, Baltimore)

ISBN: 978-1-84935-278-9
E-ISBN: 978-1-84935-279-6
Library of Congress Control Number: 2016954832

AK Press	AK Press
370 Ryan Ave. #100	33 Tower St.
Chico, CA 95973	Edinburgh EH6 7BN
USA	Scotland
www.akpress.org	www.akuk.com
akpress@akpress.org	ak@akedin.demon.co.uk

The above addresses would be delighted to provide you with the latest AK Press distribution catalog, which features books, pamphlets, zines, and stylish apparel published and/or distributed by AK Press. Alternatively, visit our websites for the complete catalog, latest news, and secure ordering.

Cover design by Josh MacPhee | Antumbra Design

Interior design by Margaret Killjoy | www.birdsbeforethestorm.net

DEDICATION

DAVID GÓMEZ VAZQUEZ (1992–2017)

THE FIRST TIME I MET DAVID, HE WAS 22 YEARS OLD—A BRIGHT EYED, SLIGHT-ly shy, and quick-stepped "compañero." We met at a workshop about organiz-ing for community health. We didn't speak much that time but I remember him earnestly jotting down notes and asking questions with a look and tone that transmitted both interest and urgency. This was one of the first collective encounters that gave birth to the Brigada de Salud Comunitaria 43, a grass-roots, community-based project and organizing space that David participated in and supported until the day of his assassination on February 11th, 2017, a few weeks shy of his turning 25. David's sense of urgency was one that we shared in the almost three years that we knew each other as friends and com-pañeros, supporting the work of the Brigada in one of the most politically, economically, and socially turbulent regions of Mexico: the state of Guerrero. A sense of urgency permeates daily life in this region and country where forced disappearance, torture, and extrajudicial assassinations, alongside worsening living, work, and health conditions, are factors that organizers contend with, strategize around, and far too often, lose their lives to. David often spoke about the need to do as much as possible while he "was still young" and still had energy. He viewed grassroots organizing as an identity and way of life. His life's path and choices reflected this deep commitment. At the age of thirteen he participated in the mobilization that pressured for the release of political prisoners detained during the anti-globalization protests in Guadalajara, his home city. He continued to participate in various spaces in Guadalajara until making the decision to move to Mexico City in 2010 at the age of 17, in or-der to participate in the vibrant and radical student movement. It was during this period that his interest grew in supporting organizing efforts in the state of Guerrero. Over the next few years he would support the organizing efforts of students at the Ayotzinapa Teachers' College and the Community Police (CRAC-PC) while remaining active in solidarity efforts in student-led spaces in Mexico City. As I got to know David, I was surprised by his dedication, especially his solid theoretical base. I admired his familiarity with various political processes and social movements from different eras of Mexican history but above all the ease with which he brought people from different organizing spaces together and participated in the construction of community-based efforts. In the various community-based organizing spaces I witnessed David in, it was evident that he inspired trust, hope, respect, and, above all, a sense of family—something we always spoke of as being fundamental to solid organizing efforts. During the most difficult days in which the weight of political repression and violence hung heavily over us, during the mourning for compañeros fallen in struggle, I could always count on David to make sure I didn't give up hope. He believed it was possible to construct community-based autonomy with a mix of socialist and anarchist principles through praxis that respected indigenous identity, local needs, history, and experience. This is the commitment that we hold to David's memory and the memory of many other compañeros we have lost. David, I can only say thank you for your energy, your ideas, your mistakes, and the time that you shared with us—part of your family rooted in struggle.

David, hermano mío, contigo seguiremos siendo pueblo, haciéndonos pueblo y estando con el pueblo. Descansa en eterna rebeldía.

Brigada de Salud Comunitaria 43
28 de febrero, 2017
México

FOREWORD

ORGANISING IN THE TWENTY-FIRST CENTURY

WHY DON'T THE POOR RISE UP? THIS QUESTION EVOKES REFLECTION AND engagement from anyone concerned with the question of organization and transformation in a world inflicted with Capitalism and blighted by Imperialism.

The title is both challenging and provocative, in the sense that it is at once a question and an assumption. But is it true that the poor do not rise up? Or do we simply not recognize their resistance and rebellions?

This book, with contributions from all over the world grounded in activism, academia, advocacy, arts, culture, community-based organizing, education, grassroots politics, media, research, human rights, and unionism, provides us with a practitioner's perspective on the range of issues that challenge us on this question.

In a world where the definition of "poor" and the erstwhile distinction between the working class and the poor has become merged in the "working poor," we are confronted with the inferred frustration in the title.

Sometimes activists and organizers slide into apathy, especially when confronted with the daily challenges and frustration in trying to organize within our communities, constituencies, and countries. We often think that our situation is peculiar, and that the grasslands of struggle are greener and more fertile in other places.

As one who contends daily with the question and challenges of organizing, I believe this book offers serious analysis and deep insight on the trials and prospects of organizing in the twenty-first century. There is a dire need for books like this, which will hopefully develop into a series of organizers' manuals on practical themes.

In this anthology of radical perspectives on contemporary struggles from around the world, contributors offer cutting edge analysis and proffer radical possibilities from research, experience, and praxis. We are offered critical pathways in exploring new ways of thinking about organization, resistance, rebellion, and revolution. This book is a testimony to the fact that there is a universal narrative in people's stories, and that our struggles are essentially similar.

"The most potent weapon in the hands of the oppressor is the mind of the oppressed."
—Steve Biko

The question of the spiritual exploitation of the poor is very close to home, especially for anyone here on the Afrikan continent. In these times of mega churches overflowing with masses of poor folk desperately searching for "salvation," the people are led to believe that salvation is lodged in a secure, albeit unidentified, location in heaven, certainly not here on earth, and therefore not worth fighting for. Thus, religion plays a critical role in subduing and demobilizing the poor into passivism and acceptance of their fate as destiny.

The constant and unrelenting peddling of hope for a better tomorrow while investing in heaven—as opposed to organising for an earthly version of paradise—are the toxic ingredients of mind numbing propaganda unleashed daily on the masses. The lesson? That resistance and rebellion are ungodly activities that will not secure the golden one-way ticket to eternity!

The new prosperity preaching on the long-awaited treasures from heaven and the virulent demonization of poverty as an affliction from the pit of hell ensures that the poor are snared in a dual trap of aspiring to become wealthy like the preacher while temporarily tolerating poverty as an affliction from Satan, certainly no fault of capitalism or imperialism!

The consequence of this religious tranquilizer is that people subscribe to the notion that it is not in their interest to rise up and smash the system; they only want a bit of the capitalist cake, rotten as it is. The icing on this spiritual cake is that suffering is a test of faith and endurance. So why struggle?

The issue and location of power is a matter of concern for anyone interested in the question of organization and revolution. Some see power as external, to be taken over or snatched from the oppressor. Others view power as internal, to be discovered within and among us, that must be organized, manifested, and unleashed on the oppressor.

We do not have enough knowledge and information on the diverse struggles waged around the world, the wealth of experience gained, and the lessons learnt from them and the numerous victories achieved. Consequently, we do not celebrate them nor gain inspiration from them to wage new struggles. The first-hand experiences and contributions shared in this collection serve as a radical attempt to reverse this trend. All Power to the People!

What is the price of resistance, and what is the price of rebellion? What is the price of memory, and how do we sustain our collective memory? How do we pass this information from one generation to the next? Have we examined the genocidal effects of trans-Saharan and trans-Atlantic enslavement, settler colonialism, and forced migration on our global communities of resistance? Are there lingering post-traumatic issues to be addressed, as we organise in the 21st Century?

In a world in which we are force-fed images of desolation and despair in the global South, this book nourishes us with counter information on the determination, self-empowerment, fortitude, and strength of the people as they wage struggle against multiple forms of oppression. We see the revolutionary potential in the unity and solidarity of erstwhile disconnected communities, albeit victims of the same violence of settler colonialism, slavery, and indentured labor migration. These essays offer a clear case of the vital need to unite our struggles and embrace the challenge of organizing beyond divisive identity politics in our quest to defeat imperialism.

The violence of police brutality unleashed daily, and the impunity of police officers, is a phenomenon that confronts us whether we are in our neo-colonial nations in the global South, or live in colonized communities in the North. The struggle for community policing is even more urgent, as we witness daylight slaughter on the streets and state-sanctioned executions of citizens by an increasingly militarised police force. How are the poor organising to protect themselves?

What is the price of rising up in impoverished communities where desperation breeds potential for revolution but the contradictions of the neo-colonial State manifest in crude, undiluted, and unrelenting violence?

As we embrace the words of Thomas Sankara that we must dare to invent the future, we are presented with the liberating option of the politics and dynamics of a women-generated moneyless economy offering a vision of a potentially capitalist-free world where people are seen as resource-full rather than resource-less, by utilising a modus-operandi of resisting capitalism on a daily basis.

"The liberation of women is not an act of charity, the result of a humanitarian or compassionate position. It is a fundamental necessity for the revolution, a guarantee of its continuity and a condition for its success."
—Samora Machel

The contradictions of the global struggle of Black women as they strive to survive, negotiate, and surmount the triple trauma of patriarchy, capitalism, and imperialism in a world infested with the twin virus of race and class oppression provides a key insight into the battle for women's humanity as a precondition for the victory and survival of any revolution. We must all sharpen and deepen our perspectives on the question of women, as the noxious roots of patriarchy are still firmly entrenched in the minds of "progressive" men, and yes, women too.

Mobilization and organization are usually seen as one and the same. Quite often we are guilty of substituting and confusing one with the other, and this is what Kwame Ture, (aka Stokely Carmichael), warned us about. In contemporary times, we see popular movements hijacked by single-issue politics, where agitation is woven around one issue. The danger is that it is easy to mobilise around a specific issue and for the system to pacify us while remaining entrenched. Without the more long-term, concrete, and enduring weapon of organization, mobilization becomes a quick fix, band-aid type solution to problems where we are in danger of mobilizing people away from organization and transformation unto the path of survival on a pillar-to-post basis.

When imperialism hijacks the struggle and infuses it with cash and the NGO epidemic, activists reincarnate as careerists, politics resurrects as a project, liberation mutates into human rights, mobilization descends into consultation, organizing struggle degenerates into organizing conferences, campaigns disintegrate into charities, potentially governmental organizations morph into non-governmental organizations, revolution is a dirty word, spoken in hush tones and replaced by respectable terms of civil society, democracy, and good governance.

O, who will bring back that old-time religion of revolution?

Drawing inspiration from historical organizers in the global struggle for Afrikan liberation like Marcus and Amy-Ashwood Garvey (Jamaica), Josina Machel (Mozambique), Kwame Nkrumah (Ghana), Malcolm X (USA), Amilcar Cabral (Guinea), Claudia Jones (Trinidad), Steve Biko (South Afrika), Ella Baker (USA), Thomas Sankara (Burkina Faso), Kwame Ture (Trinidad) and women of the South Afrikan anti-apartheid movement, we are strengthened in the knowledge that, indeed, power comes only from the organised masses.

Imagine a world where revolution is a way of life!

Affiong Limene Affiong
Bamako, Mali
December 2016

INTRODUCTION

WHY DON'T THE POOR RISE UP?

Michael Truscello and **Ajamu Nangwaya**

WHY DON'T THE POOR RISE UP?

The question is a perennial component of revolutionary thought, but it requires parsing: Who, precisely, are "the poor"? What does it mean to "rise up"? What does asking this question say about the interrogator? Of course the poor often do *rise up*, forcing full-scale revolutions on occasion, but sometimes they choose fascism as the political form of obtaining material needs or refuting popular narratives. As Erin Araujo notes in her contribution to this collection, evidence of contemporary popular leftist revolts is abundant: "Kurdish resistance in Rojava and Northern Syria, the Zapatistas in Mexico, the Landless Workers Movement in Brazil, the Piqueteros in Argentina, the autonomous region of El Alto, Bolivia, and many other large movements throughout the world." But in the Global North, successful uprisings are currently less conspicuous.

Recently, capitalist media such as *The New York Times* and *The Economist* have posed the question *why don't the poor rise up*, as if amazed that their economic system has not been met with greater resistance in the United States and Europe. The same question could and should be applied to Africa, Asia, the Caribbean, and Latin America, which are not characterized by mass uprisings against gross forms of economic exploitation of the laboring classes by domestic and international capital. In the context of unparalleled global wealth disparity, aggressive militarism, ecological catastrophe, and the perpetuation of structural racism, sexism, and ableism, the question of why the poor don't rise up provokes revolutionaries to consider the primary contemporary obstacles for mass insurrection, in addition to casting new light on examples from around the world of poor people confronting capitalism and other forms of authoritarianism.

The provocation for our anthology was a June 24, 2015 *New York Times* op-ed written by journalist and Columbia University professor Thomas B. Edsall titled, "Why Don't the Poor Rise Up?"[1] Edsall believes social movements in the United States no longer "capture the public imagination," and there is "very little support for class-based protest—what used to be called solidarity." For the extent to which this theory is true in the United States, writes Edsall, "the prospects for collective action on behalf of the poor are dim, at best." Edsall believes "there is so little rebellion against entrenched social and economic injustice" because "those bearing the most severe costs of inequality are irrelevant to the agenda-setters in [the Democratic and Republican] parties." Radicals will immediately recognize this type of liberal analysis, in which electoral parties that operate in the interests of capital are positioned as the only hope for the poor, an argument that treats the poor as people incapable of autonomy, sitting patiently while the capitalist class decides what to do with them. While disagreeing with the perception of these brokerage parties as the source of social salvation of the poor, radicals and revolutionaries must admit that the ideological hegemony of the bourgeoisie's political or philosophical liberalism and capitalist doctrine over the minds of the people accounts for the bourgeois apologists' belief that capitalist parties have a substantive role to play in transforming the poverty-stricken condition of the poor.

Naturally, anarchists do not believe justice for the poor in the United States or elsewhere will come from capitalist electoral parties, and Edsall's analysis has nothing to say about capitalism, patriarchy, colonialism, or structural racism, the principal culprits for massive economic oppression across the globe. Anarchists have always understood that the private property regime of capitalism produces poverty, and that the poor are essential to an anti-capitalist revolution. While Marx dismissed layers of the working class—the so-called *lumpenproletariat*—as useless to the revolutionary cause, Bakunin and other socialists believed the people categorized by Marx as worthless outcasts—"vagabonds, discharged soldiers, discharged jailbirds, escaped galley slaves, swindlers, mountebanks, lazzaroni, pickpockets, tricksters, gamblers, maquereaux [pimps], brothel keepers, porters, literati, organ grinders, ragpickers, knife grinders, tinkers, beggars"[2]—were integral to a social revolution. The lumpen elements, very much like Marx's valorized sections of the working class, need politicization to unleash their revolutionary potential.

However, we are not calling on revolutionary or progressive organizers to ignore the reactionary or oppositional behavior of the criminalized elements within the lumpenproletariat toward social and national liberation struggles and other progressive political developments. Yet we would be wise and prudent in heeding Frantz Fanon's call in *The Wretched of the Earth* to organize the lumpen elements and prevent the bourgeoisie from using them to undermine struggles for liberation or revolution:

> It [the lumpenproletariat] will always respond to the call to revolt, but if the insurrection thinks it can afford to ignore it, this famished underclass will pitch itself into the armed struggle and take part in the conflict, this time on the side of the oppressor. The oppressor, who never misses an opportunity to let the blacks tear each other's throats, is only too willing to exploit those characteristic flaws of the lumpenproletariat, namely the lack of political consciousness and ignorance.[3]

Under the contemporary regime of global capitalism, the ranks of the poor are expanding. Populations that are considered "surplus" to the functioning of capitalism continue to swell under the multiple threats of automation, colonial expansion, the retrenchment of white supremacy, and a host of other structural exploitations. Capitalism is lumpenizing broad swaths of the working class in the Global South and North through the proliferation of part-time work with little or no benefits and the vicious attack on the social wage as represented in the state's provision of social and income-support programs. Across the world, capitalism has been proletarianizing work-life for middle-income workers; many of these workers who were once seen as members of the so-called aristocracy of labor, and even some petit bourgeois professionals such as adjunct or precariously employed university and college educators, are experiencing high levels of job insecurity and low wages that were unthinkable even thirty years ago. These workers are falling into the ranks of people who are generally seen as poor people. Bourgeois researchers or commentators have resorted to calling these members of society *the working poor.*

The poor cannot abandon the project of building a revolutionary struggle against global capitalism, nor can the poor be abandoned by the struggle. In this anthology, we offer perspectives from around the world on the ways in which the poor are defined, the forms in which they resist, and the obstacles to mass insurrection. We value a variety of radical perspectives, and so a single type of anarchism or ideological outlook that is rooted in revolution from below does not define our collection.

We see renewed urgency for a revolutionary response to a world dominated by capitalism, in which the richest 8 billionaires have as much wealth as the poorest half of the human population[4]; as of 2015, 43.1 million Americans live in poverty,[5] and 19.4 million Americans live in "deep poverty"[6]; according to a 2009 *British Medical Journal* study, extreme income inequality in the United States prematurely kills over 880,000 people annually, more deaths than guns, auto accidents, and tobacco combined[7]; the poorest people in the poorest countries will be most adversely affected by global climate change; and the global poor continue to be disproportionately women and people of color or racialized people. The tragic reality that must be addressed specifically by revolutionaries is that the poor constitute the largest and fastest growing group victimized by capitalism; by one estimate, over 5 billion humans, about 80 percent of the global population, live in poverty.[8] Our authors bring this tragedy into focus, and articulate the primary obstacles preventing the poor from rising up in anti-authoritarian organizations.

The authors we have assembled for this collection were asked to address the question: Why don't the poor rise up? Some of our authors interrogate the category of "the poor" and its assumed homogeneity. Some of our authors offer contemporary examples of impoverished communities resisting capitalism along anarchist principles. And some of our authors examine the primary obstacles for popular insurrection, with the intention of breaking down these barriers.

Defining Poverty

Poverty is notoriously difficult to define because the definition often serves hegemonic imperatives. Capitalism and the state typically define poverty using economic metrics that deliberately deflate the number of people living in poverty, and mask the structural violence endured by people living just below or above the so-called poverty line. For example, the number of Americans living in poverty cited above, 43.1 million, assumes that *being poor* can be reduced to an income level: "The U.S. Census Bureau determines poverty status by comparing pre-tax cash income against a threshold that is set at three times the cost of a minimum food diet in 1963, updated annually for inflation using the Consumer Price Index…, and adjusted for family size, composition, and age of householder."[9] The official poverty line does not take into consideration the standard of living in the twenty-first century United States and is actually based on that of a family of four from the 1960s. Based on the per capita expansion of the United States' national income since 1969, an official poverty line that is sensitive to this economic reality would have stood at $46,651 in 2011 for a family of four.[10] However, a family of four living in the United States in 2015 would be considered poor if their income were less than $24,257, and an individual under 65 years of age with an income of $12,331 or less would be classified as poor. These income levels are obviously low, and do not account for the degraded lives of people who live on marginally greater incomes. Various studies have interrogated the algorithm that determines the poverty line, and calculated the actual number of Americans living in poverty to be 160% to 170% higher than the official figure.[11]

Critiquing official estimates of poverty are important for the struggle to illustrate the true cost of capitalism, delegitimize its self-serving narrative of being the most effective way to meet the material needs of the people, raise the awareness of a greater number of people that they are being shafted by this economic system, and win their political commitment for the anti-capitalist or socialist option. But we believe the more important problems with reducing poverty to income levels are the ways in which income levels mask structural oppressions not made explicit by income (racism, sexism, ableism, and so on), and the ideological gesture achieved by setting a minimum standard. The poverty line hides the structural violence of capitalism, such as the ecological catastrophe capitalism produces, and legitimates the deprivation and suffering of millions without containing the wealth and power accumulation of the ruling class. The poverty line says, as long as an acceptable number of people are earning an acceptable amount of money—no matter how humiliating and debilitating their work, no matter how their working and living conditions deteriorate from the distribution of resources, no matter how much the economic system deprives them of agency—the system is working.

In addition to the creation of impoverished and oppressed subjects internationally, a direct result of colonial apparatuses such as extractive industries and sweatshops, capitalism produces economic precarity, increased morbidity and mortality rates, and active forms of deprivation such as homelessness, domestically. The World Health Organization (WHO) describes "extreme poverty" as "the world's most ruthless killer and the greatest cause of suffering on earth"; the poor are more likely to suffer from a range of mental and physical health complications, leading to mortality rates many times higher than those of the rich.[12] Capitalism produces conditions of precarity in which the extremely poor have no shelter, while millions of houses stand empty; in the United States, it has been estimated that there might be as many as 6 empty houses for every 1 homeless person.[13] In Ireland, there are an estimated 13 empty homes for every homeless person.[14] Globally, it is estimated that by 2030 there will be

2 billion squatters, or 1 in 4 human beings "unlawfully" occupying an empty building or piece of land.[15] As Craig Willse argues in *The Value of Homelessness: Managing Surplus Life in the United States*, "living without housing is systemically produced and must be understood as the active taking away of shelter, as the social making of house-less lives…. Housing [in the United States] draws from already existing racial subordinations and entrenches and intensifies the death-making effects of those racisms."[16] To make people homeless, poor, and precarious, capitalism combines speculative market mechanisms with "anti-black racism, the everydayness of police occupation, and the transformation of urban space into consumption enclaves."[17] These tendencies are accelerating in the context of global urbanization, increasing wealth disparity, and the impacts of global climate change, among other forces.

As radical and revolutionary organizers engage in the contestation with the bourgeoisie over the definition and scope of poverty and the magnitude of the ranks of the poor as a demographic group in capitalist societies, we should not allow the ruling class and its academic gladiators and spin doctors among the commentariat to define the poor out of the working class. After all, capitalism still engenders a class-based society with an inherent, winner-takes-all conflict between the bourgeoisie and the members of the laboring classes. The bourgeoisie finds it ideologically necessary to shift the focus away from class struggle to the consumption struggle in the Global North to mask the fact that a working-class majority is a fact of life in these societies. In the hegemonic worldview of the bourgeoisie that is propagandized or peddled to the laboring classes, Europe, Japan, and North America have demographic majorities that are largely middle-class. It is in this context that the good professor Thomas B. Edsall would have the audacity to declare that the people bearing the brunt of capitalist class inequality and austerity are an insignificant minority. Hence, the limited appeal of "class-based projects" from the perspective of this moderate bourgeois academic.

The capitalist class and its confederates amongst the managers of the state are ideologically and politically invested in a large majority of people accepting themselves as a part of this socially contrived middle class. It is on this basis that Fanon's "wretched of the earth" forsake the appeal of "classed-based projects" because they would, existentially, foster class warfare against them by the envious, demographically insignificant working class minority. Revolutionary and radical organizers of the twenty-first century should not abandon the category "working class" or "laboring" classes for the concept "the poor," in their organizing and political education work among the oppressed. If state socialists and anarchist communists are committed to creating the classless, stateless, and self-organized (communist) society, how are they going to do so in the absence of a strong emphasis on class relations and the general class struggle, while centering non-class oppressions as they affect the working class. The neoliberal capitalist turn since the mid-1970s saw the capitalist class's repudiation of the social safety net and organized labor usher in an intensified form of class warfare and primitive accumulation of capital. The transfer of wealth from the working class to the bourgeoisie came in the form of tax cuts, decreased regulation on capitalist enterprises, reduction in the funding of social programs, and the use of labor legislation to weaken the bargaining clout of unions in the workplace. It is the preceding state of affairs that inspired a certified member of the ruling class, Warren Buffett, to declare, "There's class warfare, all right, but it's my class, the rich class, that's making war, and we're winning." If we are going to use the category *the poor* in this era of neoliberal capitalism, it should be as a synonym for the working class or laboring classes.

Neoliberal Capitalism and Poverty

The standard neoliberal capitalist response to poverty is to deny that capitalism creates poverty, and to posit more capitalism as the answer to poverty. The contemporary template for this interpretation of capitalism, poverty, and history is Columbia Professor Jeffrey D. Sachs's 2005 book *The End of Poverty: Economic Possibilities for Our Time*, complete with a foreword by rock star and liberal punchline, Bono. Sachs's analysis, now over a decade old, provides both historical and predictive inaccuracies, while claiming its goal is the UN Millennium Development Goal to halve global poverty by 2015 and end extreme poverty by 2025. He argues, for example, "extreme poverty no longer exists in today's rich countries, and is disappearing in most of the world's middle-income countries."[18] Sweatshops, instead of being institutions of capitalist exploitation and wealth transfer, "are the first rung on the ladder out of extreme poverty."[19] He especially enjoys invoking what he believes is a feminist argument for capitalism, the notion that women of the Global South are liberated by factory wages and saved from lives of "rural misery," to which they would most certainly return in the absence of the beneficent sweatshops.[20]

For Sachs, and for neoliberal capitalism at large, the wealth gains of the rich are not predicated on the financial and physiological deprivation of the poor; instead, the world of capitalism "is rather a positive-sum opportunity in which improving technologies and skills can raise living standards around the world."[21] Sachs believes "the forces of market-based modern economic growth" undermine traditional social hierarchies,[22] and that the "colonial era is truly finished."[23] However, as Keeanga-Yamahtta Taylor forcefully counters, the gains of the rich are indeed at the expense of the poor:

The essence of economic inequality is borne out in a simple fact: there are 400 billionaires in the United States and 45 million people living in poverty. These are not parallel facts; they are intersecting facts. There are 400 American billionaires *because* there are 45 million people living in poverty. Profit comes at the expense of the living wage. Corporate executives, university presidents, and capitalists in general are living the good life—*because* so many others are living a life of hardship.[24]

The tenets of neoliberal capitalism portray a fantasy in which technology transfer does nothing but spread prosperity everywhere, and the rise of Nazism in the 1930s was a consequence of "trade protectionism."[25] These are the myths of neoliberalism, which has dominated the globe for the past 50 years, and against these fictions revolutionaries must struggle for the minds of the people. Colonialism exists. Extreme poverty can be found in the largest, richest American cities. Working people create wealth, and they suffer and die in the process. Capitalism flourished more under the Nazis than it did under President Franklin Delano Roosevelt's regime.[26]

In spite of the fact that hundreds of millions of poor people know that the glossy, seductive, and self-serving propaganda of capitalism is betrayed by their lived experience of it, they are not instinctively predisposed to rise up against it. Capitalism looks like the only game in town. The inability of state socialist regimes such as the former Soviet Union and states in Eastern Europe, China, Cuba, and North Korea to produce an adequate quantity of consumer goods, as well as demonstrate themselves as economic success stories, have forced people to stick with the devil with which they are most familiar, capitalism. Revolutionaries are politically obligated to become the experts at studying the causes behind successful revolutions, and judiciously apply and adapt these lessons to the peculiarities of their local conditions. The study of revolutions is much too important to leave to non-revolutionary bourgeois academics that are sequestered in universities and are not embedded in radical social or revolutionary movements as active members.

Global North

The first half of our collection contains essays whose focus is the Global North. Praba Pilar, a diasporic Colombian artist, and Alex Wilson, an academic from the Opaskwayak Cree Nation and an organizer with Idle No More, remind us of the necessity to decolonize the "White Left," which inherits many assumptions and "epistemic violence" from the colonial powers of the Global North.

By making "hemispheric connections" between what we have divided into Global North and South, Pilar and Wilson illustrate some common ground for indigenous struggles and perform a necessary act of decolonization in the global struggle against capitalist impoverishment. The next three chapters address race and poverty in the United States. Ben Brucato and Thandisizwe Chimurenga trace the origin of the "color line" in the U.S., and its persistent division in contemporary capitalism. Brucato emphasizes the many Black proletarian uprisings (in Ferguson and Baltimore, for example) that Edsall overlooks, and argues that "a break in the cross-class alliance by a significant part of the white working class could make whiteness an unreliable guarantor of loyalty to the existing order, and provoke a crisis within it." Kali Akuno connects the expansion of surplus populations under global capitalism to the increasingly "disposable" lives of Black Americans. In response, Akuno establishes a set of principles for creating Black Autonomous Zones, "structural" objectives that "necessitate nothing less than complete social transformation." Chimurenga interrogates the "distractions" of a Black president, and the debilitating ways in which Black churches, formerly spaces for the dissemination of Black Liberation, have become dedicated to a rhetoric of "forgiveness" toward those who perpetrate violence against African Americans. Ellie Adekur Carlson also interrogates an existing institution that once served the poor, by examining the failure of contemporary trade unions to represent the needs of poor and working class people, the very principles on which unions were founded.

Jordy Cummings addresses the most debated recent development in the Global North: Donald Trump. Specifically, Cummings reminds us that sometimes when the poor rise up to contest popular narratives or meet their material needs, they choose an authoritarian option: "In the absence of a well-organized and united left, right-wing populism will be the means with which the poor rise." Cummings locates the rise of Trump and the alt-right "in the combined and uneven development of global capitalism." The next two chapters engage successful strategies for building a radical Left alternative to the populist right currently ascendant. Lesley Wood and Alex Khasnabish study social movements, and their chapters examine, respectively, the ways that charity and social work can deprive anti-poverty organizations of necessary energy and time, and the principles of effective organizing and liberating the radical imagination. As Khasnabish, who has studied the Zapatistas, writes, "Especially in dark times, the work of those committed to social justice and social change must be about building organizational capacity and cultivating the radical imagination."

Both Nathan Jun and Franco "Bifo" Berardi address the book's central question by appealing to Wilhelm Reich's famous observation: "What has to be explained is not the fact that the man who is hungry steals or the fact that the man who is exploited strikes, but why the majority of those who are hungry don't steal and why the majority of those who are exploited don't strike." Jun interrogates the role that "the so-called Christian Right plays in encouraging and perpetuating economic inequality in the United States by demonizing poverty, exalting the capitalist system, and discouraging economically vulnerable populations from resisting their own oppression." Berardi returns to the work of Jean Baudrillard to examine the implosion of the social from the time of Margaret Thatcher to the present. "The effects of the deterritorialization of labor, and of the technological fragmentation of the social body," writes Bifo, "result in the inability to create networks of solidarity and in widespread loneliness broken by sudden random explosions of rage." One of the challenges for contemporary anti-capitalist struggles, therefore, is to replace competition with empathy, to restore sociability.

Global South

The naked exploitation that takes place in the Global South tends to use indiscriminate violence against significant sections of the population. This state of affairs has a high likelihood of inspiring many people to embrace extra-constitutional approaches to deal with the economic and political elite, when things become unbearable. Many of the states are not seen as legitimate among large numbers of people, which is unlike the situation in the Global North. The collection of essays on the Global South in this anthology provides interrogative and revealing perspectives on the extent to which poor people do or don't rise up against their oppressive social and economic conditions.

Ajamu Nangwaya, a lecturer at the University of the West Indies and a community organizer, explores the factors that prevent the people of the Anglophone Caribbean from rising up against economic oppression, and offers specific actions that must be taken in order to enable the laboring classes to resist the systems of exploitation in the region. Nangwaya's chapter places a strong emphasis on the practical matter of organizing the people. Kimalee Phillip, a trade union staffer and community organizer, explores the effects of the intra-leadership bloodletting that occurred in the Grenadian Revolution, and the subsequent invasion and destruction of the revolution. The unsettled ghosts of these events are still haunting the consciousness of the living in Grenada. Erin Araujo, who lived in Chiapas for 9 years, documents the experiences of a group of women in San Cristobal de las Casas, Mexico who are resisting capitalism by sharing resources through moneyless economic transactions. David Gómez Vazquez examines the "community police" in Guerrero,

Mexico. They use the pressing need for security of their persons to establish self-defense networks and community health initiatives to deal with the predatory behavior of criminal elements, some of whom have close ties with the state and capital. Wangui Kimari looks at the murderous behavior of the Kenyan police against the people in the country's largest slum community. Despite the intense expression of structural and physical violence against the people of Mathare, Wangui finds forms of resistance in the people's acts of solidarity that have given birth to the possibility of a challenge to the hegemony of the state. Gussai H. Sheikheldin explores the absence of critical consciousness as an important factor that explains the failure of the poor to rise up against inequality and general oppression in Sudan. Anna Selmeczi and Aragorn Eloff engage in a dialogue on the possibility of social transformation in South Africa, the "protest capital of the world." They discuss Fallism and the recent student protests in South Africa, in one of the more introspective contributions to our book.

Organizing the
Twenty-first Century Resistance

The Guinea-Bissau revolutionary, organizer, and military strategist Amilcar Cabral reminds us:

> Always remember that the people do not fight for ideas, for the things that exist only in the heads of individuals. The people fight and accept the necessary sacrifices. But they do it in order to gain material advantages, to live in peace and to improve their lives, to experience progress, and to be able to guarantee a future for their children. National liberation, the struggle against colonialism, working for peace and progress, independence—all of these will be empty words without significance for the people unless they are translated into real improvements in the conditions of life.[27]

It should be noted that Cabral is not declaring that ideas are unimportant to the process of organizing the people or carrying out political mobilization. Otherwise, he would not have declared in "The Weapon of Theory," that "if it is true that a revolution can fail even though it is based on perfectly conceived theories—nobody has yet made a successful revolution without a revolutionary theory."[28] Cabral is encouraging the revolutionary organizers to be acutely aware of the concrete needs that are motivating the people to "fight and accept the necessary sacrifices" in confronting the forces of oppression. The people must see hope for a better future in the vision that is presented to them or generated from the dialogue with the revolutionary organizers. Ideas are necessary but not sufficient in the protracted struggle that will take place against capitalism, patriarchy, racism, and imperialism in the twenty-first century.

Revolutionary ideas must resonate and implicate the material needs and aspirations of the working-class and other oppressed groups in the short-term and long-term. This political alignment is a ground on which many people will find hope in the present and the future, and the necessity to make sacrifices by embracing a transgressive and active political engagement against capitalism and other forms of structural oppression. To effectively engage the poor or the laboring classes, the organizers or activists of today must reject the seductive appeal of almost exclusively using the mobilizing approach to resist capitalist, and other forms of, oppression. The mobilizing approach to resisting oppressive conditions is too reliant on the episodic spectacle of the demonstration, march, rally, or press conference that results in an inherently demobilizing imperative and low commitment and expectations, with respect to the participants in the struggle for liberation.[29] Mobilizing tactics or actions are important in the struggle to facilitate the birth of revolutions. But they tend to be used in situations wherein the oppressed are reacting to initiatives from the oppressive forces and not as a part of ongoing programmatic and counter-institution building organizing work among the dispossessed classes.

The organizing approach to fighting oppression should be the default of organizers who are committed to emancipation from below. Why should the organizing approach be given such a pride of place in the twenty-first century struggle for emancipation? One of the editors of this collection offers this defense of organizing:

> When I raised the issue of organizing the oppressed, this project is centrally focused on building the capacity of the people to become central actors on the stage of history or in the drama of emancipation. The socially marginalized are placed in organizational situations where they are equipped with the knowledge, skills and attitude to work for their own freedom and the construction of a transformed social reality.
>
> Under the organizing model the people are the principal participants and decision-makers in the organizations and movements that are working for social change. The people are not seen as entities who are so ideologically underdeveloped that they need a revolutionary vanguard or dictatorship to lead them to the "New Jerusalem." The supreme organizer

and humanist Ella Baker took the position that the masses will figure out the path to freedom in her popular assertion, "Give people light and they will find a way."[30]

It is impossible to exaggerate the importance behind enabling the people to become the architects of the process and movements for liberation. The means that we use will prejudice or highly determine the outcomes of this struggle. Means are truly ends in a state of becoming.

We will reap what we sow with respect to the strategy and tactics used to bring down the oppressive regimes of power. It is for the preceding reason that we ought to pay attention to the prefigurative politics of Mikhail Bakunin and the collectivistic structures that are necessary in the transitional program that is needed in moving from capitalism to anarchism, or the communist society (stateless, classless, and self-managed/self-organized):

> Let us enlarge our association. But at the same time, let us not forget to consolidate and reinforce it so that our solidarity, which is our whole power, grows stronger from day to day. Let us have more of this solidarity in study, in our work, in civic action, in life itself. Let us cooperate in our common enterprise to make our lives a little more supportable and less difficult. Let us, whenever possible, establish producer- [worker]-consumer cooperatives and mutual credit societies [credit unions] which, though under the present economic conditions they cannot in any real or adequate way free us, are nevertheless important inasmuch as they train workers in the practice of managing the economy and plant the precious seeds for the organization of the future.[31]

Bakunin calls on us to serve in social movement organizations and build programs that attend to the needs of the poor or the laboring classes. It is also a way to facilitate a culture of resistance in the here and now, while developing the people for life in the revolutionary, self-managed socialist society of the future.

Organizing the Political Culture of Opposition and Resistance

For a ruling-class to truly exercise hegemony or the universalizing of its views, prejudices, values, and sensibilities within the ranks of the laboring classes or dominated groups, it must do so through its cultural domination of the people in the essential or primary realms of culture. The ruling class or paramount groups are able to use the agents of socialization such as the family, religion, media, and school to make its self-serving values and interests appear true and right in the eyes and consciences of the dominated classes. However, the hegemonic ruling class does not exercise total control over the production and dissemination of all values in society, and it is in that context that counterhegemonic values, beliefs, and practices from within the cultures of a dominated class or people will find the space to engage in the war of cultural contestation or foster the cultural revolution, which is the midwife of the political revolution.

The revolutionary or radical organizers in the twenty-first century who are committed to fomenting revolutions against capitalism, imperialism, and other forms of oppression cannot ignore the culture of the oppressed, the poor, or the working class that they are seeking to organize. In Amilcar Cabral's article "National Liberation and Culture," he highlights the morbid fear that colonizers or socially dominant forces have about the culture of those they dominate:

> When Goebbels, the brain behind Nazi propaganda, heard culture being discussed, he brought out his revolver. That shows that the Nazis—who were and are the most tragic expression of imperialism and of its thirst for domination—even if they were all degenerates like Hitler, had a clear idea of the value of culture as a factor of resistance to foreign domination.[32]

The fear of the transgressive elements of the culture of the dominated is even relevant in cases where the ruling class is from the same racial, religious, or ethnic group as the poor or the dominated groups. The culture of the ruling class is normally used to indicate the social distance between the oppressed and the oppressor, and a part of the reason that the latter's economic, social, and political condition is so desperate and exacting. It is the potentially transgressive character of the people's culture to which the revolutionary or radical organizers must appeal and integrate into the political vision and praxis that is articulated in organizing with the poor or the people who are being shafted by the various systems of oppression, especially capitalism and imperialism.

Since revolutionary movements do not operate in an ideational vacuum and must appeal to ideas that are oppositional to the existing social order, the cultural revolution of values must enter the stage of history prior to the political revolution. The people must be convinced that another world is indeed possible and is worth the investment of their time, material resources, hope,

self-organization. Power to the people in practice! It is at this unit level that the people would experience direct democracy, and it would be at this level that the ultimate decision-making power would reside. Even when the community assemblies are members of federations of other assemblies, substantive power would remain at the base level of the assembly. The application of the federative principle is critical to the task of coordinating programs of common interests beyond the local sphere. Localism or a fixation with the purely local is the enemy of solidarity and mutual aid, and will not effectively prepare the people to self-manage their common affairs over a broad territory with its attendant rewards and challenges.

When we referred to the assemblies as the "counterhegemonic or counter-power oppositional organs," we hold these structures as the formations that contest the power of the liberal capitalist, political bodies (for example, municipal councils and provincial/state and national legislatures) and elected representatives (members of parliament, senators, and congresspersons). A prefigurative politics of liberation must pragmatically address the fact that the authoritarian electoral political structures are still in place and are making decisions that affect the lives of the people who are organizing in the self-organizing assemblies. The assemblies must find creative ways to impose their priorities in and on the normative political processes and structures.

The popular assemblies, as an organ of direct democracy, are relevant to organizing projects in both the Global South and the Global North. In both regions, the laboring classes, and poor people in particular, struggling under liberal capitalist democracies are becoming increasingly alienated from them. It is a noticeable problem identified by politicians and political researchers, and this disaffection with electoral politics has been coined the "democratic deficit." This act of voting with their feet has resulted in alarmingly low voter turnout. While the political class worries what the democratic deficit means for their legitimacy, as regimes are endorsed by smaller and smaller fractions of eligible voters, the revolutionary organizers should see this development as an opportunity to organize communities into assemblies. It is not only the democratic deficit that favors the assembly and preparing the people for the administration of things. It is understood that the demands or needs of the poor are not translated in policies and programs in the political system, unlike the case of the bourgeoisie whose desires are attended to by the political class.

The introduction of the assembly in territorially based communities is easier to accomplish under the organizing approach to liberation than the mobilizing approach to resistance. This is the case because the organizers are in regular, face-to-face contact with the oppressed in their communities. Further, with the deployment of Paulo Freire's "problem-posing" approach to engaging the poor in reading the world and formulating solutions based on a critical interrogation and assessment of the objective and subjective conditions, they are likely to see the value of the popular assembly as an instrument to fight for justice, equity, dignity, respect, and self-determination. The assemblies will also be the body in which decisions about the people-controlled economic institutions and their supporting structures and organizations would be determined. Therefore, these popular assemblies with their horizontal structures and relations are not talking shops, but spaces in which the revolutionary processes come alive. They would also give the participants objective lessons on the promise and challenge of self-organization in the classless, stateless, and self-organized society. Of equal importance, the assemblies will be organized, active, and revolutionary centers that equip the laboring classes with the knowledge, skills, and attitude to unflinchingly take on the responsibilities of self-managing a large territory.

Organizing the People's Needs through Economic Mutual Aid

There is a perception that socialists or members of the Left just do not know how to "manage the shop," but they are excellent at distributing the goods from the proverbial shop. When we look at the fact that the socialist states of the former Soviet Union, Eastern Europe, China, North Korea, and Cuba produced neither the high quality nor sufficient quantities of consumer goods with their central planning system, there might be some truth to the prejudicial outlook on socialists and their prowess in the economic and business arena. However, be that what it may, capitalism is not working for the working class or the poor majority across the world so twenty-first century organizers must incorporate economic programs into organizing initiatives. These economic programs must also be reflective of the prefiguative politics (economics) of liberation. It should be non-exploitative, valorize the dignity of work, sovereignty of labour over capital, and be an economic practice that is solely geared to meeting the needs of its members and/or community and not the generation of profit. Moreover, this economic practice should promote a collectivist ethos and psychological orientation, and its very essence should be a repudiation of capitalism and class exploitation.

Anarchists and state socialists have ignored building an economic alternative while living in the belly of the beast due to deep prejudices against cooperative economics. Many contemporary socialists are of the view that the ruling class would not allow collectivist economic practices to become a mortal threat to capitalism, and would use legislation to destroy the collectivistic economic

institutions. Yet they curiously do not express the same poverty of imagination when it comes to the possibility of the state and capital creating laws
to destroy autonomous, oppositional political organizations of the oppressed.
Revolutionary and radical activists take it for granted that the political and
economic initiatives would seek to neutralize the political organizations of the
socially dominated classes. It is a given within the ranks of revolutionary and
radical organizations that they are going to fight back and contest the state and
capital for power. A psychological and political orientation toward construct-
ing the collectivistic economic institution of the future communist society
must be a priority today. A prefigurative politics of economic self-management
must work in tandem with, or be a reflection of, the work of the popular assemblies that administer the common affairs of the self-organized oppositional
bloc within civil society.

Nineteenth century communists such as the anarchist Mikhail Bakunin,
and state socialist revolutionaries such as Karl Marx, had more positive or
accommodating views of economic cooperation among the working class as
expressed through labor self-managed firms and consumers and financial cooperatives such as what we now know as credit unions. Anarchists and state
socialists are politically and morally obligated to attend to the economic processes and structures that are necessary in the transitional program that will
take the oppressed from capitalism to the stateless, classless, and self-organized
society—the communist society. Bakunin saw the value of economic cooperation in the revolutionary transitional program:

> What should be the nature of the agitation and development of
> the workers of the International and what will be the means of
> these, before the social revolution, which alone can emancipate
> them fully and definitively, does so? The experience of recent
> years recommends two paths to us, one negative and the other
> positive: *resistance funds* [strike funds] *and cooperation.*
>
> By the term 'cooperation', we mean all known systems of
> *consumption*, of *mutual credit* or *labour credit*, and of *produc-
> tion.* In the application of all these systems, and even in the
> theory on which they are based, we should distinguish two op-
> posing currents: the bourgeois current and the purely socialist
> current.[38]

Bakunin offers two useful concepts (bourgeois current and purely socialist current) in organizing the laboring classes into programs and institutions
of economic cooperation. Contemporary labor self-managed firms, worker

cooperatives, and consumer cooperatives fall within the bourgeois current. They do not view themselves as instruments of the class struggle or the embryonic entities that are the building blocks of the non-capitalist society. They have simply accommodated themselves to the economic domination and ethos of capitalism.

What did Marx have to say about economic cooperation and the working class creating cooperative economic relations and structures, while living under the capitalist economic order? Marx had a positive assessment of the labor self-managed firms or "cooperative factories" and their role in the transitional program from capitalism to communism:

> The co-operative factories run by workers themselves are, within the old form, the first examples of the emergence of a new form, even though they naturally reproduce in all cases, in their present organization, all the defects of the existing system, and must reproduce them. But the opposition between capital and labour is abolished there, even if at first only in the form that the workers in association become their own capitalists, i.e., they use the means of production to valorise their labour. These factories show how, at a certain stage of development of the material forces of production, and of the social forms of production corresponding to them, a new mode of production develops and is formed naturally out of the old [...] Capitalist joint-stock companies as much as cooperative factories should be viewed as transition forms from the capitalist mode of production to the associated one, simply that in one case the opposition is abolished in a negative way, and in the other in a positive way.[39]

To avoid tackling the thorny question of the economic transitional programs and institutions through which the people might meet their needs and practice counterhegemonic values at the point of production, as well as in their communities as consumers of goods and services, would be politically irresponsible on the part of the organizers of today's movements for social emancipation. The revolutionary organizers need to engage and identify the features of Bakunin's "purely socialist current" as applied to economic cooperation or a cooperative movement that is anti-capitalist or committed to creating the (anarchist) communist society.

Below are several features that should, at a minimum, be included in the "purely socialist current" of a prefigurative politics of economic liberation based on consumer and worker cooperatives and collectivistic economic formations:

1. Cooperatives must operate as instruments of the class struggle and forces that are explicitly opposed to all forms of oppression;

2. Self-management of these economic enterprises must not just be reflected in the principles of economic cooperation but must be demonstrated in the everyday ideational, strategic, and operational leadership and decision-making practices. Worker cooperatives or labor self-managed firms are seen as economic entities that are vulnerable to *the degeneration thesis* that argues that these democratic enterprises will eventually capitulate to the authoritarian, bureaucratic management practices of capitalist corporations in order to compete and survive in the unfriendly institutional and market environment of capitalism.[40] The experience of labor alienation is the most damning indictment of capitalist companies, and this dehumanizing and exploitative phenomenon has no place in economic mutual aid.

3. The transitional program ought to create schools of economic cooperation that provide an ideological and practical preparation for the cooperators, nurturing a socialist path to labor self-management and collectivist economic development. One cannot overemphasize the important role of education in preparing the cooperators to master the "practical details of the process of deep self-management."[41] It is also essential to develop a high level of class consciousness among the cooperators and neuter the ideological hegemony of the ruling-class over the poor or the working class.

4. The application of the federative principle is paramount in organizing the people for economic self-management. Cahill quite rightly asserts that an emphasis on "community-based or local needs" should be a feature of an explicitly anarchist economic system because they are best placed to understand their social and economic predicaments.[42] However, localism could give rise to the seductive embrace of economic isolation when cooperation beyond the local would better serve the needs of the people. Regional, national, and international cooperation of the forces of economic self-management would allow them to reap economy of scale and present a more formidable challenge to the economic domination of capitalist enterprises. The development of federations that maintain strong democratic local control are important in the process of establishing the "purely socialist current" as an emerging counterhegemonic bloc.

Endnotes

1 Thomas B. Edsall, "Why Don't the Poor Rise Up?" *The New York Times*, June 24, 2015. Available online: http://www.nytimes.com/2015/06/24/opinion/why-dont-the-poor-rise-up.html?_r=0.

2 Karl Marx, *The Eighteenth Brumaire of Louis Napoleon*, Joseph Weydemeyer, trans. (New York: International Publishers, 1963), section V, paragraph 4.

3 Frantz Fanon, *The Wretched of the Earth* (New York: Grove Press, 2004), 87.

4 Katie Hope, "Eight billionaires 'as rich as world's poorest half,'" *BBC News*, January 16, 2017. Available online: http://www.bbc.com/news/business-38613488.

5 Center for Poverty Research, "What is the current poverty rate in the United States?" September 13, 2016. Available online: http://poverty.ucdavis.edu/faq/what-current-poverty-rate-united-states.

6 Center for Poverty Research, "What is 'deep poverty'?" September 13, 2016. Available online: http://poverty.ucdavis.edu/faq/what-deep-poverty.

7 Josh Holland, "High inequality results in more US deaths than to-bacco, car crashes and guns combined," *Moyers & Company*, April 19, 2014. Available online: http://billmoyers.com/2014/04/19/high-inequality-results-in-more-us-deaths-than-tobacco-car-crashes-and-guns-combined/.

8 Jason Hickel, "Exposing the great 'poverty reduction' lie," *Al Jazeera*, August 21, 2014. Available online: http://www.aljazeera.com/indepth/opinion/2014/08/exposing-great-poverty-reductio-201481211590729809.html.

9 Institute for Research on Poverty, "How is poverty measured in the United States?" Available online: http://www.irp.wisc.edu/faqs/faq2.htm.

10 Salvatore Babones, "America's Real Poverty Rate," *Inequality.org*, November 14, 2011. Accessed on January 2, 2017, http://inequality.org/americas-real-poverty-rate/.

11 See, for example, Patricia Ruggles, *Drawing the Line: Alternative Poverty Measures and Their Implications for Public Policy* (Washington, D.C.: Urban Institute Press, 1990), and Constance F. Citro and Robert T. Michael, *Measuring Poverty: A New Approach* (Washington, D.C.: National Academy Press, 1995).

12 Vijaya Murali and Femi Oyebode, "Poverty, social inequality and mental health," *Advances in Psychiatric Treatment*, 10.3 (May 2004): 216–224.

13 Tanuka Loha, "Housing: It's a Wonderful Right," *Amnesty International*, December 21, 2011. Available online: http://blog.amnestyusa.org/us/housing-its-a-wonderful-right/.

14 The Department of Housing, Planning, Community & Local Government, "Homelessness Report," December 2016. Available online: http://www.housing.gov.ie/sites/default/files/publications/files/homeless_report_-_december_2016.pdf.

15 Robert Neuwirth, *Shadow Cities: A Billion Squatters, A New Urban World* (New York: Routledge, 2016), 9.

16 Craig Willse, *The Value of Homelessness: Managing Surplus Life in the United States* (Minneapolis: University of Minnesota Press, 2015), 2.

17 Ibid., 12.

18 Jeffrey D. Sachs, *The End of Poverty: Economic Possibilities for Our Time* (New York: Penguin Books, 2005), 3.

19 Ibid., 11.

20 Ibid., 12.

21 Ibid., 16.

22 Ibid., 36.

23 Ibid., 50.

24 Keeanga-Yamahtta Taylor, *From #BlackLivesMatter to Black Liberation* (Chicago: Haymarket Books, 2016), 194.

25 Ibid., 46.

26 Corey Robin, "Capitalism and Nazism," *Jacobin*, April 23, 2014. Available online: https://www.jacobinmag.com/2014/04/capitalism-and-nazism/.

27 Lar Rudebeck, *Guinea-Bissau: A Study of Political Mobilization* (Uppsala, The Scandinavian Institute of African Studies, 1974), 91.

28 Amilcar Cabral, *Revolution in Guinea: Selected Texts* (New York: Monthly Review Press, 1969), 93. The text of this speech (The Weapon of Theory) is available online at https://www.marxists.org/subject/africa/cabral/1966/weapon-theory.htm.

29 Ajamu Nangwaya, "Ferguson, Mobilization and Organizing the Resistance," *CounterPunch*, August 19, 2014. Accessed from http://www.counterpunch.org/2014/08/19/ferguson-mobilization-and-organizing-the-resistance/.

30 Ibid.

31 Sam Dolgoff, editor and translator, *Bakunin on Anarchism* (Montreal: Black Rose Books, 1980), 173.

32 Amilcar Cabral, *Return to the Source: Selected Speeches of Amilcar Cabral* (New York: Monthly Review Press, 1973), 39.

33 John Foran, "New Political Cultures of Opposition: What Future for Revolutions?," 238. Available online: www.academia.edu/1277296/15_New_political_cultures_of_opposition.

34 John Foran, *Taking Power: On the Origin of Third World Revolutions* (New York: Cambridge University Press, 2005), 21.

35 Theda Skocpol, *States and Social Revolutions: A Comparative Analysis of France, Russia and China* (Cambridge: Cambridge University Press, 1979), 4.

36 Ibid., 41.

37 Foran, *Taking Power*, 13.

38 Cited in Tom Cahill, "Cooperatives and Anarchism: A Contemporary Perspective," in *For Anarchism: History, Theory, and Practice*, ed. David Goodway (New York: Routledge, 1989), 239.

39 Cited in Bruno Bossa, "Marx, Marxism and the Cooperative Movement," *Cambridge Journal of Economics*, 29, no. 1 (2005), 5

40 Chris Conforth, *Patterns of Co-operative Management: Beyond the Degeneration Thesis*, February1995. Accessed from https://www.academia.edu/559845/Patterns_of_cooperative_management_beyond_the_degeneration_thesis; John Storey, Imanol Basterretxea, and Graeme Salaman, (2014). *Managing and resisting 'degeneration' in employee-owned businesses: a comparative study of two large retailers in Spain and the UK.* Accessed from http://oro.open.ac.uk/40063/1/Managing%20and%20resisting%20degeneration%20in%20two%20employee%20owned%20retaileres.pdf

41 Cahill, "Cooperatives and Anarchism," 244.

42 Ibid.

THE
GLOBAL
NORTH

IDLE NO MORE

GROUNDING THE CORRIENTES OF HEMISPHERIC RESISTENCIA

Praba Pilar and **Alex Wilson**

Introduction

INDIGENOUS PEOPLES ACROSS THE AMERICAS HAVE BEEN RISING UP FOR 500 years, presenting multivalent forms of resistance to colonial violence, femicide, epistemicide, and ecocide. The many faces and instances of this resistance do not register within leftist discourse and practice, and, in fact, are often invisibilized. As Indigenous women who have actively participated in and led community resistance to colonial violence, our response to the question "Why don't the poor rise up?" is to share our own stories and the stories of our people here not as the answer to this question but as the context for our own question: "When will the Left listen?"

This article was written at the onset of the fourth anniversary of the Idle No More movement and in the eighth month of the Indigenous-led action and encampment to stop construction of the Dakota Access Pipeline on sacred ancestral lands of the Standing Rock Sioux Nation. We write from our respective cosmological and geographical locations. Praba Pilar, a Colombian Mestiza woman, now lives at the juncture of the Red and Assiniboine rivers. Alex Wilson, who is Inniniwak, lives on the Saskatchewan River Delta in the traditional territory of her people, the Opaskwayak Cree Nation.

Indigenous resistance to colonization is the enduring history and present of the Americas, and the authors are connected as participants and organizers in Idle No More, a movement that draws together and organizes activists from throughout the Americas and beyond to honor Indigenous sovereignty and to protect the land and water. A considerable physical distance separates us, but the waterways along which we live flow into Lake Winnipeg, connecting us to one of the largest watersheds in the world, reaching west to Alberta, north to the Hudson Bay, east to the Great Lakes region, and south well into the United States.

The complex structure and interactions within this river, lake, and wetlands system offer a framework for our understanding of social movements. In our communities, Indigenous peoples' cosmologies, lifeways, and resistance focus on stewardship of the waters, lands, plants, animals, and other life forms that sustain us, and are guided by and govern ourselves based on traditional ethics that value relational accountability, reciprocity, and collective and individual sovereignty. Navigating these interweaving ethical pathways have enabled our survival, as peoples, and now position us to reimagine a *pluriverse* that approaches the Zapatista's concept of a "world in which many worlds coexist."[1]

Cosmologies of the White Left

The question of why the poor do (not) rise up connects conceptually to the Left. The American political philosopher Susan Buck-Morss reminds us that the contemporary Left had its origin in European cosmology: "[T]he term 'Left' is clearly a Western category, emerging in the context of the French Revolution."[2] The Argentinian scholar of modernity and coloniality Walter Mignolo acknowledges that the Left has followed multiple trajectories and presented itself in multiple iterations (secular, theological, Marxist, European-influenced) around the globe but asserts that it can still most rightly be described as the "white Left."[3] Mignolo's naming of "the white Left" is driven by the recognition that this movement emerged from a modernity that profits from and is dependent on coloniality.

This white Left concerns us. Too often, its theorizing and work have universalized political categories that rely on and reflect exclusively European cosmologies, knowledges, and theorists. Many, it seems, have forgotten the source of the languages, practices, and legacies of the white Left. Mignolo, however, has not: "Kant's cosmopolitanism and its legacy propose the universalization of Western nativism/localism. And the Marxist Left, for better or worse, belongs to that world."[4] We acknowledge that there have been intersections (some of them meaningful and powerful) between the white Left and Indigenous resistance in the Americas. Our question is broader. We question the axes of capitalism vs. socialism/communism, which cast Indigenous people as stand-ins for the proletariat or lumpenproletariat of capitalist Europe. Other non-white Leftists have made similar challenges: "From Indian decolonial perspectives, the problem is not capitalism only, but also Occidentalism. Marx … proposed a class struggle within Occidental civilization, including the Left, which originated in the West."[5]

Decolonizing the White Left

We earlier described an ethical system that values relational accountability, reciprocity, and collective and individual sovereignty for Indigenous peoples. These ethics, which existed well before the arrival of the earliest European explorers and settlers on our lands, have persisted and enabled us to maintain our resistance to colonial violence, ecocide, and epistemicide. The interrelationships between our ethics, cosmologies, lifeways, and the waters, lands, and life forms that sustain us are as complex and critical to our survival as those between the rivers, lakes, and wetlands within the watershed where we reside. In our current political landscape, however, we must also navigate dangerously confining constructs introduced by European colonizers that function as ideological canals, locks, and dams.

An early example of these confining constructs was the "Inter Caetera," a papal bull issued by Pope Alexander VI in 1493 that laid out the justification for the Doctrine of Discovery. It established that Christian nations had a divine right (based on the bible) to grant themselves legal ownerships of any "unoccupied" lands (where unoccupied was defined as the absence of Christian people) and dominion over any peoples on those lands.

A current example of these confining constructs is the salvation narrative unconsciously reproduced by many in the white Left when they approach Indigenous or other non-European communities as allies but present solutions that have been developed in isolation, are paternalistic, and/or are inappropriate to the context. Salvation narratives are often seen as benign, but they are not. They reflect and perpetuate the early justification for colonization, i.e., that "God had directed [Europeans] to bring civilized ways and education and religion to Indigenous Peoples and to exercise paternalism and guardianship powers over them."[6]

Some in the white Left rely on codified models of hierarchical leadership, structured authority, and strategies and tactics, a construct that eradicates possibilities of deep alliance with many Indigenous people and groups who, for example, base their models on relationality or valorize community leadership rather than leadership vested in singular, celebrated figures. As Mignolo has observed, "Western Marxists belong to the same history of languages and memories as Christians, liberals, and neo-liberals. Marxism ... is an outgrowth of Western civilization."[7] For many in the white Left, it can be difficult to recognize this. The ideological constructs introduced by the European colonizers have been here long enough that they may be mistaken for natural features of the political landscape. As Indigenous women engaged in resistance, we ask those in the white Left to look more carefully, to acknowledge that colonization continues today, to make a choice to de-center the epistemic violence that accompanies it, and re-center themselves in decolonizing practices.

Hemispheric Connections

In the Southern Hemisphere of the Americas, co-author Praba comes from the largest highland plateau ecosystem in the world, the Páramo de Sumapaz of the Altiplano Cundinamarca in Colombia. Descended from the Muisca Chibcha of the Altiplano Cundiboyacense in the Cordillera Oriental of the Andes, she was forced to leave Colombia as part of a diaspora fleeing the horrors of the hemisphere's longest continuous internal war. Canada is the tenth country in which she has lived. Colombia has one of the highest rates of emigration in the Americas, with roughly one of every ten citizens living outside of the country. An even greater proportion of the population (5.8 million people within the country's total population of 48.9 million) have been internally displaced, and the majority of these are Indigenous and/or Afro-Colombian.[8]

The Toemaida military base, founded in 1954, is located in the region of Colombia where Praba spent her early years. The United States has been involved in military action in Colombia since the mid-1800s, and American soldiers are a "permanent presence at Tolemaida."[9] As noted in the report "Contribution to the Understanding of the Armed Conflict in Colombia" (Contribución al Entendimiento del Conflicto Armado en Colombia), issued by the Historic Commission of the Conflict and its Victims (Comisión Histórica del Conflicto y sus Víctimas) in February of 2015, "United States governments of the last seven decades are directly responsible for the perpetuation of the armed conflict in Colombia, in terms of how they have promoted the counterinsurgency in all of its manifestations, stimulating and training the Armed Forces with their methods of torture and elimination of those who they consider 'internal enemies' and blocking all non-military paths to solve the structural causes of the social and armed conflict."[10] The military at Tolemaida has continuously attacked the powerful Indigenous resistance in the region, and is now deliberately contaminating the water supply, dumping "battery packs, broken glass, and ceramics, slowly rotting camouflage patterned clothing and bedding, munitions boxes (labeled in English and produced in the

United States), and electrical equipment of all sorts… the water is visibly toxic green in parts, orange in others, with an oily sheen, and chemical foam."[11]

The highest coastal mountain range in the world, La Sierra Nevada de Santa Marta lies in the north of Colombia. The source of 36 rivers, the mountains feature a range of climates and abundant biodiversity. Over thousands of years, the Kogi people, who have stewarded the lands and waters, and resisted and survived colonization with their practices, beliefs, and cosmologies intact, have continuously occupied them. In 1990, the Kogi invited a British filmmaker, Alan Ereira, to work on a documentary entitled *From the Heart of the World: The Elder Brothers' Warning*. The documentary recorded the devastating climactic and environmental impacts that petroleum and resource extraction industries have had on the lands and waters of the Kogi people. Since then, the Kogi have "witnessed landslides, floods, deforestation, the drying up of lakes and rivers, the stripping bare of mountain tops, the dying of trees."[12] In response, the Kogi recently made a second film with Ereira entitled *Aluna*. In the film, they explain the complex relationship of water from the coastal areas and lagoons to glacial mountain peaks. "They want to show urgently that the damage caused by logging, mining, the building of power stations, roads and the construction of ports along the coast and at the mouths of rivers … affects what happens at the top of the mountain. Once white-capped peaks are now brown and bare, lakes are parched and the trees and vegetation vital to them are withering."[13] What do the Kogi ask for in the film? They ask for non-Indigenous people to engage with Indigenous peoples and knowledge, to protect the waterways, lands, and living creatures, and to halt ecocide.

Not far from the Kogi territory lays the Northeast desert terrain, home to the Wayúu, the largest Indigenous population in Colombia. Having survived paramilitary massacres and displacement, they are now starving and dying because their water supply has been dammed, privatized, and diverted to the El Cerrejon coal mine owned by Angloamerican, Glencore, and BHP Billiton. As reported by the mine's Director of International Relations, the mine "uses 7.1 million gallons of water a day in its 24-hour operations."[14] The International Work Group for Indigenous Affairs reports that the diversion of water, coupled with the current drought in the region, has left 37,000 Indigenous children in La Guajira malnourished and at least 5,000 dead of starvation. Armando Valbuena, the Wayúu traditional authority, identifies the actual number of deaths as "closer to 14,000, with no end in sight."[15]

The imposed nation/state borders of Venezuela and Colombia cross the territory of the Wayúu people. Both countries grossly violate Wayúu human rights. As Jakelyn Epieyu, of the Fuerza de Mujeres Wayúu relates, "I believe we live in a dictatorship of the Left in Venezuela and in Colombia the dictatorship of the Right, which has cost us blood and fire"[16] In Colombia, Indigenous and Afro-Colombians have been categorized as "a potential enemy to the identity of the nation. During the period when sociobiology and eugenics were popular ideologies of the ruling class and intellectuals of Latin America, Colombia defined the cultural base of the nation as 'white.'"[17] This politic of "blanqueamiento" (becoming white) has persisted and affects every political arena in Colombia. As Misake community leader Segundo Tombé Morales relates, "[T]he indigenous movement, as understood in a general sense, remains on the floor, remains as if we were enemies of the Colombian people, of peasants, even any person today who sees an Indigenous person on the street, is enough motive for rejection and contempt."[18]

These are not abstractions or polemical discussions. These are lived experiences generated by an excruciating war with Indigenous people in the cross hairs: "Indians are killed for defending their lands and for begging when displaced, for growing coca and for failing to grow coca, for supporting guerrillas and for failing to support guerrillas, and most of all, for daring to claim the rights Colombia grants but cannot provide."[19] The casualties include Praba's family members, some of whom were killed in the war, and others who came close to dying but somehow survived: her mother, who was picked up off the street by a military tank (leading the family to flee the country), or Praba herself, who, when visiting Colombia in 2006, travelled down a road just 15 minutes before bombs detonated, killing everyone along a 1.5 kilometre stretch.

There are over 100 Indigenous groups in Colombia. In a 2009 ruling of the Constitutional Court of Columbia, more than a third of them were identified as "at risk of extermination by the armed conflict and forced displacement."[20] Indigenous communities in Colombia are disproportionately affected by the country's internal war: "The parties to the conflict—namely, the Colombian armed forces, ultra-right paramilitary groups, and leftist guerrillas (such as the FARC and ELN)—have all been involved in crimes against Indigenous peoples."[21] Paramilitaries and armed government forces have committed massacres, assassinations, and terrorized populations, engendering displacement. Leftist guerrillas have also played a destructive role, as explained by one of the justices who helped author the Court's decision:

> First, Indigenous-owned territory often serves as the "ideal," remote place to conduct military operations. Second, parties to the conflict often incorporate Indigenous peoples into the violence through, amongst other things, recruitment, selective murders, and use of communities as human shields. Third, resource-rich ancestral lands are threatened by the extractive

economic activities related to the conflict, including mining, oil, timber, and agribusiness. And fourth, the conflict worsens the pre-existing poverty, ill-health, malnutrition, and other socio-economic disadvantages suffered by Indigenous peoples.[22]

Misak leader Pedro Antonio Calambas Cuchillo explains that Indigenous people have little choice about their involvement: "We as Indigenous people have always tried to be separate from the armed groups, both the army and the guerrilla, but often conflicts happen between them, and we are always involved by the guerrillas, specifically the FARC, and by the public force."[23]

Colombia and other nations in the Southern Hemisphere, and Canada in the Northern Hemisphere, are connected through Canadian mining corporations. On a 2014 trip to Ottawa, sponsored in part by the Assembly of First Nations (a national organization that represents First Nations throughout Canada), Colombian human and Indigenous rights advocates observed that "in their country, Canadian trade and investment is profiting from a 'genocide' against Indigenous communities as land is cleared for resource development."[24] Indigenous peoples in Canada have told the same story.

In the North, Alex emerges from Opaskwayak Cree Nation and the Saskatchewan River Delta. The name Saskatchewan comes from a Cree word, kisiskâciwanisîpiy, meaning "swift-flowing river." The Saskatchewan River Delta is a 10,000 square kilometer system of rivers, lakes, wetlands, and wildlife that acts as a filter, cleaning the water, lands, and air in the region. As one of the most biodiverse areas of Canada, it has supported and sustained Indigenous communities for more than 10,000 years through hunting, trapping, and fishing.[25] Traditional Cree knowledge traces their presence on these lands and waters back to both the last ice age and the one that preceded that. Today, the Saskatchewan River Delta is controlled and influenced by several human impacts. These include: the Manitoba Hydro dam in Grand Rapids; the EB Campbell Dam owned by SaskPower; Ducks Unlimited, a private American corporation; and phosphates from farm fertilizers and other contaminants that flow into the delta waterways.

The Cree people of this region have been defending land and waterways in the territory for many generations. Growing up in the north, Alex gathered her first knowledge about water by playing in it, testing the depths of the melt waters in spring by wading in until her boots filled, navigating the ephemeral creeks on homemade rafts in the summer, and creeping carefully out onto the ice following the first winter freeze to see if it was solid enough for skating. As she got older, her understanding of the water increased in complexity. In the Cree language of Alex's people, the word for water is *nipiy*. The first syllable in this word, *ni*, refers to "life" and is also part of the Cree word for me or myself, drawing out the relationships between people and water. The term *nipiy* also has an alternate meaning: to die or bring death. Water, they understood, is a life or death matter.

The complex system of rivers and lakes in the north that sustained Indigenous people also provided the route for European colonization of their lands. The first significant European presence in the Canadian north were fur traders, who reached that territory by traveling the waterways that Indigenous people lived along. Indigenous people had relied on trapping for survival, harvesting critical resources that fed and clothed their families. They knew where animals in their territories could be found and how to harvest them in ways that would ensure their maintained presence, carefully managing their resources to ensure the sustainability of their way of life, their lands, and waters, and the animals and plants who shared their territory. The fur trade, however, generated profound changes in Indigenous people's way of life, including a shift from sustainable stewardship of resources to a commodity-based economy, and the decimation of critical animal populations. The fur trade also opened the north to missionaries, who brought salvation narratives and a determination to replace our traditional cosmologies, spirituality, lifeways, and ethics with Christian constructs and practices.

The fur trade was the first of many damaging resource extraction activities in northern Canada, and the economy of that region now relies primarily on mining, forestry, and hydroelectric generation. The Saskatchewan River Delta was altered dramatically by the construction of two large hydroelectric dams in the 1960s. The dams constrict and manipulate the flow of water along the Saskatchewan River, displacing the natural cycles that renew the surrounding lands and sustain wildlife, and generating flooding that has displaced entire Indigenous communities from their lands. Water from the river system is also used for agriculture and as drinking water for the cities and towns that have developed along the waterways. At the same time, agricultural drainage and wastewater from urban centers have introduced fertilizers and other agricultural and industrial chemicals, waste materials, and other contaminants into the river system.

In Alex's homeland of Northern Manitoba, either Manitoba Hydro or Ducks Unlimited now controls the waterways that Indigenous people stewarded for millenia. Alex's family's traditional trapline was along the Summerberry Marsh, between Moose Lake and Opaskwayak Cree Nation. Following construction of the dams, their devastating effects were evident throughout the lands and waters they trapped, hunted, and harvested in. Settlements and gravesites were flooded. Rivers and lands they had travelled for years became unfamiliar and dangerous. Their connections to and relationships with the land, waters, furbearing animals, migratory birds, and plants were disrupted, and it was impossible to maintain traditional ways of life. Trapping quotas (including one that set limits that decreased annually on the number of muskrats her grandfather could harvest) and fishing licenses were introduced, and traditional practices such as controlled burns (a technology to renew the muskrat population in a region) were banned. For Indigenous people, this forced a shift from food sovereignty to food dependency. People were forever changed.

Idle No More

The Indigenous grassroots movement Idle No More (INM) emerged in the fall of 2012 as a contemporary iteration of ongoing resistance to colonial violence directed at Indigenous people and the waterways, lands, and living things that sustain them. It was started by four women (both Indigenous and non-Indigenous) who felt compelled to take action to affirm Indigenous sovereignty, to protect and care for the land, water, each other and all living creatures, and to address old and new colonial forms of oppression.

The movement began not long after (then) Prime Minister Harper's assertion at the 2009 G20 summit that Canada has "no history of colonization." At the time INM was emerging, an estimated 1,000 Indigenous women and girls from across Canada had either gone missing or been murdered, a number the federal government has since acknowledged is much too low, and may be as many as 4,000 women or girls. INM's emergence also closely followed the federal government introduction of legislation and legislative changes (now passed) that enabled governments and corporations to sidestep responsibilities and obligations that follow from or align with constitutionally and/or legally protected Indigenous rights, treaty-based rights and human rights. These included two omnibus bills with provisions that established procedures that would enable privatization of First Nations lands, replaced the existing Environmental Assessment Act, and excepted pipelines and power lines from the Navigable Waters Protection Act, and removed thousands of lakes, rivers, and streams from protection under that same act.

INM began as a series of teach-ins in Saskatchewan on the planned legislative changes, round dances that brought together Indigenous people and our allies in public spaces such as government buildings, malls, or intersections, and, in its first month, a National Day of Action and Solidarity on which rallies and marches to protest the impending legislation were held in cities throughout Canada, drawing anywhere from hundreds to thousands of people to each event. By transforming public spaces into political spaces, it was no longer possible for us to be invisibilized. Those around us could no longer wilfully *not* see Indigenous people and the issues they were addressing.

INM quickly grew into a global movement focused on Indigenous peoples' right to sovereignty, our responsibility to protect our people, lands, waterways, and other living things from corporate and colonial violence and destruction, and ongoing resistance to neo-colonialism and neoliberalism. These issues lay out a large expanse of common ground and a notable feature of INM has been the extent to which it has worked in solidarity with like-minded organizations and individual allies. INM also operates within a non-heirarchic leadership model that is based on the traditional ethic of relational responsibility. It has reached out (both digitally and physically) to bring people into the circle, to step into leadership by becoming political actors. As Wanda Nanibush, an INM organizer, has observed:

> We as Idle No More have put forward the voices of women, the voices of two-spirited people, and the voices of youth. This has really galvanized voices that haven't been part of this thinking or a part of democracy in Canada. Idle No More has been really amazing at raising the question of democracy and how we're going to run this country, and whose voices are really going to be at the table, to the forefront of all of our struggles...all the struggles do come together under Indigenous rights.[26]

Conclusion

The Kogi, the Wayúu, and Idle No More are connected across the Americas through the violence of colonization, through bodies—of land, water, ecosystems, living beings, animals, and humans—and through knowledges, ways of being, cosmovisions, and resistance. Those who want to join the 500 years of Indigenous resistance can work to release the locks they impose on alliance, by releasing universalized Eurocentric narratives and cosmovision, epistemic violence, and salvation narratives. When Subcomandante Marcos joined with Mayans, he had to rethink his urban Marxist perspective on Indigenous terms. He writes about the experience: "The end result was that we were not talking to an indigenous movement waiting for a savior but with an indigenous movement with a long tradition of struggle, with a significant experience, and very intelligent: a movement that was using us as its armed men."[27]

Endnotes

1   Walter D. Mignolo, "On Pluriversality," October 20, 2013, www.http://waltermignolo
    .com/on-pluriversality/.

2   Susan Buck-Morss, *Thinking Past Terror: Islamism and Critical Theory on the Left* (London: Verso, 2003), 17.

3   Walter D. Mignolo, *The Darker Side of Western Modernity: Global Futures, Decolonial Options* (Durham: Duke University Press, 2011).

4   Ibid., 330.

5   Ibid., 325.

6   Robert J. Miller, *Native America, Discovered and Conquered: Thomas Jefferson, Lewis and Clark, and Manifest Destiny* (Lincoln: University of Nebraska Press, 2008), 3–5.

7   Mignolo, *The Darker Side of Western Modernity*, 51.

8   Louise Højen, "Colombia's 'Invisible Crisis': Internally Displaced Persons," *Council on Hemispheric Affairs*, February 2, 2015, http://www.coha.org/colombias-invisible-crisis-internally-displaced-persons/.

9   Luke Finn, "Colombian Army Escalates Attack on Communities near Tolemaida Military Base," *North American Congress on Latin America (NACLA)*, May 14, 2014, http://nacla.org/blog/2014/5/14/colombian-army-escalates-attack-communities-near-tolemaida-military-base.

10 Renán Vega Cantor, "Injerencia de los Estados Unidos, Contrainsurgencia y Terrorismo de Estado." Contribución al Entendimiento del Conflicto Armado en Colombia, Comisión Histórica del Conflicto y sus Víctimas, 2015. Translation of the original Spanish by Praba Pilar. The original text states: "gobiernos de los Estados Unidos de las últimas siete décadas son responsables directos en la perpetuación del conflicto armado en Colombia, en la medida en que han promovido la contrainsurgencia en todas sus manifestaciones, estimulado y entrenado a las Fuerzas Armadas con sus métodos de tortura y eliminación de los que son considerados como «enemigos internos» y bloqueando las vías no militares de solución a las causas estructurales del conflicto social y armado."

11 Finn, "Colombian Army Escalates Attack on Communities near Tolemaida Military Base."

12 Jini Reddy, "What Colombia's Kogi people can teach us about the environment," *The Guardian*, October 29, 2013, https://www.theguardian.com/sustainable-business/colombia-kogi-environment-destruction.

13 Ibid.

14 Victoria McKenzie, "A Severe Lack of Clean Water Is Killing Indigenous Children in Colombia," *VICE*, April 20, 2015, https://www.vice.com/en_us/article/why-do-indigenous-children-in-colombia-keep-dying-of-thirst-456.

15 International Work Group for Indigenous Affairs, "Colombia: Thousands of indigenous Wayúu children dead from malnutrition," April 4, 2015, www.iwgia.org/news/search-news?news_id=1190.

16 Olimpia Palmar, "Colombia, 2014: 'Los Wayuu Vivimos la Dictadura de la Izquierda y de la Derecha.'" *Liwen Ñi Mapu & Asoc. Colectivo. Red de Noticias e Informacion Sobre Pueblos Indigenas, Derechos Humanos*, April 3, 2014, https://liwenmapu.wordpress.com/2014/04/03/colombia-2014-los-wayuu-vivimos-la-dictadura-de-la-izquierda-y-de-la-derecha/. Translation of the original Spanish by Praba Pilar. The original text states: "muy responsablemente creo que vivimos en la dictadura de Izquierda en Venezuela y en Colombia una dictadura de derecha, que nos ha costado sangre y fuego."

17 Monica Espinosa, "Ese Indiscreto Asunto de la Violencia: Modernidad, Colonialidad y Genocidio en Colombia," In *El giro decolonial: Reflexiones para una diversidad epistémica*, edited by Santiago Castro-Gómez y Ramón Grosfoguel (Bogotá: Siglo del Hombre Editores; Universidad, 2007), 284. Translation of the original Spanish by Praba Pilar. The original text states: "Hasta entrado el siglo XX, se suponía que el Indio, por su misma naturaleza 'ladina y rencorosa,' era un enemigo potencial de la identidad de la nación. En un periodo durante el cual la socio-biología y la eugenesia fueron ideologías muy populares

entre las clases dirigentes y los intelectuales en América Latina, Colombia definió la base de la cultura nacional como "blanca". Se condenó la degeneración racial de la sangre indígena y africana, y se defendió la necesidad de una higiene racial. Los indios encarnaban una especie de fatalidad premoderna."

18 John Harold Giraldo Herrera, "No somos de derecha ni de izquierda: Pedro Antonio Calambás," *Tras la Cola de la Rata*, July 29, 2012, www.traslacoladelarata. com/2012/07/29/no-somos-de-derecha-ni-de-izquierda-pedro-antonio-calambas/. Translation of the original Spanish by Praba Pilar. The original text states "Hoy, después de 35, 40 años, el movimiento indígena, como uno entiende a nivel general, queda por el piso, queda como si fuera enemigo del pueblo colombiano, del campesinado, incluso cualquier persona hoy ve un indígena en la calle y ya es motivo de rechazo, de desprecio."

19 Alison Brysk, *From Tribal Village to Global Village: Indian Rights and International Relations in Latin America* (Palo Alto: Stanford University Press, 2000), 268.

20 Alison Mintoff, "Indigenous Peoples in Colombia: The Threat of Armed Conflict and the Role of Canadian Mining Companies," *University of Toronto Faculty of Law*, http://ihrp .law.utoronto.ca/indigenous-peoples-colombia-threat-armed-conflict-and-role-canadian -mining-companies.

21 Ibid.

22 Ibid.

23 Herrera, "No somos de derecha ni de izquierda: Pedro Antonio Calambás." Translation of the original Spanish by Praba Pilar. The original text states: "nosotros como indígenas siempre hemos tratado de estar separados del tema de los grupos armados, tanto ejército como guerrilla, pero muchas veces los conflictos se dan entre ellos, y siempre salimos involucrados por la guerrilla, concretamente las Farc, y por la fuerza pública…"

24 Stuart Trew, "Free trade and genocide: Colombian activists want Canada to act," *Council of Canadians*, February 10, 2014, http://canadians.org/blog/free-trade-and-genocide-colombian-activists-want-canada-act. In 2015, the Reputation Institute ranked Canada as the most admired country with the best reputation in the world: http://www.ctvnews.ca/canada/canada-ranked-as-most-admired-country-in-the-world-report-1.2470040.

25 Partners FOR the Saskatchewan River Basin, "Human Heritage in the Basin," www .saskriverbasin.ca/images/files/Human%20Heritage%20in%20the%20Basin.pdf.

26 Wanda Nanibush, "Indigenous Peoples & Climate Change With Arthur Manuel & Naomi Klein," February 17, 2016, http://www.idlenomore.ca/ indigenous_peoples_on_climate_change.

27 Mignolo, *The Darker Side of Western Modernity*, 220.

AN AMERICAN EXCEPTION

THE COUNTER-INSURRECTIONARY
FUNCTION OF THE COLOR LINE

Ben Brucato

In Thomas Edsall's *New York Times* editorial, "Why Don't the Poor Rise Up?" he provides two categories of explanations for the absence of uprising.[1] First, to explain that poverty is no longer "grueling," he cites family planning and cheap consumer products as evidence. In this explanation, we still collectively experience the so-called affluent society that emerged in the post-war era and was expanded to include some non-whites in the wake of some successes of the Civil Rights Movement. This explanation shares some similarity with Ronald Inglehart's "post-materialist hypothesis," that in societies where basic needs are assured, citizens tend to pursue quality-of-life improvements and expand policies that pursue long-term goals and values that are more abstract than material.[2] Broadening support for "sustainability" is consistent with this hypothesis, as populations are supposedly uniting behind ensuring the continuation of a good life that is guaranteed for most—if not all—citizens. Of course, inequality persists among these affluent, comfortable, and idealistic citizens, but the lower threshold is raised enough that very few are struggling with precariousness and desperation. Freed from necessity, citizens no longer see being freed from exploitation and depravation as their cause, but rather to ensure that the benefits yielded through consumer choices are broadly shared. Moreover, they are concerned that these consumer choices have low environmental impacts so their descendants for many generations may enjoy and expand on these choices.

Edsall offers a second explanation: individualization has found citizens isolated from one another and thus underprepared to act collectively.[3] Lacking durable community organizations and social spaces, citizens retreat to social media where they are comforted to exist in an online echo chamber. Apparently, the poor are bowling alone in a post-materialist society. Now at the end of history, Edsall's bourgeoisified poor fail to issue demands in public space, but air grievances on Facebook, either resigning in cynicism, or feeling sufficiently relieved at having their concerns heard among their "friends." In the rarest of instances when the poor do issue demands, they reference only procedural issues or aim to ensure broader inclusion of diverse populations in existing institutions. What these newly included—and, still, relatively deprived—populations might do once included is, at most, an afterthought.

This conservative, Poli Sci 101 redux not only would seem unimpeachable to most *NYT* readers, but has an air of truthiness. Despite recent cutbacks in social welfare, a social safety net established in the New Deal era has grown to ensure most of the working class have access to housing, food, and healthcare. Over the past few decades, even the poorest Americans have greater access to consumer goods and the so-called digital divide has shrunk. Though income and wealth inequality has emerged as a major public concern since the emergence of Occupy Wall Street and the related Occupy Movement, expanded access for racial minorities to higher education and white-collar employment have been and remain important issues, typical of a society that has not only prioritized correcting historic racial and gender inequalities, but more importantly believes itself economically capable of doing so. Furthermore, any lack of significant rebellion among those with the lowest incomes and the least wealth would suggest they have something to lose and not enough to gain. Their lives are comfortable enough. After all, many of them have cell phones, Internet access, cable television, and name-brand clothing! They can access social media and share selfies in their fashionable attire. Unlike those in truly poor communities, they are not surrounded by death and disease.

American Exceptionalism

Edsall's question is consistent with an intellectual tradition often referred to as "American exceptionalism." What is missing from his formulation, and perhaps the reason why the answer is driven toward such conservative conclusions, is because of a crucial category shift: popular commentators and scholars in the tradition of American exceptionalism are typically concerned with understanding the political activity of *the working class*, rather than with that of *the poor*.[4] Over nearly two centuries, this intellectual tradition has been concerned with the absence of an enduring, institutionalized working class movement, movements that are present in other Western democracies.

Typical of political discourse in this century, in Edsall's formulation, class conflict is replaced by "inequality." Analyses concerned with inequality—more precisely: socio-economic stratification—deal mostly with income and wealth distributions. This approach is fundamentally different from a class analysis that proceeds from accounting for a population's economic function, or its relation to the means of production. Class analysis is concerned with the antagonism between the bourgeoisie (or capitalists, those who own the means of production and who accumulate value through exploited labor) and the working class (those who produce value through their labor). The working class *resists* the exploitation of their labor power, and the bourgeoisie *represses* this resistance. In a classic Marxist class analysis, this antagonism is the motive force of significant social change: it is the engine of history.

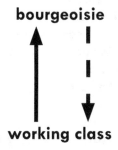

bourgeoisie

working class

Figure 1: *Marxist formulation of the antagonism between the bourgeoisie and the working class. Resistance from the working class is directed at the bourgeoisie. Repression from the bourgeoisie is directed at the working class.*

Few American exceptionalists are Marxists—some are rather anti-Marxist—but all have attempted to explain the factors that have successfully diminished class antagonism to maintain the status quo.[5] Like Marx, American exceptionalists have offered a range of explanations for why the working class in the United States was not as developed, organized, class-conscious, and radical in comparison to the working class in other advanced capitalist countries.

Commentators before Edsall included everyone from Alexis de Tocqueville, who believed the egalitarian features of U.S. politics lessened the need for working class movements, to Newt Gingrich, who believes the religious character of U.S. American life creates greater social unity.[6] Whether times of abnormal hardship were relieved by significant geographic mobility or mitigated through extreme violent repression of the working class or, if in comparison to other countries, income mobility or wages were higher, earlier exceptionalist hypotheses have tended to treat the working class as a mostly homogeneous population.

Reference to "the poor" as a population category suggests selecting from among the working class those who are compensated least, and perhaps among them those who have accumulated the least in savings and the most in debt. The trouble with this approach is that it obscures how one is positioned within the working class and overlooks their essentially antagonistic relationship with capitalists. In doing so, this approach joins other tendencies in exceptionalist commentary that Michael Goldfield shows has neglected mass mobilization, social movements, labor organizations, and radicalism.[7] Furthermore, in dividing up the working class, it looks to a dividing line that is unhelpful if the goal is to understand rebellion generally, or resistance to exploitation and domination more specifically. The focus on "the poor" as an income or wealth category diminishes needed attention to racial division among the working class, a fracture that has been fundamental to politics in the United States since the colonial era. More importantly, this move is itself a symptom of the normalization of whiteness, a means by which race is ignored through the invisibility basic to a color-blind era.

A Divided Working Class

In his study of labor in the United States, rather than asking why "the poor" have not often or successfully rebelled, Goldfield explores the causes for the exceptional weakness of labor in the United States.[8] As he establishes, "the key to understanding and solving the old conundrum of American exceptionalism—the peculiarities of American politics and the political weakness of its working class—is the interplay between class and race."[9] Taking influence from W.E.B. Du Bois and David Roediger, Goldfield attributes the weaknesses of the American working class to its division along the color line. He explains:

> Race has been the central ingredient, not merely in undermining solidarity when broad struggles have erupted, not merely in dividing workers, but also in providing an alternative white

male nonclass worldview and structure of identity that have exerted their force during both stable and confrontational times. It has provided the everyday framework in which labor has been utilized, controlled, and exploited by those who have employed it.[10]

It is not enough to consider race in terms of identity and worldview. Race is also distinct from culture, ethnicity, and biological difference, and it is more than a simple social construction.[11] Instead, race references a political category determined through the institutionalized administration of advantage and disadvantage. In the United States, two distinct political categories—"white" and "not-white"—denote who belongs to and who is excluded from the *demos*, forming what Joel Olson calls a "white democracy."[12] Du Bois referred to the advantages conferred to whites as "public and psychological wages," and Roediger as "the wages of whiteness."[13] The "nonclass worldview" Goldfield discusses is a product of psychological wages, coming from a personal sense of superiority and a lived experience of greater self-determination, both basic to white identity. These wages are public in that they determine who can collectively determine the affairs of their community.

Race is not just class tinged with color.[14] In fragmenting the working class, it builds a cross-class alliance between the white working class and the ruling class. Olson explains, "The cross-class alliance is the class foundation of the white democracy."[15] It has maintained stability for the wage system in the United States by ensuring political interests would be united by racial position rather than by class.[16] Through this alliance of working class whites with the bourgeoisie, white identity was forged and solidified, and white workers attained a unique—and *privileged*—relationship with the state.[17] The security of the U.S. American bourgeoisie has historically depended on white workers acting against their class interests and instead on the basis of their racial interests.

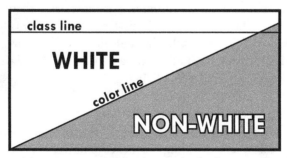

Figure 2: *The interaction of the class and color binaries that found the cross-class alliance.*[18]

The Historic Construction of the Color Line

Goldfield, Roediger, and many others (e.g., Theodore W. Allen, Noel Ignatiev) have provided elaborate analyses of key historic transitions in the United States and how these contributed to the construction and reconstruction of race.[19] There is neither the space nor the need to recount these in detail. Nonetheless, a brief recapitulation can help us to see how the color line was fabricated and refashioned, and what this means for the suppression of rebellion in the United States.

In 1619, when the first Africans arrived on the continent in bondage and were traded as chattel slaves, there was not yet a developed idea of race, and no concept of a white race.[20] In colonial Virginia during 1676, Bacon's Rebellion showed the potential for cross-racial rebellion to topple an emerging capitalist rule. The colonial administrators and early capitalists were faced with a fundamental problem regarding who would police labor. It was necessary that one part of the working class be charged with regulating the other, while remaining laborers themselves.[21] Within only decades, a concept of race and whiteness was born. Race was codified through policies like the Virginia Slave Codes of 1705, which responded to cross-racial rebellions and established a racial order in which the lowest status white person was above the highest status Black person.

This racial order was to be policed through slave patrols in the most populous colonies, particularly where enslaved Africans were becoming a majority population. The Slave Codes were crucial in establishing these first modern police forces in the first decade of the eighteenth century, and in this way, policing and race were co-productive institutions in the colonies.[22] Whites—both free and indentured—were required to police enslaved Africans, regulating movement on and between plantations. These slave patrols were initially concerned with capturing and punishing escaped slaves, but by 1721 they were charged with preventing insurrection.[23] Poor and indentured Europeans from ethnic groups and national origins that categorized them as non-white were involved in policing Blacks, and this was a crucial means by which they established their racial loyalties. In the mid-nineteenth century, fugitive slave laws required all whites—including those in states where slavery was abolished—to engage in compulsory policing of Blacks.

Olson calls the colonial period through the 1960s the *Herrenvolk* era, referencing the exclusion of non-whites from official governance.[24] During this time, whites had formal political standing in the form of citizenship, which was denied to all others. Standing reconciled political equality and freedom with the reality of slavery and the exclusion of non-whites from citizenship, thereby building white domination into U.S. American democracy.[25] During the *Herrenvolk* era, the essential principle was "democracy for whites, tyranny for everyone else."[26]

Government was crucially implicated by racializing citizenship as a perk of race, rather than of wealth.[27] Blacks were formally denied full citizenship. Citizenship was an exclusive legal standing for whites, but it was also symbolically defined by the paradigm of whiteness: to be white was to be a citizen, non-white a non-citizen. To be clear, white skin and European heritage was not a guarantee of inclusion, as immigrants like the Irish had to "work towards whiteness"—demonstrating their commitment to the cross-class alliance and often enforcing the color line with violence.[28] Prior to the abolition of slavery with the passage of the 13th Amendment in 1865 following the end of the Civil War, to be white was to be protected against being owned as property. In the following decades, both professional police forces and volunteer white citizens regulated segregation and maintained a racialized conception of public order that identified Blackness and criminality.[29] White citizen vigilantism is remembered for its wanton brutality, exemplified in lynching, and yet this was only the extreme face of the everyday intensive regulation of Blacks by white citizens.[30]

It was not until the passage of civil and voting rights legislation in 1964 and 1965—gains won by the Civil Rights and Black Liberation movements—that *de jure* racial political standing was terminated. Olson calls the following period the color-blind era.[31] Though overt racial domination and segregation remains, the color line now functions through *normalization*: white supremacy consists of probabilistic advantages that are tacit and covert, not guaranteed, codified, and persistently visible.[32] Emancipated from government policy, race is cast into the private realm. When race is acknowledged at all, it has the appearance of political neutrality and is treated as a product of personal biases. In the letter of the law, racial discrimination is produced by individuals and experienced by individuals.[33] Color-blind racism persists where whites nominally advocate racial equality while nonetheless defending and securing their privileged status.[34] Absent formal foundation in law and policy, white supremacy is conceived as prepolitical, with racial disparities explained as "the 'natural outcome' of ordinary practices and individual choices."[35]

Figure 3: *A working class fragmented along the color line and codified through racialized citizenship interrupts class-based antagonism. The repression by the bourgeoisie is directed mostly at Black proletarians, as the cross-class loyalties of white workers assures the bourgeoisie its repressive energies can be concentrated toward non-whites (especially Blacks) to efficiently maintain social* *security. That of white citizens supplements this repressive activity. Furthermore, white citizens, sheltering the state and the capitalist class against rebellion, mitigate the resistance of Blacks.*

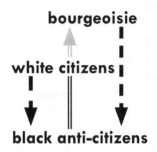

The concept of race and the practices of the state and white citizens to maintain racial domination have been fluid, admitting new members to the white race, and shifting according to political-economic conditions. What remains consistent is that by conferring advantage to one race and subordinated status to all others, race functions to encourage political docility and economic utility from whites and non-whites alike.[36] Through the cross-class alliance among whites, working class whites have functioned as auxiliaries to the bourgeoisie. Often, instead of joining the resistance of other workers, whites either actively resisted them or called upon the state to suppress resistance.

Just as whiteness defined the paradigm for those on one side of the color line, Blackness has remained the paradigm for the other. Though race encourages docility, Blacks harbor an essentially insurrectionary quality, sometimes latent, and at other times active. Though Blacks were denied citizenship, they were seen as *anti-citizens*, "enemies rather than the members of the social compact," who both threaten and consolidate that compact.[37] Defining Blacks as anti-citizens suggests a designation beyond Blackness and criminality, to instead position Blackness as a fundamental threat to social security. This identification persists, such that racial domination exists not only in the form of exploited labor, but also as a preventative measure against this segment of the working class that harbors insurrectionary potential, one absent among white workers due to their cross-class alliance. As Roediger shows, the racial order has been dependent upon maintaining a watchful eye on signs of resistance and preparedness to act on perceived threats.

Uprising and Repression, Today

Edsall's *NYT* editorial was published on June 24, 2015, almost a year after Ferguson, Missouri experienced rebellions that lasted for months, with multiple peaks in property destruction and open confrontation with police. This rebellion emerged beginning on August 9, 2014 almost exclusively from the Black residents of the hypersegregated suburb of St. Louis where and when Michael Brown was killed by Ferguson Police Officer Darren Wilson earlier that day. The rebels suffered violent repression by militarized police from Ferguson and St. Louis. Protesters joined the rebels across the nation—both physically and rhetorically—in confronting the brutality of the police. Within a week, police operations were under scrutiny by some in media and government, prompting Missouri Governor Jay Nixon to take control of policing the Ferguson rebellion.

The killing of Michael Brown and the Ferguson uprising led to the re-emergence and rapid national growth of the #BlackLivesMatter movement, an amorphous, decentralized movement led by Blacks, and with distinct leadership by Black women. It is crucial to acknowledge, however, that this movement launched after the 2012 killing of a Black teenager, Trayvon Martin, by George Zimmerman, a white citizen acting in his capacity as a private citizen and neighborhood watchman. This movement effectively linked professional police with volunteer policing and vigilantism by white citizens that together claim the lives of hundreds of non-whites every year in the United States.

Rebellion broke out in communities across the country confronting ongoing violence and terrorism from the state and white citizens against non-whites. As the Ferguson uprising continued, subsequent killings of Blacks and other people of color by police provoked protest—from Staten Island to Cleveland, and from Los Angeles to Baltimore. Another momentous example was in April 2015, when Baltimore, Maryland erupted in weeks of civil unrest following the killing of Freddie Gray by officers of the Baltimore Police Department. This rebellion seized upon the broad attention to and the momentum of the #BlackLivesMatter movement. It also relied on decades of radical organizing in this extremely segregated city. Within weeks, the rebels caused roughly $9 million in property damage, almost exclusively directed at as many as 350 businesses—only two private residences were damaged.[38] When rioters targeted businesses—almost exclusively owned by outsiders to their community and many by multinational corporations—they linked the capitalist expropriation of their community with the routine surveillance, harassment, and violence of police. These communities, while deprived of legitimate and productive economic activity, are also administered under threat of police brutality or imprisonment.

The continued mobilization and momentum of the #BlackLivesMatter movement captured the attention of various publics, alternative and mainstream media, community activists, and professional politicians. For two years, demands by activists and rebels increased attention to racial disparities in policing, sentencing, and incarceration, leading to policy reform initiatives by local, state, and federal actors. Concerns about policing and mass incarceration showed some signs of crossing historically reliable racial lines.[39] Following protests and rebellions, the Department of Justice opened 23 investigations and entered 11 consent decrees requiring reforms in Chicago, Baltimore, Cleveland, and other cities.[40]

These rebellions, and associated successful political organizing, represent the insurrectionary potential of the Black proletariat against the racial order. Both government and white citizens responded. In many cities, as in Ferguson, protests and rebellions following police brutality and killings have been met with militarized police responses. Moreover, organizers and leaders have been targeted by government surveillance that recalls the Federal Bureau of Investigation's (FBI) Counter Intelligence Program (COINTELPRO) that targeted the Civil Rights, Black Liberation, and other radical movements from the late-1950s through the mid-1970s.[41] White politicians, citizens, and media commentators called upon government to restore order and either rationalized or openly endorsed violent police responses. Shortly after the Ferguson uprising began, on-duty police officers in Ferguson, St. Louis, and elsewhere wore bracelets that read "I Am Darren Wilson."[42] The hashtag #IAmDarrenWilson initially trended on social media, with white citizens online and in the streets countering protesters. As #BlackLivesMatter increased in popularity, police and their white citizen supporters responded with #BlueLivesMatter, referencing the common color of police uniforms.

Activists aligned with #BlackLivesMatter protested at Donald J. Trump's presidential campaign rallies, where Trump urged his supporters to physically attack them.[43] Trump encouraged the crowd and police, who together accosted activists of color. Trump was openly critical of the #BlackLivesMatter movement, accusing them of promoting cop killing, and responded by affirming "Blue Lives Matter."[44] Central to the Trump campaign was a revived reference to "law and order," that recalled the anxieties of white citizens in the 1970s and 1980s over "inner city crime" and "civil unrest."[45] Trump claimed the United States is ravaged by "race riots on our streets on a monthly basis," referencing rebellions in Ferguson and Baltimore as indicative of a breakdown in social order.[46] His campaign was a direct challenge to the momentum behind demands for criminal justice reform, instead insisting on strengthening police power.

The Trump campaign bolstered surging white populism, building on links between right wing politicians and political action committees on the one hand, with grassroots conservative movements associated with the Tea Party and organized white supremacist groups, on the other. These political tendencies grew in size and resolve in response to the entrenchment of affirmative action in the 1990s and of multiculturalism throughout governmental, corporate, and educational institutions. White anxieties over perceived loss of entitlements were amplified when in 2008 a Black man, Barack Obama, was elected to the highest office in the United States government. Even though wealth inequality grew during the Obama Administration, and even though the administration deported more migrants than any before it, the worry that the state could be used to advance the interests of non-whites persisted. These anxieties combined with increased economic precarity, often linked to the financial crises of 2007 and 2008 and the enduring recession that still followed during the Trump campaign. The causes of increased precarity are many—too many to enumerate here—but this economic reality amplified fears among whites that their wages of whiteness have diminishing purchasing power.

White voters in nearly all other demographic categories solidly fell behind Trump.[47] Trump bolstered white populism with his campaign not only with promises to restore and defend order against "inner city crime," to thwart rebellions led by "thugs," to ban Muslims from entering the country, and to deport millions of Mexican and other non-white immigrants. His very style of communication represented the rejection of liberal civility and an attack on "political correctness." Trump garnered enthusiastic support from whites—not despite but because he embodied the symbol of the bully. In recent decades, anti-bullying and anti-harassment efforts from primary to higher education, and from corporate human resources officers to government bureaucrats have targeted frank expressions of racism and sexual harassment. Trump's embrace of the position of the bully and open bragging about sexually harassing and assaulting women symbolized to whites and men that they need no longer cloak their white male supremacy. If affirmative action and Obama represented the political symbol of the advancement of non-whites, Trump's bully persona represented an attack on their socio-cultural analog. It consolidated white hysteria over "trigger warnings" and "social justice warriors," allowing whites to boldly move from demands to "stop talking about race" in a "post-racial society" to relishing in the open expression of their shared sense of superiority.

Immediately after his election in November 2016, Trump tapped open racist and war-on-crime fanatic Jeff Sessions to serve as Attorney General, a symbolic affirmation of Trump's promise to squash the demands for change in policing and mass incarceration.[48] Trump selected white supremacist Steve Bannon to lead his transition team. White supremacist organizations, including the Ku Klux Klan and groups associated with the Alt Right movement, celebrated Trump's victory. Within two weeks of his election, white citizens—emboldened in their racism and xenophobia—committed at least 700 racially motivated attacks on non-whites.[49] From the highest office of the nation to individual white citizens, Trump's campaign represents a counter-insurgency against the rising status and political movement of non-whites. It seeks to set back gains from affirmative action and to halt reforms to policing and incarceration. The call for law and order will once again strengthen the resolve to solidify the racial order of white supremacy through the economic policy and the violent repression of police.

Conclusion

When Edsall asks why the poor are not rising up, he overlooks these major eruptions from Black proletarians that were everywhere on the public agenda as he wrote his editorial. His explanations for the lack of rebellion are not only standard fare among contemporary liberal commentators; his oversight is typical of the normalization of whiteness as the paradigm of all politics. This maneuver relies both on a classic identification of political activity with the behavior of citizens and on the exclusion of non-whites from citizenship, once legal (*de jure*) and now through norms (*de facto*). Edsall's question produces such conservative answers because he fails to recognize the historic motive force in American politics as a consequence of class antagonism and the fragmentation of the working class by the color line. Furthermore, by avoiding these uprisings, explanations like Edsall's reproduce the identification of Blackness with anti-citizenship, in that these rebellions are defined as being outside of the political realm.

The racial order of white supremacy and the class domination of capitalism are constantly threatened by the insurrectionary potential of anti-citizens. This potential is kept at bay by the state through the violent repression of police and the administration of poverty and segregation.[50] It is also resisted by white citizens who not only refuse cross-racial alliances to advance their interests as an economic class, but also through articulation of their cross-class alliance by mandating state violence against non-whites and active participation in racist terror.

While a successful insurrection by Black proletarians is conceivable, fundamental to the stability of capitalist domination in the United States has been the critical role played by the white working class. A break in the cross-class alliance by a significant part of the white working class could make whiteness an unreliable guarantor of loyalty to the existing order, and provoke a crisis within it. Noel Ignatiev and John Garvey ask: "What if the white skin lost its usefulness as a badge of loyalty?" They explain that the end to the institutionalized political administration of the privileges of whiteness is ensured by "a minority [of whites] willing to undertake outrageous acts of provocation."[51] The flames of white nationalist populism have been fanned by a social movement that unified behind, and fortified with, the Trump campaign, just when a popular, decentralized movement with broad participation by people of color has sustained and grown for over two years. While the white working class has been reasonably credited for Trump's successful campaign, potential remains for enough among them to break ranks from the cross-class alliance and engage in "outrageous acts" in solidarity with non-whites.

Endnotes

1   Thomas Edsall, "Why Don't The Poor Rise Up?," *The New York Times*, June 24, 2015, http://www.nytimes.com/2015/06/24/opinion/why-dont-the-poor-rise-up.html.
2   Inglehart, Ronald F. "Changing values among western publics from 1970 to 2006." *West European Politics* 31, 1–2 (2008): 130–146.
3   Edsall, "Why Don't The Poor Rise Up."
4   Michael Goldfield, *The Color of Politics: Race and the Mainsprings of American Politics* (New York, NY: The New Press, 1997).
5   Ibid.
6   Ibid.
7   Ibid.
8   Ibid.
9   Ibid., 30.
10 Ibid.
11 Joel Olson, *The Abolition of White Democracy* (Minneapolis, MN: University of Minneapolis Press, 2004), 3–9.
12 Ibid.
13 W.E.B. Du Bois, *Black Reconstruction in America: Toward a History of the Part Which Black Folk Played in the Attempt to Reconstruct Democracy in America, 1860–1880* (New York, NY: Oxford University Press, 2007); David R. Roediger, *The Wages of Whiteness: Race and the Making of the American Working Class* (New York, NY: Verso, 1991).
14 Ben Brucato, "Fabricating The Color Line in a White Democracy: From Slave Catchers to Petty Sovereigns," *Theoria: A Journal of Social and Political Theory* 61, no. 141 (2014): 30–54.
15 Olson, *The Abolition of White Democracy*, 16.
16 Ibid., 68.
17 Theodore W. Allen, *The Invention of the White Race: Racial Oppression and Social Control* (New York: Verso, 1994).
18 Adapted from Joel Olson, "Whiteness and the 99%," *Bring The Ruckus*, October 20, 2011, http://www.bringtheruckus.org/?q=node%2F146.
19 Goldfield, *The Color of Politics*; Roediger, *The Wages of Whiteness*; Theodore W. Allen, *The Invention of the White Race: Racial Oppression and Social Control* (New York: Verso, 1994); Noel Ignatiev, *How The Irish Became White* (New York, NY: Routledge, 1996).
20 Allen, *The Invention of the White Race*.
21 Noel Ignatiev, *Introduction to the United States: An Autonomist Political History* (Denver, CO: Final Conflict Publishing, 1992).
22 Brucato, "The Fabrication of the Color Line in a White Democracy."

23 Ibid. See also Sally E. Hadden, *Slave Patrols: Law and Violence in Virginia and the Carolinas* (Cambridge, MA: Harvard University Press, 2001).

24 Olson, *The Abolition of White Democracy.*

25 Ibid., 44.

26 Ibid., 71.

27 Ibid., 44.

28 David R. Roediger, *Working Toward Whiteness: How America's Immigrants Became White: The Strange Journey from Ellis Island to the Suburbs* (New York, NY: Basic Books, 2005).

29 Khalil Gibran Muhammad, *The Condemnation of Blackness* (Cambridge, MA: Harvard University Press, 2011).

30 Brucato, "The Fabrication of the Color Line in a White Democracy."

31 Olson, *The Abolition of White Democracy.*

32 Ibid.

33 Freeman, Alan David. "Legitimizing racial discrimination through antidiscrimination law: A critical review of supreme court doctrine," *Minnesota Law Review* 62 (1977): 1049.

34 Olson, *The Abolition of White Democracy.*

35 Ibid., 74.

36 Ibid.

37 Roediger, *The Wages of Whiteness*, 57; Olson, *The Abolition of White Democracy*, 43.

38 Yvonne Wenger, "Damage to businesses from Baltimore rioting estimated at about $9 million," *The Washington Post*, May 13, 2015, https://www.washingtonpost.com/local/damage-to-businesses-from-baltimore-rioting-estimated-at-9-million/2015/05/13/5848c3fe-f9a8-11e4-a13c-193b1241d51a_story.html.

39 Racial disparities in public perceptions of police have persisted for over a decade. See Frank Newport, "Black and White Attitudes Toward Police," *Gallup*, August 14, 2014, http://www.gallup.com/poll/175088/gallup-review-black-white-attitudes-toward-police.aspx. Though confidence in policing remains high, it has declined in recent years for all racial groups. It is important to note, however, that the smallest decline is observed in whites and the greatest in Blacks. See Jeffrey M. Jones, "In U.S., Confidence in Police Lowest in 22 Years," *Gallup*, June 19, 2015, http://www.gallup.com/poll/183704/confidence-police-lowest-years.aspx.

40 Eli Hager, Alysia Santo and Simone Weichselbaum, "8 Ways Jeff Sessions Could Change Criminal Justice," *The Marshall Project*, November 18, 2016, https://www.themarshallproject.org/2016/11/18/8-ways-jeff-sessions-could-change-criminal-justice.

41 Julia Craven, "Surveillance Of Black Lives Matter Movement Recalls COINTELPRO," *Huffington Post*, August 19, 2015, http://www.huffingtonpost.com/entry/surveillance-black-lives-matter-cointelpro_us_55d49dc6e4b055a6dab24008.

42 Molly Hennessy-Fiske, "Ferguson police barred from wearing 'I am Darren Wilson' bracelets," *The Los Angeles Times*, September 26, 2014, http://www.latimes.com/nation/nationnow/la-na-nn-ferguson-police-i-am-darren-wilson-bracelets-20140926-story.html.

43 Jeremy Diamond, "Trump on protester: 'Maybe he should have been roughed up,'" *CNN*, November 23, 2015, http://www.cnn.com/2015/11/22/politics/donald-trump-black-lives-matter-protester-confrontation/.

44 Perry Bacon Jr., "Trump and Other Conservatives Embrace 'Blue Lives Matter' Movement," *NBC News*, July 23, 2016, http://www.nbcnews.com/storyline/2016-conventions/trump-other-conservatives-embrace-blue-lives-matter-movement-n615156.

45 Bryce Covert, "Donald Trump's Imaginary Inner Cities," *The Nation*, November 7, 2016, https://www.thenation.com/article/donald-trumps-imaginary-inner-cities/.

46 Joel Feldmen, "Trump Says We're Having 'Race Riots' on a Monthly Basis," *Mediaite*, October 3, 2016, http://www.mediaite.com/tv/trump-says-were-having

-race-riots-on-a-monthly-basis/.

47 CNN, "Exit Polls," *CNN Politics*, November 23, 2016, http://www.cnn.com/election/
    results/exit-polls.

48 Hager, Santo and Weichselbaum, "8 Ways Jeff Sessions Could Change Criminal Justice."

49 Carter Evans, "Hate, harassment incidents spike since Trump elec-
    tion," *CBS News*, November 19, 2016, http://www.cbsnews.com/news/
    hate-harassment-incidents-spike-since-donald-trump-election/.

50 Brucato, "The Fabrication of the Color Line in a White Democracy."

51 Noel Ignatiev and John Garvey, "When Does the Unreasonable Act Make Sense?," in *Race
    Traitor* (New York, NY: Routledge, 1996), 35–37.

UNTIL WE WIN

BLACK LABOR AND LIBERATION IN THE DISPOSABLE ERA

Kali Akuno

SINCE THE REBELLION IN FERGUSON, MISSOURI IN AUGUST 2014, BLACK PEOple throughout the United States have been grappling with a number of critical questions, such as, why are Black people being hunted and killed every 28 hours or more by various operatives of the law?[1] Why don't Black people seem to matter to this society? And what can and must we do to end these attacks and liberate ourselves? There are concrete answers to these questions, answers that are firmly grounded in the capitalist dynamics that structure the brutal European settler-colonial project we live in, and how Afrikan people have historically been positioned within it.

The Value of Black Life

There was a time in the United States Empire when Afrikan people, aka Black people, were deemed to be extremely valuable to the "American project," when our lives, as it is said, "mattered." This "time" was the era of chattel slavery, when the labor provided by Afrikan people was indispensable to the

61

settler-colonial enterprise, accounting for nearly half of the commodified value produced within its holdings and exchanged in "domestic" and international markets.[2] Our ancestors were held and regarded as prize horses or bulls, something to be treated with a degree of "care" (i.e. enough to ensure that they were able to work and reproduce their labor, and produce value for their enslavers) because of their centrality to the processes of material production.

What mattered was Black labor power and how it could be harnessed and controlled, not Afrikan humanity. Afrikan humanity did not matter—it had to be denied in order to create and sustain the social rationale and systemic dynamics that allowed for the commodification of human beings. These "dynamics" included armed militias and slave patrols, iron-clad non-exception social clauses like the "one-drop" rule, the slave codes, vagrancy laws, and a complex mix of laws and social customs all aimed at oppressing, controlling, and scientifically exploiting Black life and labor to the maximum degree. This systemic need served the variants of white supremacy, colonial subjugation, and imperialism that capitalism built to govern social relations in the United States. All the fundamental systems created to control Afrikan life and labor between the 17th and 19th centuries are still in operation today, despite a few surface moderations, and serve the same basic functions.

The correlation between capital accumulation (earning a profit) and the value of Black life to the overall system have remained consistent throughout the history of the U.S. settler-colonial project, despite shifts in production regimes (from agricultural, to industrial, to service, and finance oriented), and how Black labor was deployed. The more value (profits) Black labor produces, the more Black lives are valued. The less value (profits) Black people produce, the less Black lives are valued. When Black lives are valued, they are secured enough to allow for their reproduction (at the very least), and when they are not they can and have readily been discarded and disposed of. This is the basic equation and social dynamic regarding the value of Black life to U.S. society.

The Age of Disposability

We are living and struggling through a transformative era of the global capitalist system. Over the past forty years, the expansionary dynamics of capitalism have produced a truly coordinated system of resource acquisition and controls: easily exploitable and cheap labor, and production, marketing, and consumption on a global scale. The increasingly automated and computerized dynamics of this expansion has resulted in millions, if not billions, of people being displaced through two broad processes: one, from "traditional" methods of life sustaining production (mainly farming), and the other from their "traditional" or ancestral homelands and regions (with people being forced to move to large cities and "foreign" territories to survive). As the International Labor Organization (ILO) recently reported in its *World Employment and Social Outlook 2015* paper, this displacement renders millions to structurally regulated surplus or expendable statuses.[3]

Capitalist logic does not allow for surplus populations to be sustained for long. They either must be reabsorbed into the value producing mechanisms of the system, or disposed of. Events over the past twenty (or more) years, such as the forced separation of Yugoslavia,[4] the genocide in Burundi and Rwanda,[5] the never-ending civil and international wars in Zaire/Congo and central Afrikan region,[6] and the mass displacement of farmers in Mexico[7] clearly indicate that the system does not possess the current capacity to absorb the surplus populations and maintain its equilibrium.

The dominant actors in the global economy—multinational corporations, the trans-nationalist capitalist class, and state managers—are in crisis mode trying to figure out how to best manage this massive surplus in a politically justifiable (but expedient) manner. This incapacity to manage crisis caused by capitalism itself is witnessed by numerous examples of haphazard intervention at managing the rapidly expanding number of displaced peoples, such as:

- The ongoing global food crisis (which started in the mid-2000's) in which millions are unable to afford basic food stuffs because of rising prices and climate-induced production shortages;[8]
- The corporate driven displacement of hundreds of millions of farmers and workers in the Global South (particularly in Africa and parts of Southeast Asia);[9]
- Military responses (including the building of fortified walls and blockades) to the massive migrant crisis confronting the governments of the United States, Western Europe, Australia, Malaysia, Indonesia, Singapore, etc.;[10]
- The corporate-driven attempt to confront climate change almost exclusively by market (commodity) mechanisms;[11]
- The scramble for domination of resources and labor, and the escalating number of imperialist-facilitated armed conflicts and attempts at regime change in Africa, Asia (including Central Asia), and Eastern Europe.[12]

More starkly, direct disposal experiments are also deepening and expanding against Afrikans in Colombia, Haitians in the Dominican Republic, Sub-Saharan Afrikans in Libya, Indigenous peoples in the Andean region, the Palestinians in Gaza, Adivasis in India, the Rohingyas in Myanmar and Bangladesh, and the list goes on.

Accompanying all of this is the ever-expanding level of xenophobia and violence targeted at migrants on a world scale, pitting the unevenly pacified and rewarded victims of imperialism against one another, as has been witnessed in places such as South Africa over the last decade, where attacks on migrant workers and communities have become a mainstay of political activity.

The capitalist system is demonstrating, day by day, that it no longer possesses the managerial capacity to absorb newly dislocated and displaced populations into the international working class (or proletariat), and it is becoming harder and harder for the international ruling class to sustain the provision of material benefits that have traditionally been awarded to the most loyal subjects of capitalism's global empire, namely the "native" working classes in Western Europe and settlers in projects like the United States, Canada, and Australia. When the capitalist system cannot expand and absorb, it must preserve itself by shifting towards "correction and contraction"—excluding and, if necessary, disposing of all the surpluses that cannot be absorbed or consumed at a profit. We are now clearly in an era of correction and contraction that will have genocidal consequences for the surplus populations of the world if left unaddressed. This dynamic brings us back to the U.S. and the crisis of jobs, mass incarceration, and the escalating number of extrajudicial police killings confronting Black people.

The Black Surplus Challenge/Problem and Barriers to Uprising

Afrikan, or Black, people in the United States are one of these surplus populations. Black people are no longer a central force in the productive process of the United States, in large part because those manufacturing industries that have not completely offshored their production no longer need large quantities of relatively cheap labor due to automation advances. At the same time, agricultural industries have been largely mechanized, or require even cheaper sources of super-exploited labor from migrant workers, to ensure profits.

Various campaigns to reduce the cost of Black labor in the U.S. have fundamentally failed, due to the militant resistance of Black labor and the ability of Black working class communities to "make ends meet" by engaging in and receiving survival-level resources from the underground economy, which has grown exponentially in the Black community since the 1970s. The underground economy has exploded worldwide since the 1970s, due to the growth of unregulated "grey market" service economies and the explosion of the illicit drug trade. Its expansion has created considerable "market distortions" throughout the world, as it has created new value chains, circuits of accumulation, and financing streams that helped "cook the books" of banking institutions worldwide and helped finance capital become the dominant faction of capital in the 1980s and 1990s.

The social dimensions of white supremacy regarding consumer "comfort," "trust," and "security" seriously constrain the opportunities of Black workers in service industries and retail work, as significant numbers of non-Black consumers are uncomfortable receiving direct services from Black people (save for things like custodial and security services).[13] These are the root causes of what many are calling the "Black jobs crisis." The lack of jobs for Black people translates into a lack of need for Black people, which equates into the wholesale devaluation of Black life. And anything without value in the capitalist system is disposable.

The declining "value" of Black life is not a new problem—Black people have constituted an escalating problem in search of a solution for the U.S. ruling class since the 1960s. Although the U.S. labor market started to have trouble absorbing Afrikan workers in the 1950s, the surplus problem didn't reach crisis proportions until the late 1960s, when the Black Liberation Movement started to critically impact industrial production with demands for more jobs, training, and open access to skilled and supervisorial work (which were "occupied" by white seniority, protected workers), higher wages, direct representation (through instruments like the League of Revolutionary Black Workers), constant strikes, work stoppages, other forms of industrial action, militant resistance to state and non-state forces of repression, and hundreds of urban rebellions.

This resistance occurred while the international regime of integrated production, trade management, financial integration, and currency convergence instituted by the United States after WWII, commonly called the Bretton Woods regime, fully matured and ushered in the present phase of globalization. This regime obliterated most exclusivist (or protectionist) production regimes and allowed international capital to scour the world for cheaper sources of labor and raw materials without fear of inter-imperialist rivalry and interference (as predominated during earlier periods). Thus, Black labor was hitting its stride just as capital was finding secure ways to eliminate its dependence upon it (and Western unionized labor more generally) by starting to reap the rewards of its post-WWII mega-global investments (largely centered in Western Europe, Australia, Japan, South Korea, and Taiwan).

One reward of these mega-global investments for U.S. capital was that it reduced the scale and need for domestic industrial production, which limited the ability of Black labor to disrupt the system with work stoppages, strikes, and other forms of industrial action. As U.S. capital rapidly reduced the scale of its domestic production in the 1970s and 80s, it intentionally elevated competition between white workers and Afrikan and other non-settler sources of labor for the crumbs it was still doling out. The settlers' worldview, position, and systems of entitlement possessed by the vast majority of white workers compelled them to support the overall initiatives of capital and to block the infusion of Afrikan, Xicano, Puerto Rican, and other racialized labor when there were opportunities to do so during this period. This development provided the social base for the "silent majority," "law and order," "tuff on crime," "war on drugs," and "war on gangs and thugs" campaigns that dominated the national political landscape from the late 1960s through the early 2000s, which lead to mass incarceration, racist drug laws, and militarized policing that have terrorized Afrikan (and Indigenous, Xicano, Puerto Rican, etc.) communities since the 1970s.

To deal with the crisis of Black labor redundancy and mass resistance, the ruling class responded by creating a multipronged strategy of limited incorporation, counterinsurgency, and mass containment. The stratagem of limited incorporation sought to and has partially succeeded in dividing the Black community by class, as corporations and the state have been able to take in and utilize the skills of sectors of the Black petit bourgeoisie and working class for their own benefit. The stratagem of counterinsurgency crushed, divided, and severely weakened Black organizations. And the stratagem of containment resulted in millions of Black people effectively being re-enslaved and warehoused in prisons throughout the United States' domestic empire.

This three-pronged strategy exhausted itself by the mid-2000s, as core dynamics of it (particularly the costs associated with mass incarceration and warehousing) became increasingly unprofitable and therefore unsustainable. Experiments with alternative forms of incarceration (like digitally monitored home detainment) and the spatial isolation and externalization of the Afrikan surplus population to the suburbs and exurbs currently abound, but no new comprehensive strategy has yet been devised by the ruling class to solve the problem of what to do and what politically can be done to address the Black surplus population problem. All that is clear from events like the catastrophe following Hurricane Katrina and the hundreds of Afrikans being daily, monthly, and yearly extra-judicially killed by various law enforcement agencies, is that Black life is becoming increasingly more disposable. And it is becoming more disposable because in the context of the American capitalist socio-economic system, Black life is a commodity rapidly depreciating in value, but still must be corralled and controlled.

A Potential Path of Resistance

Although Afrikan people are essentially "talking instruments" to the overlords of the capitalist system, Black people have always possessed our own agency. Since the dawn of Europe's Atlantic slave trade and the development of the mercantile plantations and chattel slavery, Black people resisted their enslavement and the systemic logic and dynamics of the capitalist system itself. The fundamental question confronting Afrikan people since their enslavement and colonization in territories held by the U.S. government is: to what extent can Black people be the agents and instruments of their own liberation and history? It is clear that merely being the object or appendage of someone else's project and history only leads to a disposable future. Black people must forge their own future and chart a clear self-determining course of action to be more than just a mere footnote in world history. Self-determination and social liberation: how do we get there? How will we take care of our own material needs (food, water, shelter, clothing, health care, defense, jobs, etc.)? How will we address the social contradictions that shape and define us, both internally and externally generated? How should we express our political independence?

There are no easy or cookie cutter answers. However, there are some general principles and dynamics that I believe are perfectly clear. Given how we have been structurally positioned as a disposable, surplus population by the United States' empire, we need to build a mass movement that focuses as much on organizing and building autonomous, self-organized, and executed social projects as it focuses on campaigns and initiatives that apply transformative pressure on the government and the forces of economic exploitation and domination. This is imperative, especially when we clearly understand the imperatives of the system we are fighting against.

The capitalist system has always required certain levels of worker "reserves" (the army of the unemployed) to control labor costs and maintain social control. But, the system must now do two things simultaneously to maintain profits: drastically reduce the cost of all labor, and ruthlessly discard millions of jobs and laborers. "You are on your own," is the only social rationale the system has the capacity to process, and its overlords insist that "there is no alternative" to the program of pain that they have to implement and administer. To the system, therefore, Black people can either accept their fate as a disposable population, or go to hell. We must therefore create our own options and do everything we can to eliminate the systemic threat that confronts us.

Autonomous projects are initiatives not supported or organized by the state or some variant of monopoly capital (finance or corporate industrial or mercantile capital). These are initiatives that directly seek to create a democratic "economy of need" by organizing sustainable institutions that satisfy people's basic needs around principles of social solidarity and participatory, or direct, democracy that intentionally put the needs of people before the needs of profit. These initiatives are built and sustained by people organizing themselves and collectivizing their resources through dues-paying membership structures, income sharing, resource sharing, time banking, etc., to amass the initial resources needed to start and sustain our initiatives. These types of projects range from organizing community farms (focused on developing the capacity to feed thousands of people), to forming people's self-defense networks, to organizing non-market housing projects, to building worker and consumer cooperatives to fulfill our material needs. To ensure that these are not mere Black capitalist enterprises, these initiatives must be built democratically from the ground up and must be owned, operated, and controlled by workers and consumers themselves. These are essentially "serve the people" or "survival programs" that help the people to sustain and attain a degree of autonomy and self-rule. Our challenge is marshaling enough resources and organizing these projects on a large enough scale to eventually meet the material needs of nearly forty million Afrikans inside America's domestic empire. And overcoming the various pressures that will be brought to bear on these institutions by the forces of capital to either criminalize and crush them during their development (via restrictions on access to finance, market access, legal security, etc.), or co-opt them and reincorporate them fully into the capitalist market if they survive and thrive.

Our pressure-exerting initiatives must be focused on creating enough democratic and social space for us to organize ourselves in a self-determined manner. We should be under no illusion that the system can be reformed; it cannot. Capitalism and its bourgeois nation-states, the U.S. government being the most dominant amongst them, have demonstrated a tremendous ability to adapt to and absorb disruptive social forces and their demands—when it has ample surpluses. The capitalist system has essentially run out of surpluses, and therefore does not possess the flexibility that it once did. Because real profits have declined since the late 1960s, capitalism has resorted to operating largely on a parasitic basis, commonly referred to as neo-liberalism, which calls for the dismantling of the social welfare state, privatizing the social resources of the state, eliminating institutions of social solidarity (like trade unions), eliminating safety standards and protections, promoting the monopoly of trade by corporations, and running financial markets like casinos.

Our objectives therefore, must be structural and necessitate nothing less than complete social transformation. To press for our goals, we must seek to exert maximum pressure by organizing mass campaigns that are strategic and tactically flexible, including mass action (protest) methods, direct action methods, boycotts, non-compliance methods, occupations, and various types of peoples', or popular, assemblies. The challenge here is to avoid becoming sidelined and subordinated to someone else's agenda—in particular that of the Democratic Party (which has been the grave of social movements for generations)—and not getting distracted by symbolic reforms or losing sight of the strategic in the pursuit of the expedient.

What the combination of these efforts will amount to is the creation of Black Autonomous Zones. These Autonomous Zones must serve as centers for collective survival, collective defense, collective self-sufficiency, and social solidarity. However, we have to be clear that while building Black Autonomous Zones is necessary, they are not sufficient in and of themselves. In addition to advancing our own autonomous development and political independence, we must build a revolutionary international movement. We are not going to transform the world on our own. As noted throughout this short work, Black people in the U.S. are not the only people confronting massive displacement, dislocation, disposability, and genocide; various peoples and sectors of the working class throughout the U.S. and the world are confronting these existential challenges and seeking concrete solutions and real allies as much as we are.

Our Autonomous Zones must link with, build with, and politically unite with oppressed, exploited, and marginalized peoples, social sectors, and social movements throughout the U.S. and the world. The Autonomous Zones must link with Indigenous communities, Xicano's, and other communities stemming from the Caribbean, and Central and South America. We must also build alliances with poor and working class whites. It is essential that we help to serve as an alternative (or at least a counterweight) to the reactionary and outright fascist socialization and influences the white working class is constantly bombarded with.

Our Autonomous Zones should seek to serve as new fronts of class struggle that unite forces that are presently separated by white supremacy, xenophobia, and other instruments of hierarchy, oppression, and hatred. The knowledge drawn from countless generations of Black oppression must become known and shared by all exploited and oppressed people. We must unite on the basis of a global anti-capitalist, anti-imperialist, and anti-colonial program that centers the liberation of Indigenous, colonized, and oppressed peoples and the total social and material emancipation of all those who labor and create the value that drives human civilization. We must do so by creating a regenerative economic system that harmonizes human production and consumption with the limits of the Earth's biosphere and the needs of all our extended relatives— the non-human species who occupy 99.9 percent of our ecosystem. This is no small task, but our survival as a people and as a species depends upon it.

The tremendous imbalance of forces in favor of capital and the instruments of imperialism largely dictates that the strategy needed to implement this program calls for the transformation of the oppressive social relationships that define our life from the "bottom up" through radical social movements. These social movements must challenge capital and the commodification of life and society at every turn, while at the same time building up its own social and material reserves for the inevitable frontal assaults that will be launched against our social movements and the people themselves by the forces of reaction. Ultimately, the forces of liberation are going to have to prepare themselves and all the progressive forces in society for a prolonged battle to destroy the repressive arms of the state as the final enforcer of bourgeois social control in the world capitalist system. As recent events in Greece painfully illustrate,[14] our international movement must simultaneously win, transform, and dismantle the capitalist state at the same time in order to secure the democratic space necessary for a revolutionary movement to accomplish the most minimal of its objectives.

Obstacles and Barriers

So, all that said, we have to question, why aren't Black people revolting in mass, everyday, all day? And, where are the Black Autonomous Zones? Why haven't they emerged?

Black working class folks do in fact revolt everyday, all day. This is manifested in a myriad of social practices, from various forms of labor sabotage, to cultural defiance and non-conformity with white bourgeois cultural norms, and more. Unfortunately, however, our resistance is typically unorganized, and not directed in a systemic fashion. And while there are numerous structural blockages to the development of our organized resistance, not least amongst them the U.S. settler-state apparatus, there are internal contradictions and limitations. One of the main limitations is psychological and social, and that is fear, deep-seated intergenerational fears that have been passed down and continuously reinforced since the capture and enslavement of our ancestors on the African continent. Large segments of the Black community live in utter fear of the state, in the form of the police, and the specter of the nightriders, be they Klansmen, White Citizens Councils, or reactionary homeowners' associations. This fear is used to council against various types of resistance, particularly organized resistance, in almost every Black household in one form or another as a survival tactic. And while this cultural practice is not foolproof, it is effective, often too effective at hindering the development of more profound and revolutionary resistance.

As for the development of Autonomous Zones, to be fair, there have been countless attempts to build Black autonomous zones in every city, borough, and parish in the U.S. where Black folks reside, for generations. But, the effort is easier said than done. The state is the main obstacle that constricts the various efforts to build autonomous zones in the form of community centers, urban farms, cultural refuges, etc. A challenge nearly as daunting is acquiring resources, particularly capital. Too often, Black organizers are incapable of generating or securing the financial capital needed to purchase the facilities they need to operate and build from.

The limitation is both structural and social, and interplays both internally and externally to the community. In the U.S. context, financial capital is highly dominated and controlled by white ruling class interests who own and control the banks, and who have devised a labyrinth of blocking mechanisms to prevent Black people and radical Black political organizations, in particular, from gaining access to much needed funds to purchase buildings, equipment, etc. And again, there are the historic fears that deeply permeate our culture and consciousness. Fears of persecution, of repression, of being burned out of our homes, farms, and businesses, and fears of making ill-fated investments in projects and institutions that aren't going to last because they will either be destroyed by violence, by systemic deprivation in the form of red-lining and depreciation, or because of corruption and internal contradictions.

Upending centuries, if not millennia, of social conditioning of accepting, accommodating, and internalizing the oppressive systems that have dominated the history of significant portions of humanity the past 20,000 years, like patriarchy and class in particular, is not an easy task. As noted by many historians, cultural change is typically the most challenging dimension of social change, and many of the barriers to revolt within the Black community are deeply rooted in our socialization and culture; which is not to condemn our culture or our people in any way, but to recognize that the process of decolonizing ourselves from the internalization of white supremacy, Eurocentrism, settler-colonialism, patriarchy, and heterosexism, and the fears, irrationalities, and individual and collective psychosis these systems stimulate, constitute real, material obstacles that we have to overcome.

Return to the Source

The intersecting, oppressive systems of capitalism, colonialism, patriarchy, imperialism, and white supremacy have consistently tried to reduce African people to objects, tools, chattel, and cheap labor. Despite the systemic impositions and constraints these systems have tried to impose, Afrikan people never lost sight of their humanity, never lost sight of their own value, and never conceded defeat.

In the age of mounting human surplus and the devaluation and disposal of life, Afrikan people are going to have to call on the strengths of our ancestors and the lessons learned in over 500 years of struggle against the systems of oppression and exploitation that beset them. Building a self-determining future based on self-respect, self-reliance, social solidarity, cooperative development, and internationalism is a way forward that offers us the chance to survive and thrive in the 21st century and beyond.

Endnotes

1   Arlene Eisen, *Operation Ghetto Storm: 2012 Annual Report on the Extrajudicial Killing of 313 Black People by Police, Security Guards and Vigilantes* (2013). Available online: http://www.operationghettostorm.org/uploads/1/9/1/1/19110795/new_all_14_11_04.pdf.

2   Edward E. Baptist, *The Half Has Never Been Told: Slavery and the Making of American Capitalism* (New York: Basic Books, 2014).

3   International Labour Organization, *World Employment and Social Outlook 2015* (Geneva: International Labour Office, 2015). Available online: http://www.ilo.org/global/research/global-reports/weso/2015-changing-nature-of-jobs/WCMS_368626/lang--en/index.htm.

4   Michael Parenti, "The Destruction of Yugoslavia," May 11, 1999. Available online: http://www.newyouth.com/archives/balkans/destruction_of_yugoslavia.html.

5   Samir Amin, "Rwanda, 20 Years Later," April 9, 2014. Available online: http://mrzine.monthlyreview.org/2014/amin090414.html.

6   Gérard Prunier, *Africa's World War: Congo, the Rwandan Genocide and the Making of a Continental Catastrophe* (Oxford: Oxford University Press, 2011).

7   David Bacon, "How U.S. Policies Fueled Mexico's Great Migration," *The Nation*, January 4, 2012. Available online: https://www.thenation.com/article/how-us-policies-fueled-mexicos-great-migration/.

8   Anup Shah, "Global Food Crisis 2008," *Global Issues*, August 10, 2008. Available online: http://www.globalissues.org/article/758/global-food-crisis-2008.

9   Brian Bienkowski, "Corporations, investors grabbing land and water overseas," *Environmental Health News*, February 12, 2013. Available online: http://www.environmentalhealthnews.org/ehs/news/2013/land-grabbing.

10 Griff Witte, "Europe plans military response to migrant crisis," *The Washington Post*, May 18, 2015. Available online: https://www.washingtonpost.com/world/europe/eu-approbes-plan-for-military-effort-to-foil-human-smuggling-networks/2015/05/18/fd95da52-fd6a-11e4-8c77-bf274685e1df_story.html?utm_term=.201950a0037b; and Eleanor Albert, "The Rohingya Migrant Crisis," *Council on Foreign Relations*, January 12, 2017. Available online: http://www.cfr.org/burmamyanmar/rohingya-migrant-crisis/p36651.

11 Friends of the Earth International, "Corporate Capture." Available online: http://www.foei.org/what-we-do/corporate-capture.

12 Paul Street, "Regime Change Madness: Hillary, Obama and murderous mayhem in the Muslim World." Available online: http://www.counterpunch.org/2016/01/08/regime-change-madness-hillary-obama-and-murderous-mayhem-in-the-muslim-world/) .

13 Gillian B. White, "Black Workers do need to be twice as good," *The Nation*, October 7, 2015. Available online: http://www.theatlantic.com/business/archive/2015/10/

why-black-workers-really-do-need-to-be-twice-as-good/409276/; and Will Evans, "When companies hire temp workers by race, Black applicants lose out," *Reveal*, January 6, 2016. Available online: https://www.revealnews.org/article/when-companies-hire-temp-workers-by-race-black-applicants-lose-out/.

14 Costas Lapavitsas, "The never-ending Greek disaster," March 7, 2016. Available online: http://costaslapavitsas2.blogspot.com/2016/03/the-never-ending-greek-disaster.html.

SOME THOUGHTS ON WHITE SUPREMACY AND JESUS AS BREAD AND CIRCUSES

Thandisizwe Chimurenga

CREATING A FUTURE WHERE ALL THOSE WHO WORK—ALL THOSE WHO MUST sell their labor, who actually produce things of value—are united based on a common interest, a common well being, a common enemy, and are in control of their labor and the forces of production is not thwarted when we acknowledge this simple truth: for the majority of U.S. history, this country has been cleaved in two: black and white. The foundation of the United States is white supremacy; it is a country founded by whites for whites; built on stolen land; with the stolen labor of a stolen people. Within the U.S., there exists a Black working class and a white working class; likewise, there are also a Black poor and a white poor. Why is it that they have not united and risen up to change their conditions? I would venture the primary reason why whites (both workers and the poor) have not united with their Black counterparts, nor felt a need to overthrow this system, is a fairly simple and straightforward one: white supremacy. It is the glue that binds all persons racialized as white, regardless of their class or any other factors. Why have Black workers and the Black poor not seen fit to rise up? That answer is a bit more involved.

White Workers

White supremacy is described by Charles Mills as "a political system, a particular power structure of formal or informal rule, socioeconomic privilege, and norms for the differential distribution of material wealth and opportunities, benefits and burdens, rights and duties."[1] That "differential distribution" is in favor of whites and against those who are not white, with special emphasis (or denials) for Black people (anti-Blackness). This system is backed by force. To be sure, white supremacy is a distraction; but it is not one that can or should be taken lightly.

W.E.B. Du Bois, writing about the South during the period of Reconstruction immediately following the Civil War that ended chattel slavery, maintained that the white working class was paid a "public and psychological wage"[2] via white supremacy. This "wage" consisted of the non-economic but tangible benefits the white working class received from the class of whites who exploited them: the planters, the land and factory-owning industrialists, bankers, and other men of means. The "public and psychological wages" are the unearned cultural currency known today as "white privilege." Du Bois asserts that:

> Considering the economic rivalry of the black and white worker in the North, it would have seemed natural that the poor white would have refused to police slaves. But two considerations led him in the opposite direction. First of all, it gave him work and some authority as overseer, slave driver, and member of the patrol system. But above and beyond this, it fed his vanity because it associated him with the masters.[3]

Black Servitude

Before the Civil War and Reconstruction, it is the 1640 trial of John Punch in the British colony of Virginia that gives us a good indicator of the beginnings of the separation of Black workers and white workers in the land that would become the United States. Punch, a Black laborer, ran away from his master along with two indentured servants, one Scottish, the other Irish. The trio were caught and, as punishment, the Scot and the Irishman were to be held for four additional years beyond their original contracted time period. Punch, however, was sentenced to servitude for the rest of his life.

Black identity, as a marker of servitude, would be further solidified about twenty years or so after Punch's sentencing. It was in 1662 that Virginia enacted a law that declared "Negro women's children to serve according to the condition of the mother." If the mother was enslaved, so was the child. Virginia law had originally declared children inherited the status of their fathers. The change in the law was undoubtedly "conceived" to offset the inevitable results of the sexual availability of Black women to white men. By 1667, church had joined with state in the branding of Black servitude in Virginia. While Christian baptisms might save the souls of enslaved Blacks, it would no longer free their bodies. Religious conversion would thus no longer be a path to freedom for Black people or Indians in the colony.

While the sentencing of John Punch may be the beginning of the separation of Black workers and white workers, the creation of "white" as an identity would not come about until after the time of Bacon's Rebellion (1676–1677). It was Bacon's Rebellion and its aftermath that sent a shudder down the collective white spine of the elite landowning class. Bacon, a land-owning newcomer to Virginia, committed the crime of basically throwing a monkey wrench into the smooth operation of the colony. Positing that all Indigenous peoples (Indians) were the enemy of the colony, he sought support to exterminate them. Such a move threatened the thus-far cordial business relationship the colony had developed with certain local Indian groups. Without the support or blessing of the governor of the Virginia colony, Bacon unilaterally declared war on all Indians on his own, raising a militia of like-minded settlers, killing the colony's allies, as well as those hostile to the colony. Such treasonous behavior on Bacon's part created rebellion between his backers and those Virginians still loyal to Britain. Like all good tacticians, both Bacon and the British rulers of the colony offered the promise of freedom to enslaved Afrikans who joined their side. Bacon's forces, however, were numerically greater. The rebellion lasted one year but its implications were far reaching. The sight—and thought—of the unity of Black and white against the crown (regardless of the reason) was too much to behold. As Howard Zinn notes:

> Only one fear was greater than the fear of black rebellion in the new American colonies. That was the fear that discontented whites would join black slaves to overthrow the existing order … masters, initially at least, perceived slaves in much the same way they had always perceived servants... shiftless, irresponsible, unfaithful, ungrateful, dishonest... And if freemen with disappointed hopes should make common cause with slaves of desperate hope, the results might be worse than anything Bacon had done.[4]

Tobacco production was the economic engine of the colony and a labor-intensive undertaking. Zinn observes that fewer and fewer immigrants from Europe were coming to the Virginia colony, which posed a dilemma: The whites that had been in the colony as indentured servants were either reaching the end of their contracts, or bettering their lot by purchasing small plots of land for themselves.[5] At the same time, the supply of Black bodies from Africa seemed to be inexhaustible. The perfect storm had thus begun to brew in Virginia.

Poor Whites

The psychological wage that Du Bois spoke of—white supremacy—unites both the white working class and the white poor against all Blacks within the United States, regardless of class. It creates an "us" versus "them" dynamic that should be seen as comical—a Hollywood concoction—were it not real. The 2016 election of Donald Trump to the U.S. Presidency is only the most recent example of the "us" versus "them" mentality. Writing for the online magazine *Resist*, Donyae Coles says that the focus on the needs of poor rural white voters in the 2016 election cycle created a narrative that glaringly left out the fact that poor people of color, some of whom also happen to live in rural areas, have some of the same needs as poor rural whites. Such "oversight" reinforces the idea that poor whites are separate—and thus, above—others:

> In discussions that center rural white voters, we are not calling on rural white people to understand their neighbors of color, let alone some distant, brown city folk. In doing this, in saying, "Oh hey, maybe we need to better listen to rural white people," we are subtly reasserting white supremacist thinking because we are treating these concerns as if they are different and more important than those of people of color in the exact same situations.
>
> White poverty is different because it lacks the structural barriers that keep the communities of POC oppressed. This lack of understanding and the persistent belief in myths about POC (the stereotypes about job stealing Mexicans and Black welfare queens, for example) keep poor white voters trapped in a cycle of voting against the very things that would help them in the long run because they don't want to help "those" people.[6]

The rural white poor were courted in the 2016 presidential election under the auspices of white supremacy. As Princeton scholar Keeanga-Yamahtta Taylor notes, poverty in the U.S. is rarely seen as white and rural: "the majority of poor people in the United States are white but the public face of American poverty is Black. It is important to point out how Blacks are over-represented among the poor, but ignoring white poverty helps to obscure the systemic roots of all poverty."[7]

For the most part the white poor and working class in the U.S. have refused to unite with their Black counterparts. Sociologist Robert L. Allen shows how every major social reform movement in the United States from the mid nineteenth century to the end of World War II (Abolitionist, Populist, Progressive, Woman's Suffrage, Labor, Socialist, Communist) was derailed due to racist ideology within its ranks.[8] This refusal on the part of whites to unite with Blacks, while beneficial to the rulers of capitalism, is deeper than being a mere ploy on the part of bosses to keep workers divided. J. Sakai posits that whites—ALL whites—have always been part of a "labor aristocracy" here in the United States; that as a settler-colonial society, it is the colonized people of color that are the true proletariat.[9] That may or may not be true. What is obvious, however, is that not wanting to work in unity with whites can never, ever, be a charge that is laid at the foot of the Black community.

The Black Body Politic

According to Glen Ford, co-founder and executive editor of the *Black Agenda Report*, African Americans within the U.S. have been the most consistently progressive constituency in the country.[10] The Black body politic has historically been the voice of conscience and reason in the areas of peace, civil liberties, and social justice. That is until the election of Barack Obama as the 44th President of the United States. Ford argues that "the cornerstones of a progressive Black historical consensus has been neutralized, and our instinctive reactions to travesties wrought by power have been short circuited."[11] In short, we lost our minds over a Black president. The hesitancy to criticize former President Barack Obama or the policies he carried out during his tenure has been well documented elsewhere. Needless to say, the election of a Black man as president of a white supremacist settler-colonial project such as the United States tapped into a psychological need of the masses of Blacks—the Black poor, working class, and the Black Elite. Speaking in *USA Today* back in 2008, Black Republican Armstrong Williams—the 2016 presidential campaign manager for Ben Carson—said, "I can honestly say I have no idea who I'm going to pull that lever for in November. And to me, that's incredible." Rising up against a country that elected a Black man as its president, a country with a history of anti-Black racism such as the U.S., was not going to happen—at least not in this go 'round. President Obama's (s)election was a distraction. But it was only one of many.

Writer Kiese Laymon penned an article for *The Guardian* that (lightly) touched on another distraction that keeps African Americans from rising up:

> We … were supposed to love white folks because they knew not what they did. We were supposed to heal them because they knew not who they were. We were supposed to forgive them because salvation awaited she or he who could withstand the wrath of the worst of white folks. We were supposed to pray for them, often at the expense of our own healthy reckoning.[12]

It was in June of 2015 that a white racist murdered nine African American churchgoers at Bethel AME in Charleston, South Carolina. A witness who lived to tell of the encounter said the killer labeled Black people as being a scourge upon the U.S. that had to be eliminated. The killer, once identified and located, was brought before a South Carolina magistrate to be arraigned. Before a trial was held, before his innocence or guilt determined, before he outlined the reasons for his crime, the relatives of his victims forgave him. Before he asked for forgiveness for murdering nine innocent African Americans, he was granted forgiveness automatically by the relatives of his victims. The killer has, to this date, never indicated that he sought or needs their forgiveness, but it was granted to him anyway. Automatically.

Black people within the U.S. have only been Christians for about 300 years or so. In that time, however, we have swallowed a gospel that not only absolves our tormenters of their crimes but also encourages us not to fight back, not to rise up but, in the words of Laymon's grandmother, "give it to God."[13] During enslavement, church services held under the watchful eyes of white masters and overseers served as covert planning meetings for freedom. The modern civil rights movement in the U.S. was nurtured in the Black church. As non-violence gave way to Black Power during the late 1960s in the U.S., Black Liberation Theology appeared as a necessary corollary. But then something happened. Under the air of conservatism that began creeping over the United States after the destruction of the Black Power/Black Liberation Movement, the Black church began to change its tune also. A strategy of confronting the rulers of society was replaced with a prosperity gospel. Individuals are supposed to have wealth. Jesus was wealthy; he simply chose to reject it. Almighty God ordained that everyone should have wealth. This wealth was not being denied to Black people, in particular, because of government policies or racism. Black progress and success was individual. (It was also promised in the Bible.) The focus of the Black church's sermons was shifted. Pharoah had been let off the hook.

Kareem Abdul-Jabbar describes this prosperity gospel as a war on the poor, noting that its adherents are typically "African Americans, evangelicals and those less educated."[14] Parishioners who subscribe to a prosperity gospel are people who are hoping on something better. Unfortunately, in the words of Abdul-Jabbar, they are being sold hope from the descendants of snake oil peddlers. The rise of a prosperity gospel coincides with Republican faith-based efforts at directing domestic policy in the U.S. The presence of flashy, wealthy Black preachers cozying up to Presidents may not be seen as different from those of flashy, wealthy white preachers. The difference lies in the history, and what their presence means for future movement and resistance.

According to Assata Shakur, "People get used to anything. The less you think about your oppression, the more your tolerance for it grows. After a while, people just think oppression is the normal state of things. But to become free, you have to be acutely aware of being a slave."[15] The words of former Black Panther and current political exile Assata Shakur are most prescient for our times. While Black people have always resisted our oppression on these shores, have always rebelled, to rise up and overthrow the capitalist system of the United States—the United States itself—is a hard pill to swallow, especially when your sacred spaces, which once preached sermons on Black Liberation and doubled as a meeting place for insurrection, now preach sermons on forgiveness and "you, too, can be rich."

Black people in the U.S. can ill afford such deliberate distractions at this point in history. To effectively rise up and replace the current world with a new, more humane and egalitarian one, we must first envision that new world. It is not, then, enough that we must believe that it will come to pass; we must believe that we are the architects and the builders that can make it come to pass. In order for that to happen, the clutter of "deliberate distractions" must be identified and neutralized.

George Jackson, revolutionary, author, and Field Marshall of the Black Panther Party, put forth a simple question: "Prestige bars any serious attack on power. Do people attack a thing they consider with awe, with a sense of its legitimacy?"[16] Jackson posed this query in 1971. An affirmative corollary to Jackson's query was put forth by another imprisoned revolutionary and writer, James "Yaki" Sayles (a.k.a. Atiba Shanna) in 1980: "To kill the prestige of the oppressive state, is, first of all, to kill the image of its legitimacy in the minds of the people…there is a need to destroy within the minds of the people the sense of awe in which they hold the oppressive state."[17]

The U.S. is an illegitimate settler-colonial state. Its prestige must be destroyed. Fortunately, the legitimacy of the U.S. as a moral and democratic beacon continues to be chipped away. The rise of the Black Lives Matter phenomenon under a Barack Obama presidential administration provided a necessary blow. The election of Donald Trump as the 45th president has also landed a most potent blow. There will be more deliberate distractions, more bread and circuses, to distract the Black body politic. These distractions will also target white workers and the white poor, as well as other people of color, immigrants, etc. Our task is to see them for what they are, and work harder to bring into fruition a society where all those who live are secure, are cared for, have their basic needs met, and control the forces that impact their daily lives. It is a monumental task. But it absolutely must be done.

Endnotes

1   Charles W. Mills, *The Racial Contract* (Ithaca: Cornell University Press, 1999), 3.

2   W.E.B. Du Bois, *Black Reconstruction in America, 1860–1880* (New York: Free Press, 1998), 700.

3   Ibid., 701.

4   Howard Zinn, *A People's History of the United States*, (New York: Harper and Row, 1980), 37.

5   Ibid.

6   Donyae Coles, "The empathy double-standard: Why poor white voters get compassion and poor Black and brown people get blame," *Resist*, December 2, 2016. Available online: https://resistmedia.org/2016/12/02/empathy-double-standard-poor-white-voters-get -compassion-poor-black-brown-people-get-blame/.

7   Keeanga-Yamahtta Taylor, *From #BlacklivesMatter to Black Liberation*, (Chicago: Haymarket Books, 2016), 49.

8   Robert L. Allen, *Black Awakening in Capitalist America: An Analytic History* (Trenton, NJ: Africa World Press, 1990).

9   J. Sakai, *Settlers: Mythology of the White Proletariat From Mayflower to Modern* (Oakland: PM Press, 2014).

10 Glen Ford, "Black Madness Under Obama: African Americans More Pro-NSA, Anti-Snowden Than Whites and Hispanics," *Black Agenda Report*, January 22, 2014. Available online: http://blackagendareport.com/content/black-madness-under-obama-african -americans-more-pro-nsa-anti-snowden-whites-and-hispanics.

11 Ibid.

12 Kiese Laymon, "Black churches taught us to forgive white people. We learned to shame ourselves," *The Guardian*, 23 June 2015. Available online: https://www.theguardian.com/ commentisfree/2015/jun/23/black-churchesforgive-white-people-shame.

13 Ibid.

14 Kareem Abdul-Jabbar, "Prosperity Gospel Is War on the Poor," *Time Magazine*, June 8, 2015. Available online: http://time.com/3912366/kareem-abdul-jabbar-prosperity-gospel/.

15 Assata Shakur, *Assata: An Autobiography* (New York: Lawrence Hill and Company, 1987), 262.

16 George Jackson, *Blood In My Eye* (Black Classic Press, 1996 (1971), 50.

17 Atiba Shanna (Yaki Sayles), *Notes from A New Afrikan P.O.W. Journal, Book 1*. (Chicago: Spear and Shield Publications, 1980), 4.

ORGANIZING WITH SOLIDARITY IN MIND

NOTES ON SOCIAL MOVEMENT UNIONISM AND CRITICAL EQUITY WORK

Ellie Adekur Carlson

In November 2015, the National branch of the Canadian Union of Public Employees (CUPE) held a convention open to delegates from locals across Canada at the Vancouver Convention Centre. Charging locals $200 for each of the 2,000 delegates in attendance, the convention—a space meant to determine the national union's social and political priorities for the coming year through social and political action groups and the electing of executive officers—was filled with extravagant gifts, socials, and production value. From the feature-film-like, professionally-edited commercials lauding the union's work and advocacy, to lavish hotel meeting spaces and penthouse parties, delegates entering these spaces looking for discussions around critical equity work and political organizing through CUPE often found themselves sidelined, even openly antagonized, for critiquing union strategy.

One particular example sticks with me from that convention: a carefully crafted resolution hit the floor to expand the National Executive Board by four seats specifically reserved for members from equity-seeking caucuses: women, LGBTQ workers, workers with disabilities, and young workers. This was a controversial resolution that organizers from each of the four equity-seeking caucuses had campaigned for throughout the course of the convention, handing out flyers and campaigning in hallways from the first day of the convention until the resolution hit the floor on the final day. Despite a week's worth of modules and impassioned convention speeches on the importance of building solidarity across sectors, organizers were met with a fierce campaign countering their work, a particularly loud group of members flooding microphones in the convention hall to express dissent. These dissenting voices spoke to concerns over favoritism. Other convention-goers cheered, arguing that "talking about our differences takes away from equality," and that "merit" should be the only consideration, not special seats created to "help people get ahead." From our seats, we listened to speakers from the growing lines at the mics:

"I'm a woman, and I find it insulting that someone would want to create a special seat for me when I'm more than capable of earning it myself. I don't need a handout."

"People earn positions on the National Executive Board. You don't get reserved seats."

"If minorities want to be on the executive board, they can run."

"Talking about our differences like this breaks our solidarity."

Suddenly narratives of solidarity, collective action, and campaigns for workers' rights began to advance without the most marginalized communities in the union hall. It became a space difficult for workers from equity-seeking backgrounds to exist in, listening to convention-goers belittle legitimate claims of systemic discrimination within union structures. Union organizers, activists, and equity representatives worked hard to counter ideas about merit and mobility in union spaces, by touching on issues of power, structural inequalities, and discrimination that has historically kept poor and working class communities from taking on leadership roles at local, provincial, and national levels of CUPE. These testimonies were consistently met with the thin logic of bootstrap development philosophies that falsely equated equality clauses to favoritism and handouts: work hard, and you will move ahead in the union.

Proponents of merit-based ideas of progress and success often neglect to think through important issues of power and privilege in union-spaces that set poor and working class members—particularly women, queer and trans workers, racialized workers, and workers living with disabilities—at a disadvantage from the beginning. The resolution to expand our national executive board was overwhelmingly opposed in the convention hall. It fell to thunderous applause and cheers from a room of largely cis-gendered, able-bodied, white, male delegates. The convention hall was then led through a rendition of "Solidarity Forever" by CUPE National's in-house band, as the rest of us were left to take in the absurdity of the moment.

This is one of my most vivid memories of union organizing. My first national convention was a staggering moment of defeat for the progressive trade unionists running the campaign for better representation on our National Executive Board. The fallout was new and confusing to me. A fierce backlash I hadn't expected, followed by the celebration of a motion shut down; a standing ovation for refusing to include these equity seats followed by "Solidarity Forever." As members in the hall sang, many organizers pushing for the equity seats sat frozen in defeat, caught somewhere between bewilderment and pain from the obvious erasure of such a tune following the failure of a resolution built on principles of inclusion. This loss reveals some of the most pressing blind spots in union organizing to date—the idea that issues of equity, inclusion, and social justice are second to merit-based, bootstrap development principles, and labor management models of unionism.

I'm interested in how trade unions founded on radical ideas of direct action, working-class power, and solidarity have become institutions replicating the same false narratives of development as employers. In labor unions like the Canadian Union of Public Employees, spaces founded on principles of working class empowerment and radical organizing shift to replicate these structural inequalities, and mark a shift in their ability to fight for the poor and working class communities represented in their membership. Principles of equity and inclusion have become afterthoughts in the labor movement's struggle for working class power. I'm interested in thinking through the work of labor unions as institutions for working class resistance, and the disconnect between the legacy of trade unions as spaces for radical action to improve the lives of the working class through direct action and creative forms of protest, and the present-day focus on collective bargaining and incremental gains as markers of strength and progress in modern labor movements. Modern trade unions replicate the hierarchies and exclusionary tactics of employers by prioritizing collective bargaining and incremental gains over radical forms of social and political mobilization. Poor and working class communities do attempt to rise up and reclaim spaces and power from employers and forces of systemic discrimination, but some of the most detrimental forces to this progressive push come in the form of institutions set up to help and represent working-class communities.

Labor Organizing through Social Movement Unionism

Conversations of social movement unionism are concerned with organizing workers outside of typical workplace issues and moving to embrace social movements and collaborative organizing between workers' rights movements and social justice work around critical equity issues.[1] Social movement unionism stands in staunch opposition to labor management models of unionism that adopt a corporate model of union operations and require local executives to operate as managers of their membership, often instituting the same structures of bureaucracy as employers and reproducing structural inequalities within their work by taking on this kind of managerial role.[2] Accordingly, the tactics of social movement unionism differ from labor management models, or business unionism. Social movement unionism is heavily influenced by the drive and dissent from radical activist communities, whereas labor management models of unionism operate as a top-down structure whereby decision-making power and capacities are concentrated with local executives and executive branches of provincial and national unions.[3]

The same bodies trade unions are meant to combat and hold accountable are able to disenfranchise workers on the basis of social locators such as race, class, and gender. Labor unions are capable of reproducing power inequalities and privilege within their governance. When these forms of inequality are reproduced through institutions tasked with representing poor and working-class communities—through local executives, decision-making capacities and the dissemination of information—only the most privileged are able to access positions of authority in labor movements. When our labor movements ignore—or actively denounce—the impact of racism, classism, sexism, and other forms of bigotry in our institutions, they invalidate the experiences of marginalization and exclusions equity-seeking groups often experience in labor organizing, despite taking on disproportionate amounts of organizing.

On Incremental Gains and Radical Organizing Potential

Disenfranchising and excluding workers from labor movements can happen directly and indirectly through representation and policy in local unions, as well as the strategies and tactics labor unions choose to adopt to hold employers accountable to workers. Whereas the politics of social justice work often allow for organizations to pursue direct forms of action such as rallies, occupations, and very contentious forms of protest, labor management models of unionism are concerned with maintaining friendly relationships with labor management bodies. Union leadership that refuses to engage in contentious negotiations with employers are not capable of defending the rights and interests of their most marginalized members. Critical equity issues—issues of access, targeted discrimination, and exclusion in our workplaces—need to be met with swift action, organizing from labor movements, and an open acknowledgment of the role of employers looking to disenfranchise poor and working-class communities. Employers are not our friends, nor should we negotiate with them as such. Employers have a vested interest in the continued marginalization of poor and working-class communities. To embrace them as friends or allies is a decision made at the expense of our most vulnerable communities.

The idea of incremental gains as tangible progress stands in direct opposition to the by-any-means-necessary tactics of radical organizing and direct action. Past ideas of radical protest—taking over the institutions we work for and reclaiming space through direct action—have been revamped by large trade-unions to, instead, focus on business unionism and labor management models whereby senior leadership and executive committees become middle men, negotiating between employers and their membership in ways that stress strong, positive relationships with employers. When dealing with employers looking to keep workers below the poverty line, and who refuse to address important issues of pay equity, biased hiring practices, and the marginalization of poor and working-class communities, prioritizing incremental gains through collective bargaining processes pushes leadership to work to sell lackluster agreements to the membership, and balance the demands of a radical left with the bottom line—the very least that's needed to convince members to capitulate to the demands of the employer.

The Corporate Executive: Managing Labor Relations

It's not uncommon for executive members to become so wrapped up in maintaining these relationships with the employer that they begin to neglect and resent the demands and interests of their members. Prioritizing strong relationships with employers over member-driven organizing and political action works to replicate the same exclusionary forms of top down leadership that employers rely on. When senior leadership in labor unions are occupied with needing to create amicable relationships with employers, they overlook the inherent conflict between employers and working-class communities represented by their unions. Factoring in executive salaries, access to union funds, and the tiered nature of relations between union executives and their membership, can make union executives an extension of the employer.

In this context, when there is no emphasis on union development, training organizers, creating support systems, or social and political action groups to challenge and improve on how local unions function, there is no growth. These practices exclude the most marginalized members—poor and working class, sex-working, BIPOC/racialized members, new immigrants, single parents and families with dependents, workers with disabilities and members disproportionately exposed to harassment and intimidation. Detached from labor management perspectives are the views and experiences of seasoned organizers in union spaces who come from marginalized communities. Because unions don't typically champion the politics and perspectives of the most marginalized, we see a lack of education and awareness in these spaces when it comes to pressing political concerns around issues of anti-Black racism, anti-poverty organizing, policing, status, and related social movements. In CUPE, we still struggle to connect Black Lives Matter and anti-racism work to union development when Black women and racialized members are threatened, harassed, and disrespected by those who think anti-racism work is a distraction from the goals of the union.

In CUPE 3902, representing teaching assistants and academic workers at the University of Toronto, for example, issues of sexual violence during the 2015 Unit 1 strike went unreported and unresolved when union reps and strike coordinators told those disclosing to "focus on the goals of the strike" and present a united front. Issues of sexual violence highlight the violence and the trauma that we inflict onto vulnerable members looking to address forms of gendered violence and discrimination in union spaces. The advice to "focus on the goals of the union" and "present a united front" is an alarming reminder of the level of violence members are asked to endure and hide in the name of "solidarity." Equity work and fighting inequality are seen as something secondary to this labor management model of union operations and a rigid focus on building a relationship with the employer by presenting a unified front. But the reality stands: if you can't walk into a union space and feel safe, secure, and heard, these elusive "goals of the strike" or "goals of the union" aren't built around you and your needs. In this way, the most marginalized communities are overlooked and pushed out because they aren't being heard.

Critical Equity Work in
Labor Movement Organizing

The work that inspired the motion at CUPE National in 2015 to push for the expansion of our National Executive Board was perceived as a threat to the structure of our union, using principles of equity, diversity, and inclusion to thwart conversations about union operations. Critical equity work and political action that is actively critical of the work of trade unions is interpreted by leadership as threatening—"breaking our solidarity"—and taking time away from the goals of the union by introducing a new, critical rhetoric of leadership and union operations. For these reasons, grassroots organizing in trade unions needs to stay critical of leadership and the operations of our unions both at the provincial and national level, as unconditional partnerships with political parties like the New Democratic Party of Canada (NDP) have become the norm. When organizations are tasked with acting as the unilateral voice of working class communities, representing us to employers and government bodies, it's important that we are able to shape, critique, and direct their work; otherwise, we risk the same forms of hierarchy and exclusion reproducing themselves in the work of our unions.

When labor movements are disconnected from the realities of their most marginalized members, they are disconnected from the roots, realities, and motivations of their most powerful, resilient, and creative organizers. Considerations of social justice, equity, and inclusion are the foundation of a strong labor movement and strong organizing. Thinking about equity and inclusion in the context of bargaining and negotiations means collective agreements do not allow particularly vulnerable groups to slip through the cracks. Equity audits and bargaining built on inclusion point to agreements prioritizing workers from equity seeking groups and strong support networks.

When leaders don't bother to invest in organizing or outreach, and actively shame people doing mobilizing work, they are scared of their members and the power of a strong, informed, organized union base. Members hold power: the power to elect officials, shape policy, determine bargaining practices and demands, as well as the power of oversight. When members are allowed to access the same information as executive committees, they are better able to hold leadership accountable. In the context of CUPE, a union whose executive is largely comprised of the same faces changing positions from year-to-year, these executive roles are coveted. Elected leaders do not want members, particularly *active,* critical, and politicized members, to participate in these spaces. Political action, direct action, member-engaged organizing strategies— these things work to shift power and authority off of executive members and onto the membership. That kind of accountability terrifies executive members, because it forces them to get political and get organizing. It highlights their use of union funds and resources, making indiscretions transparent to the members they serve: paying each other out in honorariums, using union funds to buy each other gifts, double salaries, nepotism, and secure jobs within larger divisions of CUPE.

The labor movement isn't anyone's playground for a better job opportunity—it's a political struggle for workers' rights that has the power to better the lives of some of our most vulnerable communities. When our leadership actively works against member-driven organizing and pushes for critical equity work, they silence the voices, concerns, and demands of those with the most to lose. A friendly relationship with labor relations divisions is not more valuable than engaging a membership ready to organize. It is not the job of executive officers to "sell" anything to their members. Executive officers work for us. They are elected to carry out the will of the membership, and need to be held accountable for abusing power, withholding information, and demobilizing communities. In CUPE this method of critique is dangerously conflated with anti-union sentiments, "breaking our solidarity" to include conversations of critical equity work, and detracting from "union goals" under a labor management model of unionism. The operations, strategizing, and campaigning of modern trade unions should be built on a solid foundation that prioritizes ideas of critical equity work, pushing for diverse representation from marginalized, working-class communities within our membership.

Unions replicate the work, strategies, and philosophy of employers looking to disenfranchise working class communities when they prioritize business unionism and labor management models built on incremental gains over member-driven organizing and engaged critiques of union leadership and developments. When unions shut these voices out of union development and campaigns, we get creative in our organizing. To survive, grassroots, working-class campaigns rely on action and outreach that the apolitical cannot replicate—grounded forms of member engagement, public education, and political action. These are methods that lead to many uncomfortable conversations, requiring patience, unlearning, and a dedication to building spaces for as many members as possible, but often what these member-driven initiatives reveal to us is that we must be willing to question, critique, and defy traditional notions of solidarity to build it properly and authentically.

Endnotes

1   Peter Waterman, "Social-movement unionism: A new union model for a new world order?" *Review* (Fernand Braudel Center), 16.3 (Summer 1993): 245–78.

2   Melay Abao, *Fighting Back With Social Movement Unionism: A Handbook for APL Activists.* (Quezon City, Philippines: Alliance of Progressive Labour, 2001).

3   Stephanie Ross, "Varieties of social unionism: Towards a framework for comparison," *Just Labour: A Canadian Journal of Work and Study* 11 (2007): 16–32; Jim Smith, "The corporatization of unions," *Labor Notes*, June 30, 2002. Available online: http://www.labornotes .org/2002/06/corporatization-unions.

TRUMP, THE ALT RIGHT, AND THE NEW STATE OF EXCEPTION

Jordy Cummings

Preamble—The Monster Mash

*This essay was written in the summer of 2016. Like much of the
English-speaking Left, I thought Trump didn't stand a chance
at winning the presidency. The British writer Richard Seymour,
American gadfly documentarian Michael Moore, and professor
Allan Lichtman, who predicted the previous 30 years of presidential
elections, were of the few that predicted Trump's win. Even as of
Tuesday afternoon on election day, I'd thought he was gonna tank.*

*As this preamble is being written, four days into Trump as
President-Elect, already hate-crimes have spurted up throughout the
country. Giving hope, protest movements have sprung up "from the
Redwood Forest, to the Gulfstream Waters." To put it simply, the Left,
understood broadly as the spectrum ranging from social-democrat all
the way out to anarchist, with some exceptions, understated what seems
to be an "organic crisis" of the American political system. While Donald
Trump is certainly bourgeois, he is absolutely not what the American
bourgeoisie wanted. One is reminded of Marx's* 18th Brumaire of
Louis Bonaparte, *in which the liberal bourgeoisie, at first opposing a
new authoritarianism from Napoleon's nephew, and participating with
the proletariat and intelligentsia in the 1848 revolutions, ended up
buttressing the power of a demagogue. That was preferable, of course, to
allowing a "social republic" or "dictatorship of the proletariat," as the
communist movement was calling for at the time.*

This is to say, it now seems clear that the American bourgeoisie and, as both Trump and Bernie Sanders put it, the "Political Establishment" and "Billionaire Class," were fully prepared—as the Wikileaks emails show—to lose an election rather than allow a real rising of the poor and working classes by virtue of a potential presidency for a moderate social democrat like Sanders. As is predicted in the essay, a good chunk of working-class and union-household voters went with Donald Trump.

In his seventh thesis on the philosophy of history, Walter Benjamin writes that what appears to be a "state of exception," a suspension of normal legal and juridical rule—as theorized by Nazi jurist Carl Schmitt—was actually the norm for the oppressed. What is the election of Trump, and the rising of the alt.right, but something exceptional that is really a hyper-real manifestation of tendencies laying dormant in American society, ready to pounce when neither the working classes nor bourgeoisie are strong enough to rule their state? As the Marxist Antonio Gramsci, who saw the rise of fascism, put it, "The old world is dying, and the new world struggles to be born; now is the time of monsters." It is to these monsters that we shall now turn.

IN THE ONGOING GREAT RECESSION, A RANGE OF VOICES, FROM LIBERAL TO socialist, have wondered why there has not been an "uptick" in extra-parliamentary class struggle, and often actually blame the working class itself, implicitly, given the focus on "individualism," cheap consumer goods and the like.[1] This essay will argue, contrary to popular understanding, that the poor do "rise," but not in a fashion that those on the Left may wish for. The growth of right-wing populism and appeals to class has garnered at least as much success as progressive electoral projects, from SYRIZA to Bernie Sanders. Indeed, while the Left downplays an explicit class-orientation and merely speaks about austerity and the "1%," the populist right makes explicit appeals to class and class consciousness. While the most popular American socialist in recent memory, Bernie Sanders, spoke of the "billionaire class," he counterposed it to the "people," while on the other hand, conservatives from Margaret Thatcher to Donald Trump have spoken the language of class, with Trump even calling for a "Workers' Party." Liberal and Marxist thinkers, from Georg Lukács all the way to Thomas Frank, have written off the appeal of right-wing populism as some kind of "false consciousness."[2]

This is to assume what needs to be explained, that is to say, to ignore the symbolic as well as real and perceived material gains promised to the poor and working class public by right-wing populists. In very basic terms, right-wing populism points at the compromised liberal or social-democrat promising pie-in-the-sky-in-the-bye-and-bye, and calls them crooked, dishonest or, in more polite terms, calls their plans "unrealistic." Their own tax-cutting plans, meant to split working classes by pitting private vs. public sector workers, in material terms, leaves relatively more liquid money in the pockets of voters than do liberals and social democrats. Right wing populists often will have "signature" issues for which they promise to deliver the goods; take former Toronto mayor Rob Ford and his promise of "subways, subways, subways." As someone with some experience organizing around transit access in the Greater Toronto Area, I can say that Ford's plans to build subways through poor and working class communities were far more popular than the social-democratic urbanist darling plans of "Transit City." These gains may be real, or they may be perceived. Beyond this, there are the symbolic gains, the "rising," which may well have an authoritarian, as opposed to an emancipatory, quality of "one of us," a white straight man, salt-of-the-earth, Huey Long, Donald Trump, or Nigel Farage.

In the past year, a social movement has sprung up; while predominantly popular amongst those whose income is comfortably middle class, it features—and speaks on behalf of—a healthy amount of poor and working class Americans. On the backs of the offshoring of jobs and growing gap between rich and poor in both absolute and relative wealth and income terms, in the face of epidemics of hard drugs and the economic draft turning small town boys and girls into cannon fodder, a movement of Americans from outside of the elite urban enclaves, on one hand, and the bible belt, on the other, has made its anti-systemic voice heard. The cadre of this movement, as one activist puts it, are "mostly white, mostly male middle-American radicals, who are unapologetically embracing a new identity politics that prioritises the interests of their own demographic."[3] That movement, of course, is the movement around Donald Trump, the bridging of the "alternative right" with the old-right "paleo-conservatives." The anti-systemic social movement that Donald Trump has helped coalesce predated and will outlast him, and, I argue here, needs to be seen as a distorted refraction of class struggle. It is a "rising" of the poor and working classes, but the direction of that rise ain't exactly clear. After all, what do we mean, politically, when we say "rise"? For every "rising" of the far-left, of oppressed and marginalized people, there have been far more "risings" of the right, at least in advanced capitalist countries. The Ku Klux Klan was a rising of the petit-bourgeois whites of the south, meant to defeat the governing Reconstruction authorities. Franco and Mussolini took power in "risings" of social movements that were bound together like sticks, or, in Italian, *fasci*. Let's not mistake "rising" for something inherently emancipatory!

One thing that must be kept in mind, however—and certainly has been by Trump and his advisors, without offering fundamentally transformational, anti-systemic politics—is that the "poor do rise" in support of policies that would offer less harm than technocratic neoliberalism. The simple fact that Trump promised fewer "overseas entanglements" should not be understated as part of his appeal, like India's Modi, a man who deftly plays the Chinese off of the Americans. As Ecuadorian president Rafael Correa said, while Clinton may be better for America at the moment, Trump would be better for the world; there is indeed a perception, in our post-neoconservative age, that the far right is less belligerent on the level of foreign policy. The discrediting of the neoconservative imperialist consensus, at least within "conservatism," has seen electoral losses for this worldview across the world.

The rascal philosopher Slavoj Žižek often attributes the quote "Behind every fascism, there is a failed revolution" to Walter Benjamin.[4] Whether or not Benjamin ever directly made this point, it is certainly the implication of his "Concept of History" essay.[5] After all, Hitler's rise came after the left destroyed itself, starting with Social Democracy's sell-out of the 1919 communist revolution, all the way through fractious spreads and adventurist turns throughout the 1920s and culminating in tragic disagreements during the Communist "Third Period" in which the slogan was "After Hitler, then Us." At this time, Socialists, anarchists, Communists, Bundists, Trotskyists, and so on, were all, literally, knives drawn, shooting each other in the street—and the two largest forces on the Left and the Labor movement, the Communists and the Social Democrats, refused to form a United Front against fascism.[6] Similar, if geographically specific trajectories took place in other rises of historical fascism and right-wing authoritarianism, from the hoodwinking of anarcho-syndicalism by Italian fascism to the hollow popular-front "resistance" mounted by France and Spain against fascist uprising or occupation.[7] One can even generalize this to the rise of nationalist populism in Eastern Europe following the collapse of state-communism.

In the absence of a well-organized and united left, right-wing populism will be the means with which the poor rise. Religion can only promise so much, and destitution tends to lend itself to wanting earthly salvation, especially in an era of mass consumption. Of course, this is not to say that the Left can hothouse revolutionary social conditions in which the popular masses have no excuse but to revolt against their conditions, such as was the case, for example, with the first sparks of the Arab Spring in Tunisia. Nor is it even to say that it is the most destitute of the working classes that lead revolutionary movements: If we are to expand "the poor" to "the poor and working classes," we can understand how the poorest casual day-laborer as well as the well-paid, highly-skilled metalworkers, the latter of whom took a leading role, were protagonistic players in the Russian revolutions of 1917. Nor is this a fuzzy call for "left unity" that often ends in lowest-common-denominator coalitions or liquidating into tragic experiments like SYRIZA or the Bernie Sanders campaign, both of which showed thirst for left-wing change drowned out by both structural imperatives and cowardice. There was and is no iron law that reformists have to sell out, but it just so happens that they often do.

Egalitarianism or Anti-Capitalism?

In his *New York Times* editorial that this book is addressing, the liberal journalist and academic Thomas Edsall points out that "those bearing the most severe costs of inequality are irrelevant to the agenda-setters in both [Democratic and Republican] parties. They are political orphans in the new order. They may have a voice in urban politics, but on the national scene they no longer fit into the schema of the left or the right."[8] Since the writing of his editorial in early summer 2015, major candidates from both political parties, Bernie Sanders for the Democrats and Donald Trump for the Republicans, attempted to shift the narrative to encompass those on "the losing end of globalization," so to speak. The former failed, and, as is likely inscribed in his "popular front" left-social democratic worldview, largely capitulated after having some tiny influence on a non-binding party platform. The latter succeeded largely due to contingent circumstances of the party's establishment picking too many candidates, as much of the advanced segments of capital, notably the FIRE (Finance, Insurance, and Real Estate) and tech sectors, were already dead-set on Hillary Clinton going back some years, as has been shown in her numerous speeches articulating her "private" pro-finance view to bankers and those at other financial institutions. A larger key, however, to Trump's success was his articulation of the emerging worldview of the "alternative right," combined with firm opposition to neoliberal free-trade policies and even "American exceptionalism."

Another key issue with Edsall's formulation, however, is understanding the lack of working class or sub-altern rising in the United States (and Canada). This is to reduce the problem with post-crisis (and indeed any) capitalism to merely "inequality," as if inequality were a causal mechanism of itself; of course, inequality breeds inequality, but inequality is a necessary component to the reproduction of capitalist social property relations and the need for what Karl Marx called a "Reserve army of labour." And further, the categorization of "the poor" as opposed to "the working class(es)," who are on a sharp trajectory towards poverty, in particular amongst millennials, seems to imply a precious image of panhandlers, for whom we have a *noblesse oblige* to "do something about."[9] It is not inequality that is the problem; it is capitalism; and it is not merely the poor who must rise; it is the working class as a whole. While, as Edsall mentions and is also written about elsewhere in this book, African Americans have been engaging in militant challenges to the status quo, most working class white people have not been doing so. Meanwhile, in just four hours in formerly prosperous West Virginia, no fewer than twenty six people overdosed on Oxycontin.[10] From the 1990s onwards, big agribusiness has encroached on the land of small-holding farmers and ranchers. The leadership of the labor movement, with some exceptions, have gotten so comfortable with concession bargaining that for many unions strikes are an exception, not the norm.

The "wages of whiteness," the social wage of not being victimized due to skin color, is certainly a determining factor in explaining the quiescence of the white working class to struggle on class lines, to "rise" in a progressive and anti-racist direction. Yet even these wages have depreciated and/or been outsourced. Edsall mentions the cheapening of consumer goods and, implicitly, the availability of cheap credit, misreading the purpose of Keynesianism priming the pump with private debt.[11] Certainly the cheapening of consumer goods is an effect, not a cause, of inequality. The labor movement has had very few recent tangible victories, in particular within the private sector, and even those victories have been in largely "modern" industries like technology, e.g. the Communications Workers of America (CWA) victory at Verizon. Whole sectors like trucking and logistics are either not unionized or without fighting rank and file cultures. All of this, leading to job attrition and casualization, is overdetermined by the development of a collaborating, staff-led, and distant union bureaucracy, comfortable in both the U.S. and Canada (with some exceptions) to being nothing more than a "stakeholder" in the "democratic process." So, is it any surprise that we see formations like "Teamsters for Trump"?[12] It's to be expected that, of course, police and border-police unions, if we can call them "unions," were all out for Big Don. Yet one top union bureaucrat said to the *New York Times*, "There is deep economic anxiety among our members and the people we're trying to organize that I believe Donald Trump's message is tapping into."[13] And, in comparison with the dullness of a labor meeting or the fractiousness of the far left, a new movement has appeared, even calling for a "Worker's Party."[14]

Fun Fascism

In Rainer Werner Fassbinder's masterpiece *Ali: Fear Eats the Soul,* the fifty-something German woman, Emmi, and her young Arab migrant lover, Ali, are all set for a fancy dinner out. They sit down to eat at an old fashioned and traditional "German/Italian" restaurant. Emmi is effusive, "Hitler used to eat here." This is followed immediately by an awkward moment. Here is a working-class German woman, tossed aside by her embourgeoisified offspring, who has, awkwardly but touchingly, fallen in love with a migrant who finds in her the embodiment of a spirit of hospitality that lies beneath the surface of depersonalized, capitalist, mid-seventies West Germany. She was so excited to go to a "high class" restaurant (actually quite pedestrian seeming, to the audience), because it was once the favorite of her Führer.[15] She is a lovely human being, and anti-racist. Yet fascism clearly brought her joy, not unlike the joy portrayed in Fellini's *Amarcord,* in its carnivalesque glory.

Fascism, and its relative within the liberal-democratic camp, right-wing populism, needs to be understood, as the historian Dylan Riley points out, as "Authoritarian Democracy."[16] The point may come as a surprise to those liberals and anti-capitalists alike who see democracy, either in its parliamentary, Soviet, or even council form, as predicated upon the instantiation of the popular will of the masses by way of *selective participation*, often merely voting. The normative essence of the very word "democracy" seems to be done violence by terming right-wing populism and fascism to be democratic. Yet, in theoretical terms, fascism and right-wing populism lay claim, quite explicitly, to the popular will, to the interests of the poor and working classes, as against a corrupt, venal, and decrepit establishment, an establishment that may or may not be under undue influence by foreigners and the "speculative" or "financial" side of capitalist property relations. This needs to be juxtaposed with simple "reactionary" or "conservative" politics, which promise "stability" and "law and order."

Fascism promises fearless law and the most orderliness of order (trains-a-runnin' on time), but much more, and to be honest, to most true-believers in fascism, these are "noble lies," the truth of fascism is its democratic—and enjoyable—core. This is as true to the German farmer and Italian artisan who felt forgotten by the Left and sold out by the bourgeoisie as it is for the 4Chan posting, diverse, and queer-friendly but deliberately offensive "for the lulz" denizens of the today's Alt Right, as well as their more extreme L.A.R.P.ing comrades amongst the many and sundry militia groups, Putin-admiring "neo-reactionaries." This is to say that when liberals and socialists alike are aghast at how Donald Trump—and to be more specific, Trump's "base" whom he plays to, are "anti-democratic," their opposition is merely to what some of us call "bourgeois democracy." Looking further afield, one sees, beyond the electoral machinations of far-right parties and "strong-men" from the Front National in France to the Golden Dawn in Greece, from Putin's social base in Russia to the BJP in India, reflections and refractions on existing social movements, largely comprised of the poor: the lower working classes, the lumpen, and the petit-bourgeoisie. In other words, the *poor do rise*.

Physiognomy of the Alternative Right

As was mentioned, the Alt Right are the key movers of this movement. The Alt Right is largely an online movement of millennials, which can lead us to deduce that a majority may have come from bourgeois backgrounds but have little to no economic hope, and are working service sector jobs or perhaps selling pot and "flipping" on Ebay. Unlike other players within the Trump movement, the Alt Right are not often thought of as a working class-based movement, partially because they often appear to be ostentatiously wealthy, a movement for "rich kids of Instagram." As pointed out by Alt Right informal leaders Milo Yiannopolous (largely referred to by the honorific of his first name) and Allum Bokharri, a queer man and an Iranian man, for the majority of this subset of outsiders, coming together on old-fashioned web discussion sites like 4Chan and Reddit, this was politics "for the lulz," that is to say for the sheer enjoyment of it.[17] As Bokhari and Milo point out, "Long before the alt-right, 4channers turned trolling the national media into an in-house sport." Yet this movement, largely male, started to coalesce in response to the increasing influence of feminism, or what they called "misandry" in online spaces, especially in video games. "Gamergate," targeting well-known feminist online personalities, notably Aneta Sarkeesian, known for her YouTube videos on misogynist tropes in computer games, was the coming-out party for this crowd. Admittedly, this crowd has a minority, known as "1488ers," that are neo-Nazis. But, say Milo and company, they are harmless and realize they have been hegemonized by queer reactionaries of color. Aside from constituting the backbone of the "Men's Rights Activism" movement, this crowd is attempting to fight against an "onslaught of SJWs" (Social Justice Warriors) in countercultural enclaves from science fiction to, most recently, the 2016 summer blockbuster remake of *Ghostbusters*. A bullying campaign against star Leslie Jones on social media ended with Milo himself getting banned from Twitter, no small feat considering that Jihadi groups still can post.

Milo and others have pointed out the very real affinities the Alt Right share with the far-left, in particular the sixties New Left. Indeed, it is quite reasonable to point out that young people get involved with the Alt Right for the same reason that young people got involved with the New Left, especially in its later "adventurist" years.[18] Politics could be *fun, it could be far out.* Or, in contemporary parlance, politics could be *for the lulz.* On a deeper level, the left-critique of cultural appropriation and embrace of "identity politics" has the script flipped. Alt Right types proudly admit the affinity, as seen above, calling their movement one specifically based on the opposition to the cultural appropriation of European traditional culture.[19] Going beyond the Internet subculture, then, one sees a wide ferment of far-right social movements. There are the neo-reactionaries who argue against democracy and for monarchy. Their inveighing against Whig models of history brings to mind Walter Benjamin, while at the same time blaming Benjamin's Frankfurt School friends and "Cultural Marxism" for a decline in Western Civilization.[20] There are the militia members who openly compare themselves to Black Panthers, while some of their comrades sit, heavily armed, outside a NAACP chapter. It should be noted as well, given Trump's aforementioned call for a "Workers' Party," that in the words of Marxist sociologist Charlie Post, "Although Trump is a capitalist, he does not represent any significant segment of his class."[21] Post points out that, whether practicable or not, the Republican establishment, committed as they are to the programs of big business, both "Main Street" and "Wall Street," from the Chamber of Commerce to the Business Roundtable, fear Trump's ideas, whether protectionist or nativist. Capital wants rationalized migration, not deportation. Does this mean that Trump is an anti-capitalist? Far from it. Yet the imaginary of the Trump movement doesn't see capital as intrinsically connected—indeed, capital can be constrained by strongmen, controlled by states, in the interests of the people. The truth behind Trump's persistent and admiring statements about Putin and Saddam Hussein, as well as his oft-satirized early campaign theme of "China.... I love China," is his belief that he, like those states, could, in a properly Machiavellian sense, have the virtue to tame fortune.

Like with other cases of right-wing populism, progressives often point out that, numerically speaking, the majority of Trump's supporters are not working class (all the while denouncing the working class as either uneducated idiots, the labor aristocracy, or both). Yet while pointing out that much of Trump's support comes from the "new middle classes," Post points out that half of Trump's supporters earn less than $50,000 a year.[22] Even more of them, however, come from upper middle-class white men without a college or university degree—shopkeepers, salespeople, the classic "new middle class," who may, on a relative level, still be economically secure, but correctly see their own position on the verge of proletarianization. Post also provides an important reminder that Trump, while displaying signs of fascism, is not, in the last instance, a fascist. "Fascism becomes a mass movement with the potential of taking political power when left-wing movements threaten but fail to take power and capitalist classes continue to fear challenges from below."[23] Trump has not displayed any indication that he wants to overturn representative democracy, and his admiration for dictators is really nothing new in American politics.

Winning them over, or defeating them? What is to be done.

It is mythical to believe that the Left will always—inexorably—be where people turn at times of crisis, or that "rising" will occur within the shared definition of everyone from left-liberals (like Edsall) to the far-left. Right-wing populism of the Trump variety, or regional variations ranging from the relatively anti-racist former Toronto Mayor Rob Ford to the brutally racist Greek Golden Dawn, not only promises redemption from the depredations of what instead of capitalism they call "globalism," but it also—sometimes explicitly, sometimes implicitly—ties this to a sense of "greatness." This is almost intangible, a Lacanian "Objet Petit A"—greatness being what once was, and what will be, but does not exist now. In the face of the success of this populism, it may be suggested that the Left should offer its own populism, its own "cognitive mapping" that would address the same very-real sources of alienation that attract poor and working class, even middle-class white men to the Trump movement and others of its type. Merely providing another form of populism, of rhetoric that addresses particular interests in a universal frame as opposed to universal interests in a particular frame, such as in the case with modern social democrats from Hugo Chávez to Bernie Sanders, is insufficient. Rather, it gives us pointers that the poor who can be mobilized on behalf of reaction can also be mobilized against the "one percent" or the "oligarchs." The question, however, is to mobilize as a working class against a ruling class, and this question relies less on populism than on a vision of a future that is imminent within the present.

What this notion gets right is that the right is successful in the face of left failure, but as opposed to understanding that, as Corey Robin shows, the right has always learned its tactics from the Left, not vice-versa.[24] Developing a "counter-hegemonic discourse" against another "counter-hegemonic discourse" is not only insufficient, it is a waste of time. What is necessary in such circumstances is a concrete analysis of a concrete situation: What are the sources of modern grievances? What kind of political program, in the short and medium term, can win over potential recruits to the far-left? What other parts of the far-right should be seen as enemies, not as potential recruits to an anti-capitalist project? These are questions without easy answers, but it is useful at the very least to clear up detritus, not to concentrate, as liberals like Edsall, social democrats like Sanders and Chavez, and right-wingers like the Breitbart crowd all agree, on surface phenomenon like "elites" or "bankers."

Blaming "elites" or "bankers" has the inner logic of classical anti-Semitic conspiracy theory. More importantly, however, it ignores the absolute necessity—not centrality, but necessity—of finance to modern capitalism, and indeed to capitalism historically. Finance, after all, predates capitalism. Yet it serves a purpose, not merely in facilitating the chaotic planning of the social relation we call "the market," but of allowing itself to be seen as analytically distinct from capitalist social relations as a whole. Without the financial sector, since the decline in growth that has existed at least since the turn of the millennium, and in some accounts since the seventies, there would be no wealth-generation. With this in mind, there is not much difference between Trump and the right's lauding of "makers" as opposed to hedge-fund managers with Sanders's own (more sophisticated) critique of hedge fund managers counterposed with "progressive" or "soulful" entrepreneurs like Ben & Jerry's Ice Cream or "small businesses," the former of which is a gigantic corporation, the latter of which are often far more exploitive of the poor and working classes than are Wal-Marts. To simplify, it is easy to attack individuals, and even sectors—such as finance—and point to them as the problem that can be excised, like a cancer, from the body politic. It is far more difficult to identify and examine capitalism structurally, as a set of social-property relations. Whether from the left or the right, going after a particular sector mystifies capitalist social relations, and does nothing to develop capacities to fight a system, instead of "banksters."

The role of masculinity and whiteness overdetermine but don't define a guiding element of the Trump movement. This leads some on the Left to say that this element has been led into the arms of the right by "identity politics" and so forth. While there is some truth to the fact that the Left, at least until 2008 and the economic crisis, did make a retreat from class and talking about capitalism, this won't do. The misogyny, more than the racism (though not much more), is perhaps the singular guiding element to the Alt Right and its "Men's Rights Activists" (MRA). And on what the MRA crowd has called "men's issues," the Left has not said enough, if anything. As opposed to talking about prison rape, for example, people joke about it. More seriously, the epidemic of white male suicide and opiate abuse, concomitant with the decline of the "industrial working class" and the dominance of organized labor by the often female and Black-led public sector, health care and service unions. This increase in the reserve army of the unemployed, in its gendered component, has not been sufficiently analyzed. Certainly, there are those who take MRA positions, then, that are lost causes, enemies, in other words. But others can perhaps be won over with arguments that allow them to understand their lot in life in relation to capitalism as a whole, which takes seriously their grievances but channels them toward the real problem.

It is precisely in the combined and uneven development of global capitalism that we need to situate the specificity of the reactionary attitudes that emanate, often quite spontaneously and without holding personal prejudices, from the American white working class. The misogyny is rooted in shifts within the labor market, combined with the feeling of being disempowered by women, "cuckolded," and thus, as anti-feminists, they refer to feminist men as "cucks." Yet this reaction is rooted in something concrete. In turn, while there is absolutely no direct relationship between the downward mobility of the white working classes and immigration, both are intrinsically related as component parts of the process of the reproduction of capitalism. It may not be *rational* for white working class people to, like *South Park* satirizies, cry out "they took our jobs" and "build that wall." On a certain level, perhaps disavowed, they know that this process—the process of capitalist social relations and its continued disruption, to use a buzzword, is as inexorable as the factories themselves going to Mexico or China.

Anti-Black racism and Islamophobia seem simultaneously less pronounced and more primordial, depending on what segment of the overall Trump movement one considers. On one hand, there is a cheering on "law enforcement" and the whole "Blue Lives Matter" spiel in the face of police violence. On the other hand, while claiming Black Lives Matter is a "George Soros front," Alex Jones and other right-wing personalities have spoken about the militarization of police, an issue upon which Trump and his base seem to differ. Trump's Islamophobia is in many ways an articulation of what is already U.S. policy. All potential immigrants to the United States coming from majority-Islamic parts of the world are "vetted." The Muslim community is under heavy, regular surveillance, and the government depends a great deal on comprador Imams and "community leaders" to inform and monitor their own communities, much like the FBI would hire anti-communist Jews in the thirties and forties.

Many on the Left would, to return to an earlier point, imply that this growth in the use of prejudiced rhetoric needs a shift in the "hegemonic discourse," or in other terms "political education" and "consciousness raising" among white people, or even "privilege checking." Yet if the Sanders campaign, with its inherent and imminent flaws, showed anything, it's that multiracial coalitions can be built around issues of common concern on a material basis. These struggles have to come from below, and cannot be merely hothoused, or will end up in dissipation. It is far less implausible for assemblies of non-unionized workers and the unemployed to unite under the banner of class struggles than it is to imagine the effort of politically educating the masses of the

American white male working classes, shopfloor by shopfloor, filling station by filling station. The Left, as noted, has either bemoaned the old, traditional working class's lack of militancy, and/or labeled it compromised or a "labor aristocracy." But, in reality, the Left has not been able to engage this segment of the population, in the United States or in Canada. This is not, however, to say that there has been no upheaval.

There was indeed a cycle of protest, of struggle, from 2011 onwards, albeit unevenly. From the Wisconsin uprising to Occupy to the strike by Chicago schoolteachers, the recent victory at Verizon, movements that rise up from below have ebbed and flowed. These struggles, it should be noted, have largely dissipated, while the peace movement is dead. The only social movement with any social weight in the United States right now is Black Lives Matter, which is by nature coalition politics—though the radical left wing of BLM recently put out an excellent policy document.[25] The very thought of systemic change, as opposed to reforms, has been erased from the activist vocabulary. This is not helped by a presidential candidate, for whatever good work he did in challenging and exposing the Democratic Party, calling his program of moderate Scandinavian social democracy a "political revolution," while claiming no opposition to President Obama's most egregious policies—especially his drone program.

The long and short of it is, as Adolph Reed pointed out in 2015, there is no Left in the United States. The Left has not fared well, with a few European exceptions, in the last decade, but on the other hand, people tend to respond, at least electorally, to arguments using broadly "left" themes: inequality, the environment, and social justice. Liberals like Justin Trudeau and Alexis Tsipras won elections on promises of opposing austerity and investing in infrastructure. Yet especially in circumstances where the working classes and poor can look back, even less than a generation, and see people doing better than they are today, it is a situation of profound sadness and anger, the type of sadness and anger that could be channeled into a revolutionary anti-capitalist political project. But alas, revolutionary anti-capitalists are few and far between, and reformism has been exposed as an emperor with no clothes.

So, we have Trump. As the saying goes, the band sucks, but the fans are worse.

Postscript:
Make Racists Afraid Again

In Elia Kazan's A Face in the Crowd, *a country and western musician and rowdy drunk, Lonesome Rhodes, goes from being an advertising spokesperson, 50s version of a reality TV star, to a veritable political kingmaker, rousing the rabble with populist fury, until, while on a "hot mic," he is heard talking about his fans and followers as "guinea pigs," as dupes. Perhaps this was on the minds of some as a "hot mic" recording of Donald Trump suddenly appeared, a scant few weeks before election day, in which, put simply, Trump brags about being a sexual predator.*

This didn't do him in.

Instead, Trump was able to counterpunch, and, not unlike Bill Clinton, throw his survivors under the bus. Meanwhile, as the Hillary Clinton campaign went for "moderate republicans," having pretty much given up on the industrial (and not just "white") working class in the Midwest. The working class and the poor rose up on election day, and voted in Donald Trump.

Trump talks a lot about making America great again, and it is not unlikely that soon this vision will shift to one in which he denounces the racism of his followers. But the alt.right is bigger than Trump and they have a foothold in Trumpland by way of Steve Bannon, who has a seat in the administration. Racists and misogynists and homophobes are emboldened everywhere. Trans folks, people of color, queers, Muslims, Jews, and others have been attacked, while protests have been immediately mischaracterized, including labeling Black Lives Matter protesters "Terrorists."

The time has come, then, to Make Racists Afraid Again. As Trump fails to carry through his program, his followers will be demoralized. Will they turn (alt) right? Or will they listen to radical left arguments? Time will tell, but we need to MAKE RACISTS AFRAID AGAIN! Only then will we move beyond this state of exception.

Endnotes

1 Thomas B. Edsall, "Why Don't the Poor Rise Up?" *New York Times*, June 24, 2015. Available online, http://www.nytimes.com/2015/06/24/opinion/why-dont-the-poor-rise -up.html

2 Thomas Frank, *What's the Matter with Kansas* (New York: Henry Holt, 2004); Georg Lukács, *History and Class Consciousness: Studies in Marxist Dialectics* (Cambridge: MIT Press, 1971).

3 Allum Bokhari and Milo Yiannopoulos, "An Establishment Conservative's Guide to the Alt-Right" *Breitbart*, March 29, 2016. Available online, http://www.breitbart.com/ tech/2016/03/29/an-establishment-conservatives-guide-to-the-alt-right/.

4 Slavoj Žižek, "Only a radicalised left can save Europe," *New Statesman*, June 25, 2014. Available online, http://www.newstatesman.com/politics/2014/06/ slavoj-i-ek-only-radicalised-left-can-save-europe.

5   Walter Benjamin, *Illuminations*, ed. Hannah Arrendt (New York: Schocken, 1968): 253–264.

6   Matthew Worley, *In Search of Revolution: International Communist Parties in the Third Period* (London: IB Tauris, 2004).

7   Dylan Riley and George Souvlis, "Fascism and Democracy: What Gramsci can tell us about the relationship between fascism and liberalism—and the rise of Donald Trump." *Jacobin*, August 19 2016. Available online, https://www.jacobinmag.com/2016/08/ trump-clinton-fascism-authoritarian-democracy/.

8   Edsall, "Why don't the Poor Rise Up."

9   Shaun Scott "Millenials Are Not Here to Save Us" *Jacobin,* February 18 2016. Available online, https://www.jacobinmag.com/2016/02/ millennials-election-baby-boomers-revolution-capitalism/.

10 Laura Built, "One West Virginia city responds to 26 heroin overdoses in only 4 hours: 'This is an epidemic of monumental proportions'" *New York Daily News*, August 17, 2016. Available online, http://www.nydailynews.com/news/national/ west-virginia-city-26-heroin-overdoses-4-hours-article-1.2754742.

11 Robert Brenner, *The Economics of Global Turbulence: The Advanced Capitalist Economies from Long Boom to Long Downturn, 1945–2005* (London: Verso, 2006).

12 Facebook Page, "Teamsters for Trump," August 23, 2016. https://www.facebook.com/ teamstersfortrump/.

13 Noam Schieber, "Unions Lean Democratic, but Donald Trump Gets Members' Attention," *New York Times*, Jan 19, 2016. Available online, http://www.nytimes .com/2016/01/30/business/donald-trump-unions.html.

14 Nick Gass, "Trump: GOP will become 'worker's party' under me" *Politico,* May 26, 2016. Available online, http://www.politico.com/story/2016/05/ trump-gop-workers-party-223598#ixzz4IAWq8n31.

15 Rainer Werner Fassbinder (dir/wr.) *Ali: Fear Eats the Soul* (1974) Berlin: Filmverlag der Autoren.

16 Dylan Riley and George Souvlis, "Fascism and Democracy: What Gramsci can tell us about the relationship between fascism and liberalism—and the rise of Donald Trump."

17 Bokharri and Yiannopolous, "An Establishment Conservative's Guide to the Alt-Right."

18 Ibid.

19 Lawrence Murray, "Multiculturalism in Action: #OurCulturesAreNotCostumes," *The Right Stuff*, November 1, 2015. Available online, http://therightstuff.biz/2015/11/01/ multiculturalism-in-action-ourculturesarenotcostumes/.

20 Nick Land, *The Dark Enlightenment*. Available online, http://www.thedarkenlightenment .com/the-dark-enlightenment-by-nick-land/.

21 Charlie Post, "The Trump Problem," *Jacobin*, April 4, 2016. Available online, https://www .jacobinmag.com/2016/04/donald-trump-republican-party-primary-president/.

22 Ibid.

23 Ibid.

24 Corey Robin, *The Reactionary Mind: Conservatism from Edmund Burke to Sarah Palin* (Oxford: Oxford University Press, 2011).

25 Movement for Black Lives, Platform. Summer 2016. Available online, https://policy.m4bl .org/platform/.

NOT CO-OPTATION
NOR CHARITY

ANTI-POVERTY ORGANIZING
IN CANADA AND THE U.S.

Lesley Wood

- In 2004, fifteen families in East Harlem, New York City formed the Movimiento por Justicia del Barrio. Since that time, 900 members in 85 buildings have joined them, 80% of them women. They have managed to stop evictions by different landlords, with no members losing their home. Modeling themselves on the Zapatistas of Mexico, they have built a strong, supportive community and culture of resistance.[1]

- In 2010 during the Vancouver Winter Olympics, hundreds of poor residents of the Downtown East Side (mostly women) and anti-authoritarian housing activists built a tent village intended "to defend an autonomous, decentralized, and self-determined space amidst a climate of intense state security. It was an affirmation of community, deemed "paradise" by several residents. As a direct result of the month-long grassroots campaign and the popular support for the Tent Village amongst incredibly diverse communities and social justice groups, the government housed over 80 homeless Tent Village residents."[2]

The poor are rising up in Canada and the U.S., but not yet en masse. Why not? Poor people are on the front lines of struggle, but their movements face particular challenges when they push for deep systemic change. The claim that social isolation stops people from rising up cannot explain why in some times and in some places, poor people's mobilization succeeds, and at other times fails to take root.[3]

We know that mobilization is not an automatic result of suffering.[4] Indeed, it is rarely the poorest or most oppressed who fill the streets and meetings. It is more likely to be those who perceive a shift and an injustice. The best models argue that mobilization comes when people interpret and understand a situation as unfair. Often there is some sort of a triggering event. Movements are particularly likely to emerge when authorities are in crisis or conflict.[5] If people begin to see themselves as in such a shared situation, sometimes due to organizing efforts, and understand action to be possible and valuable, mobilization is likely to follow.[6]

Poor people are rising up, particularly around four issues:

1. Opposition to gentrification and the related threat to affordable housing, public services, and accessible spaces is a major battle taking place in the largest urban centers in Canada and the U.S.. In global cities such as New York City, San Francisco, Vancouver, Montreal, and Toronto, poor people are being pushed out of the downtown core by gentrification. Activists Harsha Walia and Dave Diewert define gentrification as "the social, economic, and cultural transformation of a predominantly low-income neighbourhood through the deliberate influx of upscale residential and commercial development."[7] Urban theorist Neil Smith notes, "As a generalized urban strategy, gentrification weaves together the interests of city managers, developers and landlords, corporate employers and cultural and educational institutions."[8] The lack of affordable housing is serious. In Canada, about 3.3 million households (25.2%) spent 30% or more of their total income on shelter.[9] In the U.S., over half of renters spend 30% or more.[10]

2. Policing and prisons. Poor people go to jail. Families lose breadwinners. Black and indigenous people are most frequently affected by the criminal justice system. In 2016, the movement associated with Black Lives Matter is front-page news. The movement around how police brutality and its racism and violence are affecting poor communities is significant and growing.

3. Work. In recent years, there are renewed campaigns to establish a $15 minimum wage,[11] livable wages, against precarious jobs, internships,

and for improved working conditions in a range of occupations, including sex work. As in the past, poor people are mobilizing around crappy work conditions, the lack of good jobs, and the lack of jobs generally. Large national campaigns and smaller efforts abound.

4. Austerity budgets that cut social assistance and public services. Campaigns around work are converging with campaigns around cuts to social assistance and public services. In Canada and the U.S., this has been particularly visible in Quebec, where alliances between grassroots efforts and the union and student movements exist.

In addition to these areas, movements around land claims, immigration, violence against women and trans folks, for affordable childcare, and food security keep on marching. These are major struggles within which poor people are deeply engaged. Although we are seeing important victories, gentrification continues apace, social assistance rates are stagnant, young Black and indigenous people are being killed and imprisoned, and work remains precarious.

The gap between rich and poor is increasing, and poverty is getting worse. In Canada, 14.2% of the population live in poverty. The wealthiest 20% of the population control 67.4% of the wealth and the poorest 20% are in debt, controlling less than 0% of the wealth.[12] This poverty particularly affects racialized families. One in five racialized families live in poverty in Canada, as opposed to one in twenty non-racialized families. Food bank usage across Canada is 26% higher than it was in 2008. Almost one in every five households spends over 50% of their income on rent, which puts them at risk of homelessness.[13]

In the U.S., there are similar statistics. 14.8% of U.S. Americans live in poverty.[14] This is 26.2% for African Americans, 23.6% for Hispanics (sic), 28.3% of Native Americans, versus the relatively small percentage of 10.1% of whites. 28.5% of people with disabilities live in poverty, higher than any racial category. The economic crisis that accelerated in 2008, and the Occupy movement that followed, called into question the increasing levels of inequality. There was a brief moment when it seemed that neoliberal capitalism might be reconsidered. But instead, we saw governments saving the bank's bottom line by adopting austerity budgets that sucked social services dry.

Poor people's movements continue to mobilize and fight back, but aren't strong enough to stop this trend. How are they challenging the status quo? These movements are working on two fronts: making improvements in people's lives through challenging oppressive systems and institutions; and second, maintaining and increasing the power of poor people to control their own lives.

The most effective strategy for these dual goals is debated. Seeking to get beyond disorganized revolt, many movement analysts emphasize the need to build strong, strategic organizations. This often means obtaining resources and building infrastructure and alliances with authorities and other groups. However, Piven and Cloward find that the emphasis on building organizations and institutions tends to lead towards stagnation, bureaucratization, and oligarchy.[15] This does not mean there is no role for leadership, but that this leadership should be mobilizing people to disrupt.[16] Saul Alinsky notes that poor people's organizations don't have access to many resources, and must "build power from flesh and blood."[17] This power is most effective when it disrupts, as shown by Bill Gamson's classic study of hundreds of movement organizations. This disruptive power is most effective when poor people's movements are rooted in and led by people in poor communities, when alliances are diverse, providing human and material resources and skills.[18] Conditions do matter: poor people's movements (like other movements) are most successful at having their demands met by elites when those elites are divided and in flux.[19] Disruptive power never builds without opposition, or without internal divisions. As the Toronto group Ontario Coalition Against Poverty (OCAP) says, "they call it struggle for a reason."

Sucking Energy

There are many reasons why poor people's movements today are not as powerful as they might be. Capitalism and colonialism divide and delude, cities isolate, commodities distract, lack of resources limit, organizations stagnate, violence traumatizes, culture demeans. This paper points to two ways that poor people's movements are coopted and drained by the tactical dilemmas of social movements themselves. These traps are: consultation without control, and casework as charity or social work.

The first, consultations around "poverty reduction," are benign. What could be wrong about being asked, as a poor people's movement, to participate in discussions of what needs to change? Over the past twenty years, politicians and non-governmental organizations organized these consultations within the internationally celebrated framework of poverty reduction. This approach emerged in the wake of widespread critique of structural adjustment policies of the IMF and World Bank. The earlier attempts to stimulate economic growth through cutting social spending had caused widespread social and economic damage.[20] In response to criticism, these institutions embraced new ways of working that emphasized local control and "participation" in the development process. Although intended for low-income countries as a condition for receiving IMF loans, the framework has shaped anti-poverty initiatives in the Global North.[21] By 2010 every province and many municipalities in Canada had a poverty reduction strategy, most with some consultative process. While most U.S. states (with the exception of Connecticut) do not use the language of poverty reduction, large NGOs like American Progress and Children's Defense continue to urge governments to adopt the framework. The Child Poverty Reduction Act of 2015 was assigned to a Congressional Committee, but has seemingly little hope of passing.

Poverty reduction consultations contain struggle by drawing well-meaning activists and poor people into meetings where the goal is a liberal one of inclusion in the existing system. In a parallel process, Nancy Fraser argues that once transformative, radical movements end up pushing for "recognition" rather than redistribution.[22] To be seen as legitimate by the authorities and by some sectors of the population, movements participate, and this becomes the goal. In these spaces, even pointed critiques of capitalist wealth accumulation are seen as "unproductive." Such processes, and the time that they take, direct energy away from mobilization, and have two main limitations: first, they offer consultation, not control; and second, they limit the analysis of the problem and the potential solutions. Let's consider these one by one.

In Ontario and Quebec, government social service and NGOs invited grassroots anti-poverty activists to consult around poverty reduction. The more institutionalized social service sector and NGOs encouraged grassroots activists to attend and "bring their expertise." There were multiple rounds of consultation, which led to the drafting of strategies, and in the case of Quebec, legislation.[23] However, such inclusion was a trap. If a group agreed to attend, its energy was redirected away from disruption toward meetings and wordsmithing. In Ontario, although the activists argued that there needed to be an increase in the social assistance rates of at least $100 per month, this demand was ignored and seen as "unreasonable." In Ontario, the poverty reduction strategy became the more politically palatable "child poverty reduction strategy." OCAP was skeptical of the process. A.J. Withers argued, "we know what the problems are. Welfare and disability rates are too low, we need more affordable housing, and we need the housing we have to be in good repair."[24] Put Food in the Budget quoted OCAP's John Clarke, "The main political capital provided by this approach is that it creates the illusion that the 'complex problem' of poverty is being duly considered, solutions sought and the 'stakeholders' consulted. Through this procedure, community anger can be safely channeled, expectations put on hold, and 'solutions' presented that don't conflict with, and even facilitate, the prevailing agenda."[25]

Although certain benefits have been expanded and programs established, consultations haven't led to significant reductions in poverty. As the Poverty Free Ontario report noted, "The social assistance reform process drags on as any

LESLEY WOOD

momentum offered by the Ontario Government's Poverty Reduction Strategy recedes into distant memory. The Strategy did nothing for adults on social assistance when released in 2008, except promise a reform process that would address their intolerable living conditions."[26] Without control, these consultations co-opt movements. Gamson's *The Strategy of Social Protest* speaks of four different potential outcomes of social movements. If the goals of social movements are (a) recognition and (b) material gains, there are four possibilities: 1. Success 2. Failure 3. Cooptation 4. Pre-emption.[27] Cooptation occurs when there is recognition, but no material gains. This has largely been the outcome of poverty reduction consultations. Those consulting are brought into spaces of power, but they fail to achieve material improvements for their base. This is one of the dangers that Frances Fox Piven and Richard Cloward wrote about in *Poor People's Movements*.[28] Examining the Welfare Rights Movement of the 1970s in the United States, they noted that when poor people's movements gain recognition, the recognition their leaders receive make them vulnerable to co-optation.

Another limitation of anti-poverty consultations is that they aren't able to consider systemic issues. While they examine housing and benefits policies that can be tinkered with, they bracket capitalism itself. Access to housing and benefits make a serious material difference in people's lives, but what is considered "reasonable" and "open for discussion" in consultations is limited. The possibility of talking about "wealth reduction" of the elite is avoided. Poverty is presented as a social problem, but wealth consolidation is not. In these two ways, constrained consultation without real influence can drain movements of their rebellious spirit and power.

Beyond Charity or Social Work

A second trap that today's anti-poverty movements face is the drift away from grassroots mobilization toward charity or social work. As Piven and Cloward's *Poor People's Movements* argues, movement organizations often try to solve the needs of their constituency through casework and advocacy. Getting people what they need to survive by helping them to negotiate housing and social assistance systems is important work. First, it builds the community's trust in the organization or campaign, if you are able to stop an eviction, obtain welfare benefits, or improve a living situation. Second, it gives people a sense of their own power, which will strengthen the movement in the long run. Third, it gives the organization that is doing this, legitimacy in the eyes of the broader public, and thus broader alliances.

However, there are risks in casework. If your campaign is rooted in poor communities, the desire to respond to the needs of that community can be intense. It is difficult to refuse to advocate for a member of the community in need, even though the particular case may not further the broader campaign. This is particularly likely if the anti-poverty activists are primarily middle class and worried about being "disconnected" from the community they are working in. If the casework becomes disconnected from the campaign work and activists neglect their goals of changing the system, casework can lead the group into becoming a social service or social work project. Capp Larsen from the Halifax Coalition Against Poverty notes: "The link between campaign and advocacy work is really important. If you're doing a lot of advocacy work, it's just one battle after another.... That's not going to change the way the system works."[29]

Similarly, Jeanne Fay, a lifelong anti-poverty activist in Halifax explains:

> What happens is that the institutions of power, social work, law, what have you, suck up our energy so we are not doing the door knocking and organizing that needs to be done. Organizing is a full-time job, and it is really hard to do when you are also doing individual casework. Nonetheless, the only way the system will change is if people can organize enough so the politicians listen up and take this more seriously.[30]

Indeed, casework can sap the rebellious spirit from anti-poverty organizing. In order to avoid these pitfalls, OCAP drew on Piven and Cloward's insights about the welfare rights movements of the 1960s and 1970s, and the unemployed workers' movements of the 1930s, to develop direct action casework, a strategy that aims to avoid the drift toward social-work-oriented casework. This approach has three principles: first, to combine legal work with disruptive action; second, not to duplicate the work of legal clinics or other agencies; and third, to forward political goals but never compromise the interests of those you are working with in the process.[31] This model spread widely, to the London (UK) Coalition Against Poverty, Seattle Solidarity Network, Halifax Coalition Against Poverty, and beyond.

Direct action casework aims both to put pressure on the authorities, and to build the power of poor people through keeping casework collective. As Piven and Cloward explain:

> The most effective tactic was to stage group actions on grievances. A group of recipients descended on the welfare center to hold a demonstration, demanding that all grievances be settled before the group left, with the threat that a sit-in would follow

if the demand were not met. These actions generally succeeded, for with the ghettos of the cities seething, welfare officials feared confrontations.[32]

When anti-poverty organizing can avoid these pitfalls of cooptation and social work, it has significant potential. We can see this across Canada and the U.S.. The following examples of poor people's movements have transformed individual cases into shared struggle, and have avoided cooptation and distraction. They have won material gains and built popular power.

- The Boston organization City Life/Vida Urbana launched a Post-Foreclosure Eviction Defense campaign in 2007.[33] Part of the national Right to the City network, City Life blocked over twenty evictions from foreclosed buildings. "They organize tenants in buildings where the landlord has more than 6 units and doesn't owner-occupy. They emphasize training and collective direct action. 'Are you fighting to stay in your home?' They ask; 'Join us at one of our weekly meetings, where you can speak with an organizer and lawyer, and meet others that are fighting the same battles!'"[34] In this way through hundreds of eviction blockades, other direct actions, and court settlements, over 100 Boston families have won the right to remain in their homes.[35] They argue for "protagonismo," and showing how direct action gives people a sense of their own power.

- In 2005, Toronto anti-poverty activists from OCAP began to mobilize around a little-known government benefit, the Special Diet Allowance. This benefit provided welfare recipients with extra money for food if they were designated as having health needs that required it. Working with supportive doctors and nurses, OCAP organized mass clinics where hundreds of people completed their forms, allowing poor people to access the extra money. Despite the government maneuvering to change the system, the amount of money people received from the benefit increased from $57.6 million in 2004 to $257.3 million in 2013.[36]

To eliminate poverty, we need to stop exploitation and the hoarding of money, resources, and opportunities by the wealthy and their defenders.[37] This is not going to happen in the current capitalist system. In the meantime, we need powerful movements that will stop evictions, expand social programs, and reduce income inequality. To do this, we need to avoid pitfalls of cooptation and charity. This means avoiding consultations when they don't lead to real influence or power. This means refusing to deal only with the symptoms of poverty, without challenging those responsible and their institutions. Activists in Boston, Toronto, New York, Miami, and Vancouver built movements that are collective, strategic, equitable/anti-oppressive, and reflexive. And they are winning.

Endnotes

1   Jessica Davies, "Movement for Justice in El Barrio: Ten Years of Struggle for Another Possible World," *Upside Down World,* March 3, 2015. Available online: http://upside-downworld.org/main/news-briefs-archives-68/5229-movement-for-justice-in-el-barrio-ten-years-of-struggle-for-another-possible-world.

2   Harsha Walia, "2011: Reflecting on Social Movement Successes in Canada," *Canadian Dimension,* October 30, 2011. Available online: https://canadiandimension.com/articles/view/2011-reflecting-on-social-movement-successes-in-canada.

3   Thomas B. Edsall, "Why Don't the Poor Rise Up?" *New York Times,* June 24, 2015. Available online: http://www.nytimes.com/2015/06/24/opinion/why-dont-the-poor-rise-up.html.

4   Neil Smelser, *Theory of Collective Behavior* (New York: Free Press, 1962).

5   Sidney G. Tarrow, *Power in Movement,* 3rd edition (New York: Cambridge University Press, 2011), 160.

6   Charles Kurzman, "Structural opportunity and perceived opportunity in social-movement theory: the Iranian revolution of 1979," *American Sociological Review* (1996): 153–170. David S. Meyer and Debra C. Minkoff, "Conceptualizing political opportunity," *Social Forces* 82, no. 4 (2004): 1457–1492.

7   Harsha Walia and Dave Deiwert. "Moving on up: Gentrification in Vancouver's Downtown Eastside," *Rabble.ca,* February 24, 2012. Available online: http://rabble.ca/news/2012/02/moving-gentrification-vancouvers-downtown-eastside.

8   Neil Smith, "Neil Smith: Gentrification in Berlin and the Revanchist State," October 20, 2007, Einstellung der §129(a)-Verfahren - sofort! Available online: https://einstellung.so36.net/en/ps/524.

9   Threshold defined by the Canada Mortgage and Housing Corporation (CMHC) to measure housing affordability.

10 National Low Income Housing Coalition, *Out of Reach 2013.* March 12, 2013. Available online: http://nlihc.org/sites/default/files/oor/2013_OOR.pdf.

11 Of course, $15 is not a living wage in most large cities.

12 Broadbent Institute, *The Wealth Gap: Perceptions and Misconceptions in Canada.* December 2014. Available online: https://d3n8a8pro7vhmx.cloudfront.net/broadbent/pages/31/attachments/original/1430002077/The_Wealth_Gap.pdf?1430002077.

13 "Just the Facts." *Canada Without Poverty.* Available online: http://www.cwp-csp.ca/poverty/just-the-facts/.

14 Carmen DeNavas-Walt and Bernadette D. Proctor, "Income and Poverty in the United States: 2014," United States Department of Labor, September 2015. Available online: https://www.census.gov/content/dam/Census/library/publications/2015/demo/p60-252.pdf.

15 Frances Fox Piven and Richard Cloward. *Poor People's Movements: Why They Succeed, How They Fail* (New York: Vintage, 1977).

16 William A. Gamson, *The Strategy of Social Protest* (Homewood, IL: Dorsey, 1975).

17 Saul Alinsky, *Rules for Radicals: A Pragmatic Primer for Realistic Radicals* (London: Vintage, 1989).

18 Marshall Ganz, "Resources and resourcefulness: Strategic capacity in the unionization of California agriculture, 1959–1966," *American Journal of Sociology* (2000): 1003–1062.

19 Sidney G. Tarrow, *Power in Movement: Social Movements and Contentious Politics* (New York: Cambridge University Press, 2011); Charles Tilly and Lesley J. Wood, *Social Movements 1768–2012* (New York: Routledge, 2012).

20 World Development Movement, "One Size For All: A Study of IMF and World Bank Poverty Reduction Strategies," *Global Justice Now*, September 2005. Available online: http://www.globaljustice.org.uk/resources/one-size-all-study-imf-and-world-bank-poverty-reduction-strategies.

21 Tony Addison, "Revenue Mobilization for Poverty Reduction: What We Know, What We Need to Know," in *What Works for the Poorest? Poverty Reduction Programs for the World's Ultra-Poor*, David Lawson, David Hulme, Imran Matin, and Karen Moore, eds. (Rugby, UK: Practical Action Publishing, 2010), 253–262.

22 Nancy Fraser, *Fortunes of Feminism: From State-Managed Capitalism to Neoliberal Crisis* (London: Verso, 2013).

23 Geranda Notten, "Does public consultation reduce poverty?" CLEP (Collective for a Law on the Elimination of Poverty)," May 27, 2015. Available online: http://www.onpovertyreduction.ca/2015/05/public-consultation/.

24 Ontario Coalition Against Poverty, "OCAP Not Participating in Sham Consultations: Minister Matthews lies to legitimize secret 'poverty meetings,'" June 18, 2008. Available online: http://www.ocap.ca/node/489.

25 Ontario Coalition Against Poverty, "The Austerity Agenda in Sheep's Clothing," *Socialist Project*, January 20, 2016. Available online: http://www.socialistproject.ca/bullet/1209.php.

26 Poverty Free Ontario, "PFO Bulletin #9: Social Assistance Review Paper #2. Missed Opportunity, Even Backsliding, as Austerity Agenda Looms," *Poverty Free Ontario*, February 6, 2012. Available online: http://www.povertyfreeontario.ca/category/social-assistance-review/.

27 William Gamson, *The Strategy of Social Protest* (Homewood, IL: The Dorsey Press, 1975).

28 Frances Fox Piven and Richard Cloward, *Poor People's Movements*.

29 The Halifax Coalition Against Poverty, "Eastern Promises: A Discussion with the Halifax Coalition Against Poverty," *Upping the Anti*, 6 (April 2008): 152–160. Available online: http://uppingtheanti.org/journal/article/06-eastern-promises/.

30 Robert Devet, "It is very dangerous to bring your own agenda." *Halifax Media Coop*, December 29, 2015. Available online: http://halifax.mediacoop.ca/story/it-very-dangerous-bring-your-own-agenda/34324.

31 Ontario Coalition Against Poverty, *Direct Action Casework Manual*. 2003. Available online: http://cril.mitotedigital.org/sites/default/files/content/ocap_casework_manual.pdf.

32 Frances Fox Piven and Richard Cloward, *Poor People's Movements*, 297.

33 City Life/Vida Urbana, "About Us." Available online: http://www.clvu.org/about_us.

34 City Life/Vida Urbana, Home Page. Available online: http://www.clvu.org/.

35 City Life/Vida Urbana 40th anniversary celebration. Available online: http://www.brownpapertickets.com/event/338254.

36 Ontario Coalition Against Poverty, "The Fight for the Special Diet Made a Difference that Hasn't Been Wiped Out!" *Special Diet*, last modified July 5, 2013: https://ocaptoronto.wordpress.com/node/1231.

37 Charles Tilly, *Durable Inequality* (Berkeley: University of California Press, 1999).

CULTIVATING THE RADICAL IMAGINATION IN THE NORTH OF THE AMERICAS

Alex Khasnabish

"Why don't the poor rise up?" During times of capitalist crisis, it seems this question is never far from the lips of liberal pundits, professional observers of social movements, journalists, and a host of other well-meaning social commentators and concerned (middle class) members of the public. In the wake of the 2008 financial crisis, particularly across the global north, this question seemed to ring out again and again as a historically unprecedented transfer of public wealth to private hands was engineered by political elites to make up for the business-as-usual of global capitalism and its functionaries. A simple answer to this question is, of course, that they do. While history written by the powerful goes to very great lengths to expunge these events, examples of the exploited and oppressed rebelling against those who make their lives unliveable are legion.[1] Basic social rights and entitlements often grouped under the umbrella of the welfare state owe their existence—increasingly impoverished and hollowed-out though it may be—not to the enlightened and gracious nature of elites but to the dedicated, tenacious, and decidedly conflictual collective action undertaken by a host of social justice organizations. The fact that these radical histories are suppressed and replaced by myths that stress social progress as distilling from the benevolent paternalism of elites is a critical part of the story I want to tell here. The colonization and enclosure of people's capacity to envision ways of living otherwise is a core dynamic in understanding mechanisms of social control and presenting the status quo as inevitable.

Why don't the poor rise up? What does it mean to frame the question in this way? Given its popularity, it's worth asking some questions about the question itself. Who's asking the question? Is it an exhortation? A complaint? A plea? What do those asking the question imagine would happen if the poor did, indeed, rise up? While the question could be strictly analytical, seeking to understand the complexities of social change, more often than not it's little more than rhetoric. Much like catastrophism—the fervent belief that crisis and collapse will usher in the conditions necessary to realize radical social change, doing what we seemingly cannot do for ourselves[2]—this question is really an invocation seeking to summon an actor ("the poor") and an event (the uprising) capable of doing the daunting work of revolutionary social transformation. It's also awash in liberal sentiment and a manifestation of capitalist alienation. This isn't a question asked by "the poor" themselves or, in fact, by anyone with any real experience in social movement organizing. It's not about why *we* don't rise up, it's about why *they* don't rise up. The question betrays that the one asking it concedes from the outset that their life is infinitely complicated and complex but it's *so simple* to see why the poor ought to rise up and do the dirty work of social justice struggle, so *why don't they?* Much like the language and imagination of "allyship," questions like this always rely on an endless deferral of responsibility on the part of the socially privileged speaker.[3] Implicated in the question and its asking is the belief that somehow "the poor" have so little to lose that they may as well dash themselves against the increasingly formidable rocks of the security state. The larger imagination at work here is one of mysterious and spontaneous forces that operate beyond human intentionality. The question betrays a fundamental misunderstanding of how social change actually happens because it treats it and society as something abstract and ideological, rather than lived, material, and run through by the imagination.

Then there is the question about who "the poor" actually are. Who is the collective actor being summoned here? This quasi-class reductionist formulation occludes the actual operation of oppression. "The poor" are not some unitary, undifferentiated group; if they are a "they," they are heterogeneous. Finally, to ask "why don't the poor rise up?" gives short shrift to the cognitive and affective work of living under white supremacist, patriarchal capitalism. Material conditions of suffering are all too often not sufficient fuel for social movements or revolutionary struggles. Movements don't just explode or emerge, they are built and maintained, organized and animated, and they come at a cost—do this, not that, invest energy and hope here and not else-where; to say nothing of the costs involved in more conflictual action against power holders. People also have to perceive a problem that can be addressed by collective action; grievances are not enough in and of themselves to generate movements, nor is the observable presence of inequality or injustice. These factors must be made meaningful to people. How do people come to collec-tively understand what is possible through struggle? How are these struggles propelled? What animates them?

So, if the oppressed and exploited actually do often resist, rebel, and seek to revolutionize the terms and conditions of their existence, and if the ques-tion about why "the poor" don't "rise up" tells us more about the one ask-ing the question than it does about the possibility of radical collective action and social change, why are robust, powerful, and resilient mass movements for radical social change so conspicuous in their absence in the global north? What most convincingly explains their absence and what factors contribute to building and maintaining them? Rather than rendering the answers to these questions in abstract terms, I turn here to my own experience as an academ-ically-based social researcher with deep and abiding commitments to radical social change. Specifically, I want to briefly explore the critical lessons about grassroots organizing for radical social change over the long haul and the dif-ficult but vital work of fomenting the radical imagination. To do so, I turn to two key examples: the Zapatista movement based in Chiapas, Mexico; and the solidarity research with activists and organizers carried out since 2010 by the Radical Imagination Project in Halifax, Nova Scotia, Canada (K'jipuktuk, Mi'Kma'ki) by myself and my project co-director, Max Haiven. These two examples shed important light on the critical question of when and how ex-ploited and oppressed people organize collectively to change their world, and how and why such attempts are neutralized.

Enough!

On January 1, 1994 two important events happened: the North American Free Trade Agreement (NAFTA) came into force, binding Canada, the United States, and Mexico together in what was, at the time, the largest and most significant neoliberal capitalist compact in the world; and the Zapatista Army of National Liberation (*Ejército Zapatista de Liberación Nacional*, EZLN) emerged publicly in Chiapas, a state in Mexico's far southeast, and declared war on the Mexican federal executive and the army. The two events were relat-ed. I have written much about the Zapatistas, the roots of their rebellion, and its transnational resonance elsewhere, and due to constraints of time, space, and topic I won't rehash this here.[4] Instead, I only want to highlight what the Zapatistas' struggle for "democracy, justice, and liberty" means to the discussion at hand and the lessons it offers for other attempts at radical social change.

For many activists who came of age during the alter-globalization movement, the story of the Zapatistas is a familiar one. It is now largely axiomatic to state that the wave of anticapitalist, transnationally networked, radically democratic struggles associated with the alterglobalization "movement of movements" would not have coalesced in the way that it did without the Zapatista uprising.[5] At a time when the U.S. loomed as the lone remaining global superpower, neoliberal capitalism and its trappings of liberal democracy were globally ascendant and the landscape of alternatives seemed woefully barren, the Zapatista uprising seemed like an impossibly bright spark for many. While the uprising was militarily contained by the Mexican military very quickly, the tremendous cry of solidarity and support from millions of Mexicans compelled the government to declare a unilateral ceasefire and enter protracted negotiations with the EZLN.

Comprised of Indigenous peasants from several different Mayan language groups drawn from the highlands, canyons, and jungles of Chiapas, the insurgents of the EZLN along with their base communities were immediately recognized as amongst the very poorest and most disenfranchised in Mexico.[6] Affirming their indigenousness and their Mexicanness, the Zapatistas refused to play the part of yet another iteration in a long line of Latin American guerrilla insurgencies. From their first public statements, the Zapatistas situated their uprising in the context of 500 years of resistance to genocide, colonialism, imperialism, racism, and capitalism. They disavowed the desire to seize the bureaucratic apparatus of the state and to impose their vision of revolution on everyone else. They also refused to lay down their arms while simultaneously eschewing further military action as a way to bring about radical social change in Mexico. In part this move was, of course, simply pragmatic, as the EZLN was woefully outgunned compared to the Mexican army. Nevertheless, their persistence as an insurgent force willing to defend territory and lives with force if necessary, alongside the enthusiastic, dialogic engagement with "national and international civil society" as they began connecting struggles, proved inspiring and potent from a strategic perspective.[7] Embarking on a struggle now into its third decade, the Zapatistas have always centered the autonomy of their movement and the building of autonomous relations of good governance among their communities in rebel territory in Chiapas within a larger frame of an anticapitalist, radically democratic, and interconnected struggle to build a world "capable of holding many worlds."[8] They have won incredible victories and faced bitter defeats. The defeats have come, most often, at the hands of the state's repressive forces and those that it arms and abets. The movement's victories are found in the realization of existing relations of autonomous governance and the material and socio-political conditions upon which they rely across nearly a third of the state of Chiapas. While the EZLN remains an armed organization, the Zapatista base communities have built clinics, schools, governance structures, and an economy that is accountable to the communities themselves and run according to the radically democratic, anticapitalist principles of the Zapatista struggle.

How can we account for the resilience of the Zapatista movement? At a time in world history when neoliberal ideologues were shrilly proclaiming the "end of history" and the unquestioned ascendance of globalized capitalism and its liberal democratic ornamentations, the Zapatista uprising seemed to many to be an anachronism, and a doomed one at that. There are three key factors that have been central to the resilience and power of the Zapatista movement: the Zapatistas' deep commitment to grassroots organizing for the long haul; the elaboration of the movement as built on living communities in and of resistance; and the resonance of Zapatismo (the political philosophy and practice of the Zapatista movement) as a radical political imaginary that broke with worn leftist ideologies and the bankruptcy of the status quo.

For many northern activists and observers who found themselves profoundly inspired by the Zapatistas, the story of this struggle often begins on January 1, 1994. While the date of the uprising and its connection to the Zapatistas' declaration that NAFTA represented a "death sentence" to the Indigenous peoples of Mexico are indeed hugely significant, a focus on the uprising too often obscures the careful, arduous, and challenging work—much of which had to be carried out clandestinely—of organizing the EZLN and the Zapatista base communities themselves. This phase of struggle begins fully ten years before the uprising itself.[9] But even starting the story here doesn't tell us enough. The modern day Zapatistas are run through by multiple radical histories, including guerrilla insurgencies both rural and urban in Mexico dating to the mid-20th century; Indigenous resistance to genocide and colonialism stretching back five centuries; peasant, worker, and student organizing independent of the state and its attempts at cooptation; the brutally supressed but most radically liberatory strands of the Mexican Revolution (1910–1917); and diverse, robust, and frustrated attempts at organizing for social justice by nonviolent means at regional, state, and national levels in every decade since the end of the Mexican Revolution.[10] This is no mere argument to consider the movement in context of other radical and revolutionary struggles in Mexico, although that is, of course, important. Rather, there are clear threads—sometimes individuals, sometimes organizations, sometimes imaginations and ideas—connecting the Zapatista movement to radical struggles across time and space. This radical ecology has been essential to the endurance of the Zapatista struggle, and is an important lesson for radicals elsewhere. While our eyes may be drawn to exceptional, dramatic, and inspiring examples of movement success, such success is only possible in the midst of a fertile field of experiments in organizing for radical social change. Isolation is nothing less than a recipe for defeat.

When revolutionary cadres arrived in Chiapas by way of Mexico City in the early 1980s with the goal of organizing the peasantry for revolution, they did so as members of a revolutionary organization known as the Forces of National Liberation working from an explicitly Marxist understanding of exploitation and a revolutionary horizon traced by that ideology. Among this small group is the man who would eventually become Subcomandante Insurgente Marcos, one of the Zapatistas' key spokespeople and military strategists. Reflecting on these early days, Marcos has recounted not only how challenging life as a clandestine revolutionary was but how little resonance the analysis and ideological line the urban revolutionaries brought with them had in the Indigenous southeast. This wasn't because Indigenous peasants in Chiapas were somehow incapable of understanding their own exploited and oppressed state, but because the worldview of that analytical line made no sense in the terms of their own experience. Before they could go to work in the communities, these urban revolutionaries had to learn about the Indigenous realities alive in Chiapas and submit themselves to them. This involved not only pragmatic issues such as learning Mayan languages but coming to understand the lifeways, lived experiences, and conceptions of reality embodied by the communities. In the process, as Marcos and many other Zapatista leaders have affirmed over the years, these urban revolutionaries and their ideologies were challenged and transformed, and the possibility for the emergence of what would become the Zapatista struggle was established.

Over the next decade, the EZLN would grow by taking root in communities confronted by a host of systemic violence and inequalities. In fact, the EZLN's first phase was organizing armed self-defense units to protect communities against the brutal repression meted out by the state and wealthy landowners.[11] Rather than beginning with grand revolutionary goals of total social transformation, the Zapatista movement's origin lies in the everyday, enduring realities of life in the base communities themselves. It is vital to understand that the EZLN entered a social and political terrain already shaped by numerous other processes and actors, and deeply marked by profound social injustices and rich traditions of struggle against them. It is impossible to do justice to this context here, but it is necessary to acknowledge it in order to highlight the fact that Zapatismo and the EZLN built upon this foundation rather than starting something entirely new. The Mexican political context has, at least since the Mexican Revolution, been marked by an elite strategy of social control and "progress" through the cooptation or, failing that, repression of popular movements. By the 1980s, the neoliberal capitalist transformation of the state significantly undercut the co-optative capacities of elites by hollowing out their ability to distribute material benefits, however limited, in exchange for compliance. The result was a fracturing of the social pact that elites had engineered in the aftermath of the Revolution that essentially brought popular demobilization through state inclusion and a measure of material benefit—or at least the faint hope of it. The Zapatista uprising was not spontaneous; rather, it was one outcome of a protracted process of dedicated, difficult, and often dangerous organizing for social justice that had all too often been frustrated.

While the EZLN had to be organized clandestinely as an armed and insurgent organization, the real roots of Zapatismo and the source of its strength are in its base communities. The EZLN remains an armed, belligerent force but it has not engaged in any significant offensive action since the January 1994 uprising. In fact, it can be argued that following the government's unilaterally declared ceasefire on January 12, 1994, it has been civil Zapatismo that has led the way rather than the EZLN itself. This is not an argument for the primacy of nonviolent struggle; instead, what I am pointing to here is the central role played by people collectively struggling even as they live their lives together. Indeed, one of the primary sources of the Zapatistas' strength is that they have hundreds of thousands of people—from the very youngest to the elders—engaged in building lived alternatives to the status quo. These are not subcultural, ephemeral scenes; they are living communities of and in resistance. This focus on collective life takes seriously social reproduction, which too many northern activists have failed to wrestle with effectively. It has become a truism in relation to the Zapatista struggle that the first uprising did not occur on January 1, 1994 but a year earlier when the EZLN ratified the Women's Revolutionary Law which codified the Zapatistas' commitment to confronting and overturning many of the entrenched patriarchal injustices at work in their—and so many other—communities.[12] Alongside this, the Zapatistas' revolutionary work has involved building schools, clinics, centers of autonomous and democratic governance, textile and coffee production infrastructure, and more. These are not spaces to "drop out"; they are the lifeblood of a living struggle for radical social change. Unlike so much activism, the Zapatistas' struggle isn't episodic, nor is it an activity or place set off from daily life. And while Zapatista territory is certainly not an unconflicted anarcho-communist utopia free of contradiction or enduring power inequalities, as a movement the Zapatistas have found a way to integrate a bold, long-term, anticapital-ist, radically-democratic vision of social change with a recognition that any movement worth its salt must be able to meet the daily needs of those who make it up.

The significance of Zapatismo as a radical political imaginary that broke with the failed experiments and bankruptcies of the left and right cannot be overstated. Powerful movements are not merely vehicles for the grievances of the oppressed and exploited, they must also be animated by collective imagina-tions of what else is possible, of how we might live otherwise. While no longer regarded, rightly or wrongly, as being at the forefront of a wave of radical strug-gle as they were at the turn of the millennium, the Zapatistas have indelibly marked the fabric of radical politics on a global scale. While it seems a strange thing to say in an age when so many recent movement-based challenges to the status quo have centrally concerned themselves with the absence or erosion of democratic practice, and Indigenous people's struggles are seen as being at the forefront of social and ecological justice struggles, at the time of their emer-gence the Zapatistas offered an irresistible antidote to the political hegemonies of both left and right. The Zapatistas compelled many to think deeply about concepts like justice, democracy, and liberty, and did so in engaging and fre-quently eloquent ways.

To me, the timing of the Zapatista uprising remains incredible. At a mo-ment in world history when bold alternatives to neoliberal capitalist status quo seemed nearly impossible, the Zapatistas rose up in a remote corner of Mexico and reminded us all that dignity would not be so easily surrendered. From a tactical perspective, the uprising seemed suicidal, and the Zapatistas' mili-tary command—Marcos included—did not support it. And yet, as historian Adolfo Gilly so penetratingly notes, members of the Zapatista base commu-nities, the Zapatista rank-and-file, measured the necessity of rebellion "against the arc of their own lives."[13] As Chris Dixon has insightfully remarked, activ-ists and organizers too often get lost in debating principles and forget about plans.[14] Dixon isn't calling for a politics that erases ideological difference: far from it; rather, he reminds us not to get lost in abstraction. Their feet planted firmly on the soil of their territory in rebellion, the Zapatistas have remained committed to radically democratic, anticapitalist social change while building a revolution committed to meeting needs in the here-and-now.

Liberating the Radical Imagination

The Zapatista movement offers important insights about how and under what circumstances exploited and oppressed peoples rise up to reclaim their lives.

This is not to suggest that there is a template or a set of objective factors that need to be realized to see this kind of mass organization in any given context. If anything should be clear from the analysis I offer above, it is that context is vital to movements, not just by way of explaining them, but also to their very existence. Farther north in the Americas, powerful, durable, and robust mass movements for social change remain ephemeral. While eruptions of social movement activity are not uncommon, cultivating a fertile movement ecology that is capable of enduring and making radical social change over the long term has proven much more elusive. This is true of Halifax, Nova Scotia, a city on Canada's east coast where I live and work. In 2010 this boom-and-bust cycle of activism combined with the broader absence of radical mass movements capable of contesting the elite austerity agenda in the wake of capitalism's most recent global crisis led me and Max Haiven to found the Radical Imagination Project a social movement research project committed to convoking the radical imagination that is the spark of radical movements for social change alongside of activists and organizers in the city.[15] As academics working within the neoliberalized confines of the university but with histories of and enduring commitments to organizing for radical social change, we wanted to find a way to put the resources of the university to work with movements to accomplish something they could not or were not already doing for themselves.[16]

We have described our project in detail elsewhere, but for my purposes here it is enough to highlight some of its key features as they relate to making social change from the grassroots.[17] First, the project has always operated according to principles quite different than most academically-based social movement research. Rather than attempting to generate "reliable data" and endlessly engage in the self-aggrandizing, academic-capital-generating work of commenting on social movements for an audience of other academic specialists, we have from the outset used the project as a process to generate encounters where people have the opportunity to discuss and think through how we might collectively live otherwise. As Robin Kelley has so poetically and powerfully argued in his work on the Black radical imagination, "[r]evolutionary dreams erupt out of political engagement; collective social movements are incubators of new knowledge."[18] As the Zapatista example shows so well, powerful movements do not spend their lives in the airy heights of victory or mired in defeat, instead they exist in that everyday space of social reproduction as they attend to the daily work of maintaining themselves.[19] While it is understandable that our eyes are often drawn to the movement moments of high drama—a massive protest event, a dramatic confrontation with elites and their agents of repression, a symbolic event bringing struggles together to show strength and solidarity—these are also the most ephemeral, superficial, and least useful places to imagine contributing to building radical struggle. Rather than focusing on events and tactics, the Radical Imagination Project has sought to open up space, process, and time for activists, organizers, and interested but uninitiated others to collectively explore bold visions of political possibility. A discussion of the methods used to accomplish this is tangential to the question of why the oppressed and exploited rise up; instead, I will explore the link between impoverished imaginations of the politically possible, and the difficulties confronting mass organizing for radical social justice in the north of the Americas today.

It seems an obvious point, but it bears reiterating nonetheless: if people do not believe things can be different, then they are not going to give of their energy, time, and effort. This is not to say people need a fully developed blueprint of some future society to work to change this one for the better. Rather, as social movement scholar Eric Selbin has so astutely noted, stories of past struggles told and retold in different ways serve a vital role in keeping people's imaginations attuned to the possibility of change even in dark times.[20] This is, perhaps, one of the most significant obstacles to organizing people for social change today, especially in places like Canada and the United States where capitalist modernity suffuses the fabric of daily life so profoundly. As autonomist Marxist scholar John Holloway discusses, one of the most potent weapons of capitalism is the powerful alienation it produces.[21] Not only does capitalism violently separate those who produce wealth from the means of production, it separates people from their ability to even conceive of themselves doing collective, social activity. Capitalism produces cascading alienation, and the state bureaucracy of Western modernity doubles down on it as people in the belly of the neoliberal capitalist beast come to see every social need, every contribution, every interaction, as mediated and validated through either bureaucratic institutions or the market. It is surely not a new observation to note that capitalism produces alienation, but the point I want to make here is that one of the manifestations of this alienation is the withering of people's ability even to imagine that there could be an alternative to the status quo. Without radical visions of possibility, reformist tinkering with the architecture of exploitation and oppression becomes the political horizon for many.

These effects are not merely cognitive, either. In fact, this is a question of imagination and lived realities. If the imagination is not a thing we have but something we do together, and if it is the spark of radical social movements, then it should be clear that the imagination is not an abstraction, it is something that we live into being. The Zapatistas are, once again, a case in point here. Marcos's communiqués, Zapatista declarations, and political performance all play a vital role in articulating and circulating Zapatismo as a transnationalized imaginary of radical political possibility. But the roots of

Zapatismo lie deep in the soil of rebel territory, in the simple fact that the Zapatistas build their struggle daily together, and they have built social, political, economic, and cultural institutions, practices, and infrastructure that sustains them. This is something that northern movements almost never do. While people may come together as defectors from the status quo, we rarely manage to constitute more than subcultural scenes or episodic eruptions of anger or dismay at the status quo. Unless and until movements can build capacity that allows them to sustain the lives of the people who make them up without depending on the market or state to do so, they will remain rejections of, rather than alternatives to, the status quo.

The liberation of the radical imagination and the development of movement capacities to do the work of social reproduction are both challenging tasks. In 2010 we began the Radical Imagination Project as a way of engaging self-identified radical activists in Halifax in hopes of providing a space and a process to work through the deep rifts, malaise, and not infrequently bitter sectarianism that characterized the radical social justice scene in the city. As the project has moved through different phases and points of focus, we have sought to engage a broader public concerned with issues of social justice, many of whom are not yet active in movement-related work. Through interviews and focus groups, public meetings and film screenings, speaker's events and activist skill-sharing workshops, free schools, and the circulation of radical ideas and analysis across a variety of media and venues, we have played a small part in attempting to break the enclosure of our movements and our radical imagination by white supremacist, patriarchal capitalism in our corner of the Anglophone North Atlantic world. But to call any of these interventions successes would be to overstate our contribution and to misunderstand the way that radical change happens. While the narrative of tipping point moments and dramatic breaks is seductive and inspiring, it is little more than a daydream fantasizing about ways to do end-runs around the arduous, uncertain work of learning to live differently together. There is no short cut to this, no silver bullet or magical elixir that will produce the movements we so urgently need. Crisis will not deliver us from ourselves, either; it will only give us over to those among us most ready and willing to use it as alibi for their own totalitarian ambitions.[22]

So why don't the poor rise up? The exploited and oppressed don't rise up when there seems to be no better alternative to be struggled for. They don't rise up at the behest of those who refuse to risk their own security, status, and material benefits, ill gotten through their enduring complicity with the current order. They don't rise up when the conditions of social life have become so decomposed that our connections to and responsibilities for one another no longer have meaning outside of the smallest circle of intimate relations or capitalist coordinates of value. And, perhaps most importantly, they don't rise up because "rising up" is a fantasy, a cathartic exercise that substitutes a quasi-magical subject appearing on the stage of history almost as if from nowhere to save us all from ourselves.

Drawing on lessons learned from my engagement with the Zapatista movement and the Radical Imagination Project, I have sought to offer here a few basic insights about what makes for robust, durable, and powerful movements built to change the world from the grassroots up. I make no claims to novelty here, nor do I suggest any of these or the larger argument of which they are a part is any kind of panacea for the ills wrought by the exploitative, oppressive system of relations in which we exist now. If these insights have merit, the credit belongs to the dedicated activists and organizers with whom I've had the privilege to work over the years, and whose knowledge and wisdom my own work is committed to circulating. If they don't, the errors lie with me. For those of us committed to radical social change—that is anticapitalist, decolonial, and radically democratic and collectively liberatory—our moment can seem dark indeed. But while the work of organizing for radical social justice and social change must be understood as happening over the long haul, there is no science for predicting rebellious or even revolutionary moments of opportunity. Hope lives in these unexpected and surprising moments and spaces; our task is to be ready to take advantage of them when they do come. Especially in dark times, the work of those committed to social justice and social change must be about building organizational capacity and cultivating the radical imagination. There simply is no substitute.

Endnotes

1   See, for example, Silvia Federici, *Caliban and the Witch: Women, the Body and Primitive Accumulation* (Brooklyn: Autonomedia, 2004); C. L. R James, *The Black Jacobins: Toussaint L'Ouverture and the San Domingo Revolution* (New York: Vintage Books, 1989); Peter Linebaugh, *The Magna Carta Manifesto: Liberties and Commons for All* (Berkeley: University of California Press, 2008); Peter Linebaugh and Marcus Rediker, *The Many-Headed Hydra: Sailors, Slaves, Commoners, and the Hidden History of the Revolutionary Atlantic* (Boston: Beacon Press, 2000), http://site.ebrary.com/id/10014732; Ian McKay, *Rebels, Reds, Radicals: Rethinking Canada's Left History* (Toronto: Between the Lines, 2005); Scott Neigh, *Resisting the State: Canadian History through the Stories of Activists* (Halifax: Fernwood Pub, 2012); Marcus Rediker, *Villains of All Nations: Atlantic Pirates in the Golden Age* (Boston: Beacon Press, 2004); Howard Zinn, *A People's History of the United States: 1492–Present* (New York: Harper Perennial Modern Classics, 2005).

2   Sasha Lilley et al., *Catastrophism: The Apocalyptic Politics of Collapse and Rebirth* (Oakland, Calif: PM Press, 2012).

3   See Cindy Milstein, *Taking Sides: Revolutionary Solidarity and the Poverty of Liberalism* (Oakland: AK Press, 2015).

4   Alex Khasnabish, *Zapatismo beyond Borders: New Imaginations of Political Possibility* (Toronto: University of Toronto Press, 2008); Alex Khasnabish, *Zapatistas: Rebellion from the Grassroots to the Global* (London: Zed Press, 2010).

5   See, for example, Paul Kingsnorth, *One No, Many Yeses: A Journey to the Heart of the Global Resistance Movement* (London: Free Press, 2004); Naomi Klein, "Rebellion in Chiapas," in *Fences and Windows: Dispatches from the Front Lines of the Globalization Debate* (Toronto: Vintage Canada, 2002), 208–23; Midnight Notes, ed., *Auroras of the Zapatistas: Local and Global Struggles of the Fourth World War* (Brooklyn: Autonomedia, 2001); Notes from Nowhere, ed., *We Are Everywhere: The Irresistible Rise of Global Anticapitalism* (New York: Verso, 2003); Rebecca Solnit, *Hope in the Dark: Untold Histories, Wild Possibilities* (New York: Nation Books, 2004).

6   Adolfo Gilly, "Chiapas and the Rebellion of the Enchanted World," in *Rural Revolt in Mexico: US Intervention and the Domain of Subaltern Politics*, ed. Daniel Nugent (Durham: Duke University Press, 1998).

7   Subcomandante Insurgente Marcos, *Our Word Is Our Weapon: Selected Writings*, ed. Juana Ponce de León (New York: Seven Stories Press, 2002).

8   See Gloria Muñoz Ramírez, *The Fire & the Word: A History of the Zapatista Movement* (San Francisco: City Lights Books, 2008).

9   George Collier, *Basta!: Land and the Zapatista Rebellion in Chiapas*, Rev. ed. (Oakland: Food First Books, 1999); Muñoz Ramírez, *The Fire & the Word: A History of the Zapatista Movement*; John Womack, *Rebellion in Chiapas: An Historical Reader* (New York: New Press, 1999).

10 Collier, *Basta!*; Khasnabish, *Zapatistas*; Muñoz Ramírez, *The Fire & the Word*; Womack, *Rebellion in Chiapas*.

11 Gilly, "Chiapas and the Rebellion of the Enchanted World"; Muñoz Ramírez, *The Fire & the Word: A History of the Zapatista Movement*; Womack, *Rebellion in Chiapas*.

12 Ejército Zapatista de Liberación Nacional, "Women's Revolutionary Law" (Zapatista Index, 1993), http://flag.blackened.net/revolt/mexico/ezln/womlaw.html; Rosalva Aída Hernández Castillo, "Between Hope and Adversity: The Struggle of Organized Women in Chiapas since the Zapatista Uprising," *Journal of Latin American Anthropology* 3, no. 1 (1997): 102–20; Elena Poniatowska, "Women's Battle for Respect Inch by Inch," in *The Zapatista Reader*, ed. Tom Hayden (New York: Thunder's Mouth Press, 2002), 55–57; Lynn Stephen, *Zapata Lives!: Histories and Cultural Politics in Southern Mexico* (Berkeley: University of California Press, 2002).

13 Gilly, "Chiapas and the Rebellion of the Enchanted World," 303.

14 Chris Dixon, *Another Politics: Talking across Today's Transformative Movements* (Berkeley: University of California Press, 2014).

15 More at: radicalimagination.org.

16 Alex Khasnabish and Max Haiven, "Convoking the Radical Imagination: Social Movement Research, Dialogic Methodologies, and Scholarly Vocations," *Cultural Studies<=>Critical Methodologies* 12, no. 5 (July 11, 2012): 408–21, doi:10.1177/1532708612453126.

17 Max Haiven and Alex Khasnabish, *The Radical Imagination: Social Movement Research in the Age of Austerity* (Halifax; London: Zed Books/Fernwood Pub., 2014).

18 Robin Kelley, *Freedom Dreams: The Black Radical Imagination* (Boston: Beacon Press, 2002), 8.

19 Max Haiven and Alex Khasnabish, "Between Success and Failure: Dwelling with Social Movements in the Hiatus," *Interface: A Journal for and about Social Movements* 5, no. 2 (2013): 472–98.

20 Eric Selbin, *Revolution, Rebellion, Resistance: The Power of Story* (London; New York: Zed Books, 2010).
21 John Holloway, *Change the World without Taking Power: The Meaning of Revolution Today* (London: Pluto Press, 2002); John Holloway, *Crack Capitalism*, (London: Pluto, 2010).
22 Lilley et al., *Catastrophism*.

ON THE SPIRITUAL EXPLOITATION OF THE POOR

Nathan Jun

"The gospel tells us, cries the priest, that there will always be poor people, *Pauperes semper habebitis vobiscum*, and that property, consequently in so far as it is a privilege and makes poor people, is sacred. Poverty is necessary to the exercise of evangelical charity; at the banquet of this world here below there cannot be room for all."
—Pierre-Joseph Proudhon[1]

Introduction

IN THIS CHAPTER I DISCUSS THE ROLE THAT THE SO-CALLED CHRISTIAN RIGHT plays in encouraging and perpetuating economic inequality in the United States by demonizing poverty, exalting the capitalist system, and discouraging economically vulnerable populations from resisting their own oppression. In so doing I aim to defend two distinct but related theses. The first is that the Christian Right's beliefs about and behavior toward the poor follows from an underlying political theology which, while it has a substantive affinity with secular capitalist ideologies and, indeed, with capitalism itself, is neither solely nor even chiefly *determined* by them. The second is that although the Christian Right's oppression of the poor intersects and overlaps with capitalist exploitation, it is not simply an extension or variation of the same.

Religions can and do have genuine power independent of ruling classes, which means that they can and do exist independently of, and prior to, the particular modes of production that give rise to ruling classes in the first place. Thus, although religions frequently play a role in generating forms of false consciousness that disempower the oppressed, they do not always do so for the sake of ruling economic interests, or as a mechanical consequence of underlying economic structures. On the contrary, religions often proceed in a perfectly autonomous fashion in their efforts to promote their own interests and to advance their most fundamental theological and political commitments. To the extent that such efforts require, or at least result in, the oppression or exploitation of the poor and other marginalized groups, this oppression or exploitation is altogether distinct from the kind that occurs under capitalism even if they happen to coincide. All of this suggests that eradicating the capitalist mode of production does not necessarily eliminate capitalist ideologies like the Christian Right—a notion that has significant ramifications for the struggle against economic oppression in the United States and around the world.

Religion and False Consciousness

"What has to be explained," wrote Wilhelm Reich, "is not the fact that the man who is hungry steals or the fact that the man who is exploited strikes, but why the majority of those who are hungry don't steal and why the majority of those who are exploited don't strike."[2] For Marx, as is well known, this phenomenon is a straightforward consequence of the ideological "superstructures" of capitalist society—that is, by the various social, political, legal, and cultural institutions that generate beliefs, attitudes, and other "forms of social consciousness."[3] Because the "real foundation" of these superstructures is the underlying "economic structure of society," the "general character" of the forms of consciousness they create is determined by "the mode of production in material life."[4] This implies that the major institutions of capitalist society tend to produce ideas that reinforce capitalist economic structures and, by extension, the power of the capitalist class. Because this effect comes at the expense of the working classes, however, its achievement requires them to accept "a number of closely related illusions"[5] that domesticate their "potentially revolutionary impulses"[6] and, more generally, "prevent [them] from behaving as their interests would otherwise dictate."[7] It is precisely such illusions—which Marx terms "false consciousness"—that account for the persistent failure of oppressed people to resist their own oppression in the way Reich describes.

Religion is unique among social institutions in its ability to shape "people's interpretation of the world" and to influence their "beliefs, goals, emotions, and behaviors, as well as… their interactions on both interpersonal and intergroup (national and international) levels."[8] This ability derives, in the first place, from the superior authority religion claims for itself on the basis of its alleged ability to disclose "*transcendent* reality."[9] Furthermore, by purporting to have privileged awareness of, and access to, a higher dimension of being that is not subject to the limitations and imperfections of ordinary material existence, religion presents itself as a source of absolute or universal truth.[10] In this way it obscures its embeddedness within concrete empirical circumstances, making it appear as something other than a human invention.[11] This enables it to function as an especially powerful form of false consciousness—an "opium," as Marx put it, that inures "the oppressed creature" to the "real wretchedness" of his situation while simultaneously concealing its true cause.[12]

Marx's theory of ideology has been routinely criticized on the grounds that it "tends to ignore many aspects of religion, to oversimplify a complex phenomenon, and to make sweeping generalizations."[13] My own misgivings concern its tendency to reduce all oppression to economic oppression, on the one hand, and its failure to acknowledge the relative autonomy of different forms of social consciousness, on the other. On Marx's account, the various components of the capitalist superstructure are oppressive only insofar as they abet capitalist exploitation of poor and working class people via the production of false consciousness. This suggests that the use of religion to more effectively oppress them is simply a variation of economic exploitation. Putting aside the fact that religions can and do oppress women, racial and ethnic minorities, LGBT people, and the like for reasons that have nothing to do with their class position, it is simply not the case that religions rationalize exploitation and other forms of oppression solely or even chiefly for the sake, or at the explicit or implicit behest, of the ruling class, nor that they are "determined" by the "mode of production of the material conditions of life"—at least not if "determined" means *caused to exist or to take some one particular form rather than another.*

This is not to deny that religions play a role in reinforcing existing economic structures and promoting ideological agendas that serve the interests of one class at the expense of others, nor that existing power structures have the capacity to *condition* or *influence* religions in various ways. Ruling classes have supported and even deliberately co-opted religions that reinforce (or have the capacity to reinforce) their wealth and power. This is evident, for example, in the case of "civil religion," whereby a ruling class uses religion to "sanctif[y] existing political values into common creed for all society."[14] But religions have also sought to reinforce their own power by means of what Benjamin Lynerd calls "political theology"—i.e., "the practice of extracting political values from [the] religious beliefs... of existing faith traditions."[15] In some cases this occurs by default, as when a religion's beliefs just happen to coincide with ruling interests; in others, it requires existing beliefs to be altered or new beliefs to be created for the explicit purpose of currying favor with the ruling class.

The Christian Right: A Brief Overview

The term "Christian Right" refers to a political, social, and religious movement comprising a "loose alliance of politically motivated and mobilized Christian conservatives who have played a significant role in American politics since the late 1970s."[16] Motivated by a desire to "restore the 'Christian' character of American culture [and] to provide a 'Christian' solution for the... problems of society,"[17] the movement is known for aggressively promoting a host of extreme right-wing causes including, but not limited to, "mak[ing] abortion illegal, fighting against gay rights (particularly gay marriage), supporting prayer in school, advocating 'abstinence only' sex education, opposing stem cell research, curtailing welfare spending, opposing gun control, and celebrating the war on terrorism."[18] This agenda reflects an underlying "political theology"—that is, a set of political beliefs, values, and principles that are derived (or purport to be derived) from a particular religious worldview. Although the Christian Right has always included a wide variety of perspectives ranging from Pentecostalism to Roman Catholicism, its political theology is rooted in the particular form of American evangelical Christianity from which it evolved historically.

The definition of "evangelical Christianity" (or "evangelicalism") is a matter of considerable dispute even among those who identify as "evangelicals." The American theologian Roger Olson, for example, has argued that the term has no fewer than "seven distinct though occasionally overlapping meanings," all of which "are legitimized by either broad historical usage or common contemporary usage."[19] For purposes of this chapter, I understand evangelicalism to refer to a broad theological orientation "situated [chiefly] in the Reformed and Wesleyan traditions" of Protestant Christianity that arose "during the eighteenth century in Great Britain and its colonies."[20] The four "defining qualities" of this orientation are usually described as *conversionism* (the belief that Christianity involves being "born again" in Christ), *crucicentrism* (the belief that salvation is made possible by Christ's death and resurrection), *biblicism* (the belief that the Bible is the inspired word of God and, by extension, the sole and absolute foundation of truth), and *activism* (the belief that Christians should actively encourage the conversion of non-Christians).[21]

According to this account, evangelicalism encompasses "a diverse group of individuals, congregations, denominations, and nondenominational ministries"[22] including "holiness churches, Pentecostals, traditionalist Methodists, all sorts of Baptists, Presbyterians, Black churches in all these traditions, fundamentalists, [and] pietist groups… to name only some of the most prominent types."[23] As George Marsden notes, however, it also refers "to a self-conscious interdenominational movement with leaders, publications, and institutions with which many subgroups identify."[24] A distinction must be drawn, accordingly, between American evangelicalism *as such*—which has historically "reflect[ed] a range of theological, political, and social convictions"[25]—and the ideologically and theologically conservative evangelical movement to which Marsden refers. Strictly speaking, it is the latter rather than the former from which "the Christian Right" emerged.

As an offshoot of the modern evangelical movement, the Religious Right in the United States traces its origins to Anglo-American fundamentalism—an "interdenominational crusade for the total restoration … of the faith" that arose "from both the Wesley holiness and Higher Life Reformer traditions… in the post-Civil War period."[26] As Matthew Sutton notes, the fundamentalists "feared that churchly conservatives had lost the authentic radicalism of New Testament Christianity" and "viewed liberal Protestantism and movements like the Social Gospel as troubling distortions of Christianity that had seemingly transformed religion into… shallow nostrum[s] for curing temporal problems."[27] Believing that global conditions augured the imminent return of Christ, they adopted a severe asceticism and militant outlook that isolated them from the American cultural mainstream.

The historical consensus is that modern evangelicalism emerged from a split with the fundamentalist movement that occurred in the 1940s and 1950s. During this time, a new generation of Christian leaders emerged that rejected the movement's cultural isolationism, its anti-intellectualism, and its "emphasis on personal ethical prohibitions at the expense of a positive social program."[28] These self-described "neo-evangelicals"—including such notables as Billy Graham—sought to provide an "alternative to both Protestant liberalism and the more extreme forms of fundamentalism"[29] by forging interdenominational alliances and creating a "unified… social and cultural program" that would "evangelize the nation" from within "the respectable centers of American life."[30] Propelled by the mid-century religious revival, the newly-minted movement grew steadily throughout the 1950s as tens of thousands of Americans abandoned mainline churches in order to be "born again."

Although its leaders "were… staunchly anti-Communist and supported Washington's militant Cold War foreign policy,"[31] the evangelical movement of this period is often characterized as an apolitical phenomenon whose chief focus was "evangelism and denominational concerns" rather than "overt political involvement"[32] and whose success had more to do with popular large-scale revivals, "door-to-door evangelism, extensive publication programs, and close-knit congregational structures"[33] than conscious efforts to manipulate the levers of political power. In reality, it had always held a firm commitment to right-wing social, political, and economic policies[34] and enjoyed a closely-knit and mutually beneficial relationship with the Republican Party and its main constituencies from the very beginning of its existence.[35] As early as the 1930s, evangelicals like James Fitfield were making common cause with prominent business leaders in their shared opposition to the New Deal. As Kevin Kruse notes:

> Fitfield convinced the industrialists that… [evangelicals] could be the means of regaining the upper hand in their war against Roosevelt [because] they could give voice to the same conservative complaints… but without any suspicion that they were motivated solely by self-interest.[36]

In so doing they could successfully refute the claim—beloved of liberal Democrats and liberal Christians alike—"that business had somehow sinned and the welfare state was doing God's work."[37]

Unlike the business leaders, who actually *were* motivated by self-interest rather than religious faith, evangelicals like Fitfield opposed the New Deal mainly because they saw it as a stepping stone to Communism and thus as "a perversion of Christian doctrine."[38] The same was true, by extension, of the Social Gospel and other forms of liberal Protestantism that regarded "caring for the poor and needy" rather than "the salvation of the individual" as "the central tenet of Christianity."[39] As Kruse writes, "If any political and economic system fit with the religious teachings of Christ, it would have to be rooted in a similarly individualistic ethos. Nothing better exemplified these values, [the evangelicals] insisted, than the capitalist system of free enterprise."[40]

Although this "militantly conservative political stance" did not originate in the 1960s, as many accounts claim, it unquestionably intensified in response to the political, social, and cultural upheaval of that era as well as the "internal crisis" this upheaval precipitated within the evangelical movement.[41] As rank-and-file evangelicals became increasingly divided over civil rights, the Vietnam War, and other issues, the leadership ramped up its "unreservedly pronationalist and procapitalist positions"[42] and slowly reneged on its earlier commitment to interdenominational unity by ginning up a backlash against the prevailing trends of liberalism, ecumenism, and pluralism within the mainline churches. As Neil Young writes:

> They decried the breakdown of the traditional heterosexual family; fretted about changing gender roles and the strength of the

women's movement and feminism; denounced sexual permis-
siveness, abortion liberalization, and the normalization of homo-
sexuality; and inveighed against government encroachments on
individual rights, free enterprise, and religious liberty.[43]

By the early 1970s the militantly conservative establishment had won the
day. Swiftly pushing the movement in an even more openly political direction,
figures such as Francis Schaeffer, Anita Bryant, Jerry Falwell, and Pat Robertson
openly aligned themselves with the far-right wing of the Republican Party
and mobilized their followers to take up political activism. In so doing, they
led the way in transforming evangelical Christianity into one of the largest,
most well-organized, and most influential grassroots political movements in
American history: the Christian Right.

In the nearly forty years since Ronald Reagan's election—an event that
is widely acknowledged as the beginning of its ascendancy—the Christian
Right has spent millions of dollars on the formation of political action com-
mittees (e.g., the Moral Majority, the Christian Coalition, the American
Family Association, etc.), "think tanks" (e.g., Focus on the Family, the Family
Research Council, etc.),[44] educational institutions (e.g., Liberty University,
Regent University, etc.), and media outlets (e.g., *Christianity Today*, the
Christian Broadcasting Network, etc.). Throughout this period the number
of evangelical churches in the United States grew explosively as membership
in the more liberal mainline denominations began to decline.[45] By 2016 the
number of self-identified evangelical Christians in the United States had risen
to 94 million, approximately 27% of the population, making them the single
largest religious constituency in the country[46] and, second only to Mormons,
the single largest Republican voting bloc.[47] With the support of its capacious
and well-funded infrastructure, the Religious Right has skillfully deployed this
bloc to lobby for conservative causes and elect untold numbers of conservative
candidates to political office. In so doing, it has become one of the most formidable forces in right-wing politics as well as in American cultural and religious
life—not by accident, as some have claimed, but by a deliberate design that is
coeval with the modern evangelical movement itself.

The Christian Right and
Capitalist Political Theology

On the surface the Christian Right's militant commitment to and advocacy of
right-wing economic policies appears glaringly out of place in the context of
a religious tradition that has historically recognized justice for the poor as one

of its most significant and enduring concerns.[48] Indeed, even a cursory examination of the Bible makes clear that both the Old and the New Testaments place far more emphasis on combating the sins of "injustice and oppression" than "intemperance, unchastity, [or] the sins of the tongue."[49] This is not to say, of course, that all Christians share the same beliefs regarding wealth and poverty—only that caring for the poor and "the conditions in which they live" has been a recurring point of emphasis in every Christian tradition, including evangelicalism.[50] Also puzzling is the enthusiastic support given to the Christian Right's free market agenda by its largest constituency, a group that is less educated and more economically underprivileged than the population at large and thus more likely to be directly harmed by it.[51]

Standard accounts of the Christian Right have responded to these and other seeming paradoxes in various ways, the most common of which is to regard it as an aberration that needs to be to decoupled both historically and theologically from the broader evangelical tradition whence it emerges, and even from Christianity itself.[52] This is evident, for example, in the aforementioned tendency to claim that the pre-1970s evangelical movement was basically apolitical—or, at the very least, that never espoused anything approaching the Christian Right's fanatically pro-capitalist positions—in which case the Christian Right is little more than a Johnny-come-lately bastardization of evangelical Christianity.

Even if this is accurate, it remains an open question *how* and *why* the Christian Right came into existence when it did, as well as *how* and *why* it managed to achieve such considerable success since that time. Typical answers to these questions are framed in terms of contingent historical, social, political, and even demographic factors that have nothing to do with theology. Some attempt to situate the Christian Right in the context of the wave of militant anti-Communism that swept across the United States in response to the tensions of the Cold War. Others portray it as part of a broader political, social, and cultural backlash against the excesses of the 1960s, or as the product of a tactical or pragmatic alliance between evangelical Christians and secular business interests "for the sake of advanc[ing] their own respective agendas."[53]

Although all such accounts contain grains of truth, they are essentially of a piece with the (vulgar) Marxist account described at the outset in their insistence that the character of the Christian Right, to say nothing of its very existence, is determined solely by external forces. This is a mistake. More than a century ago, Max Weber argued in his landmark study *The Protestant Ethic* that certain iterations of Protestantism—including those that gave rise to evangelicalism—developed unique political theologies that ascribed unprecedented value to the individual and, as such, exhibited a natural affinity with the classical liberal philosophies that encapsulate the capitalist ethos. This helps explain why the modern evangelical movement was not only fervently anti-Communist, but also vociferously and unqualifiedly supportive of free-market capitalism. The latter, after all, was not true of most professing Christians who opposed Communism both during and after the Cold War.

The Roman Catholic Church, for example, repeatedly characterized *laissez-faire* capitalism and capital "C" Communism as different iterations of a single worldview—"materialist humanism"—that denies "the essential transcendence of humanity," inflicts grave harm upon "individual person[s] and... social purpose," and run "contrary to the order established by God and... the purpose which He has assigned to earthly goods."[54] The Church rejected Communism, accordingly, on the same grounds that it rejected capitalism—that is, for failing to acknowledge the sovereignty of God and the dignity of the human person. Like the Catholic Church, the evangelical movement opposed Communism chiefly on the grounds that it "denies or ignores the existence of the supernatural"—including, obviously, the existence of spiritual saviors; that it "focuses all attention on man, rather than on man's relation to God"; and that it actively seeks to replace religion with an all-powerful state that seeks to provide a purely temporal form of salvation.[55] In the Church's case, however, this did not translate to a uniform repudiation of Communism's "social and economic programmes," many of which are broadly resonant with Catholic teaching, nor to a uniform acceptance of free-market alternatives.[56] The reason it did in the evangelicals' case is that their political theology lacks the organicism and social holism characteristic of Catholic social thought, attaching far greater importance to individual freedom and responsibility. That a hyper-individualistic political theology that "weds the gospel of individual conversion to the Lockean social contract"[57] would oppose collectivism and affirm the value of limited government and private property is not in the least surprising.

All of this is by way of saying that the Christian Right wasn't born out of a capitalist conspiracy to hijack an otherwise benign religious movement. On the contrary, the reason it exists and has the particular character it does is because it developed from a religious tradition that has always had "an intellectual affinity [with]... the American brand of right-wing politics."[58] It is, accordingly, a logical extension of, rather than a deviation from, the political theology of American evangelical Christianity—a political theology that, even though it coincides with and actively abets capitalism and its allies, is independent of and undetermined by them.

This suggests that a distinction must be drawn between otherwise diverse ideologies whose political, social, and economic values happen to coincide, and the various ways these ideologies intersect and interact with one another. As some have noted, the Christian Right lends considerable financial and political support to political parties and business interests that harm poor and working class people through their policies. It also provides the kind of false consciousness that serves as a spiritual rationalization for such policies and ensures the acquiescence of their victims. In the Marxist formulation, this would suggest that the Christian Right is simply a component of the ideological superstructure and, as such, operates solely for the sake of maintaining the capitalist system and not for its own ends. As such, its activity is entirely heteronomous and its role in reproducing the capitalist mode of production is only indirect. As I argued above, this is not an accurate reflection of the Christian Right's motives and activities. Although its values coincide with those of all other ideologies that play a role in reproducing capitalism, they are not strictly identical to or dependent on the values of capitalism itself. Indeed, the only intrinsically valuable end that capitalism recognizes is its own reproduction; all other ends are only valued as means. The mere fact that the Christian Right's activities are conducive to this end does not imply that they are carried solely or even principally for its sake. It values the reproduction of capitalism, but only as a means to attaining independently existing values derived from its political theology.

When the Christian Right oppresses the poor, therefore, it is not doing so "indirectly." It is not merely facilitating or providing the conditions of possibility for some sort of "genuine" capitalist oppression, nor is it merely serving as a proxy. This is true, again, even if the reproduction of capitalism is a consequence of its activities. The poor, like many marginal and disempowered groups, are victims of several different kinds of oppressive structures that prey upon them for different reasons. In practice this combined onslaught may appear as a single oppressive effect, but this doesn't mean that the effect in question is precipitated by a single cause. Whatever else one can say about the "true believers," they are not acting solely for the sake of reproducing capitalism; by their own lights, they are acting pursuant to religious values. If they are exploiting poor people in the process, they are not doing so *merely* out of self-interest or a desire to generate profit—they are merely following what they take to be the will of God.

Endnotes

1   Pierre-Joseph Proudhon, *Property Is Theft! A Pierre-Joseph Proudhon Anthology*, Iain McKay, ed. (Oakland: AK Press, 2011), 356.
2   Wilhelm Reich, *The Mass Psychology of Fascism*, ed. Mary Higgins and Chester Raphael (New York: Farrar, Straus and Giroux, 1970), 19.

3   See Karl Marx, *A Contribution to the Critique of Political Economy*, trans. N.I. Stone (Chicago: Charles H. Kerr & Company, 1904), 11.

4   Ibid.

5   John Plamenatz, *Ideology* (London: Macmillan, 1971), 24.

6   Raymond Belliotti, *Power: Oppression, Subservience, and Resistance* (Albany, NY: SUNY Press, 2016), 16.

7   Michael Rosen, *On Voluntary Servitude: False Consciousness and the Theory of Ideology* (London: Polity Press, 1996), 1.

8   Israela Silberman, "Religions as a Meaning System: Implications for the New Millenium," *Journal of Social Issues* 61:4 (2005), 641–663: 644.

9   Jo-Ann Tsang, et al., "Psychometric and Rationalization Accounts of the Religion-Forgiveness Discrepancy," *Journal of Social Issues* 61:4 (2005), 785–805: 789. Emphasis mine.

10 Karl Marx, "A Contribution to the Critique of Hegel's Philosophy of Right: Introduction," in *Early Political Writings*, ed. Joseph O'Malley (Cambridge: Cambridge University Press, 1994), 57–70.

11 Ibid., 57–70.

12 Ibid.

13 Malcolm Hamilton, *The Sociology of Religion: Theoretical and Comparative Perspectives* (London: Routledge, 2012), 88.

14 Benjamin Lynerd, *Republican Theology: The Civil Religion of American Evangelicals* (Oxford: Oxford University Press, 2014), 35.

15 Ibid.

16 Aaron Haberman, "The Christian Right," in *Religion and Politics in America*, ed. Frank Smith (Westport, CT: Greenwood Publishing, 2016), 146–151: 146.

17 Lynne Arnault, "Praying for a Godly Fumigation: Disgust and the New Religious Right," in *Global Feminist Ethics*, ed. Rebecca Whisnant and Peggy DesAutels (Lanham, MD: Rowman and Littlefield, 2001), 217–242: 220.

18 Phil Zuckerman, et al., eds., *The Nonreligious: Understanding Secular People and Societies* (Oxford: Oxford University Press, 2016), 98.

19 Roger Olson, *The Westminster Handbook to Evangelical Theology* (Louisville, KY: Westminster John Knox Press, 2004), 3.

20 M.A. Noll, et al., eds., *Evangelicalism: Comparative Studies of Popular Protestantism in North America, the British Isles, and Beyond, 1700–1990* (Oxford: Oxford University Press, 1994), 6.

21 David Bebbington, "Enlightenment and Revival in Eighteenth-Century England," in *Modern Christian Revivals*, ed. Edith Blumhofer and Randall Balmer (Chicago: University of Illinois Press, 1993), 17–41: 21.

22 Candy Brown and Mark Silk, eds., *The Future of Evangelicalism in America* (New York: Columbia University Press, 2016), 6.

23 George Marsden, *Understanding Fundamentalism and Evangelicalism* (Grand Rapids, MI: William B. Eerdmans Publishing, 1993), 5.

24 Ibid.

25 Brown and Silk, 6.

26 Matthew Sutton, *American Apocalypse: A History of Modern Evangelicalism* (Cambridge, MA: Harvard University Press, 2014), 3, x.

27 Ibid., 14.

28 Marsden, 72.

29 Bruce Schulman and Julian Zelizer, *Rightward Bound: Making America Conservative in the 1970s* (Cambridge, MA: Harvard University Press, 2008), 32.

30 Marsden, 73–74.
31 Ibid.
32 Ibid.
33 Schulman and Zelizer, 33.
34 See Lynerd, especially chapters 1 and 2.
35 For a detailed history of this relationship, see Kevin Kruse, *One Nation Under God: How Corporate America Invented Christian America* (New York: Basic Books, 2015).
36 Ibid., 7.
37 Ibid.
38 Ibid.
39 Ibid.
40 Ibid.
41 Marsden, 74.
42 Ibid.
43 Neil Young, *We Gather Together: The Religious Right and the Problem of Interfaith Politics* (Oxford: Oxford University Press, 2015), 3.
44 Michael Katz, *The Price of Citizenship* (New York: Macmillan, 2002), 21.
45 Ibid.
46 Available online: http://www.pewforum.org/religious-landscape-study/religious-tradition/evangelical-protestant/.
47 Available online: http://www.people-press.org/2015/04/07/a-deep-dive-into-party-affiliation/.
48 Schulman and Zelizer, 2.
49 Lynerd, 150.
50 Berend DeVries, *Champions of the Poor: The Economic Consequences of Judeo-Christian Values* (Washington, D.C.: Georgetown University Press, 1998), 5.
51 According to the Pew Religious Forum, 35% of self-identified evangelical Christians earn household incomes of less than $30,000 per year and only 14 percent hold college degrees. See http://www.pewforum.org/religious-landscape-study/religious-tradition/evangelical-protestant/.
52 See, for example, Gregory Boyd, *The Myth of a Christian Nation* (Grand Rapids, MI: Zondervan, 2005); Jim Wallis, *God's Politics: Why the Right Gets it Wrong and the Left Doesn't Get It* (New York: HarperOne, 2005).
53 Lynerd, 5.
54 Edward Norman, *The Roman Catholic Church* (Berkeley, CA: University of California Press, 2007), 171–172.
55 Richard Pierard, *The Unequal Yoke: Evangelical Christianity and Political Conservatism* (Philadelphia: Lippincott, 1970), 100.
56 Indeed, the Liberation Theology movement of the 1960s articulated its message of radical social and economic justice in explicitly Marxist language. As Norman notes, liberation theology "grew out of sympathy for working-class movements in the cities of Latin America, and for racial equality in South Africa" and sought to identify the Christian Gospel with the political aspirations of the oppressed classes" (174).
57 Lynerd, 35.
58 Ibid., 18.

SOCIETY WITHOUT SOCIABILITY

LATE NOTES ABOUT MARGARET THATCHER AND JEAN BAUDRILLARD

Franco "Bifo" Berardi

IN *THE MASS PSYCHOLOGY OF FASCISM*, WILHELM REICH WRITES THAT THE troubling question is not why people go on strike and revolt, but the other way around: Why do people not go on strike all the time?[1] Why do people not rebel against oppression? Today, after the rise and fall of the Communist hope in the last century, there are many answers to this question. People are unable and unwilling to revolt because they do not find the way to autonomy and solidarity, because of precariousness, anxiousness, and competition, which are the main features of the present organization of work. The effects of the de-territorialization of labor, and of the technological fragmentation of the social body, result in the inability to create networks of solidarity and in widespread loneliness broken by sudden random explosions of rage.

A second answer may be based on the dissolution of the physical identity of power. Power is nowhere and everywhere, internalized and inscribed in the techno-linguistic automatisms called governance. Recent waves of rebellion have proved unable to focus on a physical center of financial domination because a physical center does not exist. The precarisation of labor, which implies the end of a territorial proximity of labor, physical isolation, and the widespread sentiment of anxious competition among workers, has provoked the dissolution of social solidarity that was predicted in the works of Jean Baudrillard since the second part of the 1970s. In those years of transition from the industrial civilization to the digital civilization, changes occurred in the conceptual field and in the disciplinary organization of knowledge. This disciplinary reshuffling reflects the transformation that took place in the decades of the neoliberal reformation, which obviously intersects with digital technology.

The dissolving of the masses

In the book *Dark Fiber*, Geert Lovink observes that the academic study of mass psychology is abandoned in the 1980s, and replaced by a wide range of disciplines: sociology, psychology, cybernetic science, cultural studies, and media theory.[2] I don't want to investigate the academic motivations and implications of this disappearance and replacement. I want to focus on the real disappearance of the modern masses as a homogeneous body in society.

Masses are actually fading, almost vanishing, when the emergence of the post-mass media technology for network-communication dispels the crowd, turning it into a sprawl of connecting atoms, and the process of precarisation of labor disintegrates the physical proximity of workers. Social precarity indeed can be described as a condition in which workers are continuously moving positions, so that nobody will meet anybody twice in the same place. Cooperation without physical proximity is the condition of existential loneliness coupled with all-pervading productivity.

Workers do not perceive themselves anymore as the parts of a living community; they are rather compelled to compete in a condition of loneliness. Although they are exploited in the same way by the same capitalist entity, they are no longer a social class because in their material condition they can no longer produce collective self-consciousness and the spontaneous solidarity of a living community of people who live in the same place and share the same destiny. They are no longer "masses" because their random coming together in the subway, on the highway, and in similar places of transit is random and temporary.

Mass psychology dissolves because the masses themselves are dissolving, at least in the social mind's self-perception. The concept of "masses" is ambiguous and hard to define, as Baudrillard wrote at the end of the 1970s.[3] Furthermore, the concept of "masses" diverges from the Marxian concept of "social class," the aggregation of people who share interests, behavior, and consciousness. The existence of a working class is not an ontological truth: it is the effect of a shared imagination and consciousness. It is a mythology, in the strong sense of the word: a narration about the present and about the possible future. That narration vanished altogether with the social conditions of industrial production, and with the end of the physical massification of workers in factories. In the last three decades, the cultural conditions for class self-perception have been destroyed by the post-industrial transformation of capitalism. The dissolution of this massive dimension of society can be linked to the utter individualization and competitive disposition of workers in the age of precarisation.

Energy, desire, and simulation

In the late '70s, when I read Baudrillard's texts in which he discusses the end of the social, I felt a mix of attraction and repulsion. I rejected the idea that social conflict may disappear, but his writings were illuminating something that I could perceive in the emerging subcultures of the time. The Italian political landscape in 1976 and 1977 was marked by the insurgence of the youth: students and unemployed young people occupied universities all over the country, and a wave of squat openings and protests took place. The rebels established a network of independent radio-stations: they were speaking a new language, which had little in common with the old Marxist-Leninist jargon. The new language was reminiscent of the Dadaist art avant-garde, and also of the contemporary punk culture.

This movement, which is generally referred to as "autonomia," was rising in a new cultural context: in that period the Italian Communist Party was slowly absorbed in the power system, and staged an alliance with the ruling party called Democrazia Cristiana. The focus of the revolt was both against capitalist rule and communist authoritarianism, and the energy of that movement was an expression of the emerging creativity of the intellectual composition of labor. The concept of desire, which we extracted from books by Deleuze and Guattari, was a perfect translation of that energy. That movement, however, was double-sided: it was also influenced by the leftist imagination from the 20th Century, proclaiming the possibility of a communist transformation of daily life. Simultaneously, it was searching for new forms of singularity and creative expression, but at heart it was haunted by the premonition of a techno-totalitarian order to come.

At a certain point, after the riots of March 1977 (particularly intense in Rome and in Bologna), after the wave of repression that the Italian State launched at the movement, after the surfacing of armed groups like the Red Brigades, the libertarian soul of the movement, inherited from the '60s American hippie culture, melted with a dark perception that there was no future.

In those years, I read the books of Guattari, Deleuze, and of Jean Baudrillard, whose visions were radically distinct. That ambivalence, however, was for me the intellectual source of two divergent imaginations, which were simultaneously helping me understand the unfolding process at that time. Guattari's message was all about the inexhaustible energy of desire in the process of subjectivation. In the books that he wrote in the second part of the decade, Baudrillard replaced desire by the seductive force of simulation, and replaced the concept of subjectivation by the concept of implosion of the masses: "Everything changes with the device of simulation: collapse of poles, orbital circulation of models (this is also the matrix of every implosive process)."[4] And he continues:

> Bombarded with stimuli, messages and texts, the masses are simply an opaque, blind stratum, like those clusters of stellar gas known only through analysis of their light spectrum—radiation spectrum equivalent to statistics and surveys—but precisely: it can no longer be a question of expression or representation, but only of the simulation of an ever inexpressible and unexpressed social.[5]

Guattari was attracted by the technological rhizome of information, and foresaw the creation of a proliferating network as a tool for liberation. Baudrillard expressed awareness of the dark side of the network: the dissipation of social energy, the implosion of subjectivity, and the subjection of mental activity to the logic of simulation. Guattari was interested in the concept of network (*reseau*) because he saw in it a process of self-organization of social actors and the condition of a media-activist movement, but Baudrillard anticipated the effects of the new post-social power that was emerging under the umbrella of neoliberalism, and was taking the form of a network rather than the old form of the hierarchical pyramid.

Social autonomy and neoliberal deregulation both developed in the same period and to some extent imply each other. The concept of a rhizome is a conceptual map of the explosion of modern disciplinary society, but it is also the cartography of the process of capitalist deregulation, which paved the way to the precarisation of work and to the dissolution of social solidarity.

The neoliberal destruction of sociability

Baudrillard wrote the book *In the Shadow of Silent Majorities* at the end of the '70s, when Margaret Thatcher seized power in the Tory Party and began the triumphal progress that prepared her victory in the national elections in 1979, and launched the project that we have come to know as neoliberalism. Baudrillard's texts (*In The Shadow of Silent Majorities* and *Fatal Strategies*) can be compared with some interviews with Margaret Thatcher from the '80s. Echoing Baudrillard's concepts in an interview of 1987, she said:

> What irritated me about the whole direction of politics in the last 30 years is that it's always been towards the collectivist society. People have forgotten about the personal security. And they say: do I count, do I matter? To which the short answer is, yes. And therefore, it isn't that I set out on economic policies; it's that I set out really to change the approach, and changing the economics is the means of changing that approach. If you change the approach you really are after the heart and soul of the nation. Economics are the method; the object is to change the heart and soul.[6]

The final goal of Thatcher's revolution was not economic, but political, ethical, almost spiritual, we might say. The neoliberal reformation was finally intended to inscribe competition in the very soul of social life, up to the point of destroying society itself. This cultural intention of the neoliberal reformation was clearly described by Michel Foucault in his 1979–1980 seminar published as *The Birth of Biopolitics*: the subjection of individual activity to the spirit of the enterprise, the overall recoding of human activity in terms of economic rentability, the insertion of competition into the neural circuits of daily life. These are the trends that Foucault foresaw and described in that seminar.

Not only the economic profit, but also the cult of the individual as economic worrier, the harsh perception of a fundamental loneliness of humans, the cynical concession that war is the only possible relation among living organisms in the path of evolution: this is the final intention of the neoliberal reformation. Margaret Thatcher also says:

> There is no such thing [as society]. There are individual men and women, and there are families. And no government can do anything except through people, and people must look to themselves first.[7]

Thatcher's concept is interesting but not accurate. Society is not disappearing; sociability is dissolving, not society. During the last thirty years, society has been transformed into a sort of blind system of inescapable obligations and interdependences; a prison-like condition of togetherness in which empathy is cancelled and solidarity is forbidden. The social world has been transformed into a worldwide system of automatic connections in which individuals cannot experience *conjunction* but only *functional connection* with other individuals. The process of cooperation does not stop; it is transformed into a process of abstract recombination of info-fractals that only the Code can decipher and transform into economic value. The mutual interaction is not cancelled, but empathy is replaced by competition. Social life proceeds, more frantic than ever: the living conscious organism is penetrated by dead unconscious mathematical functions.

Endnotes

1   Wilhelm Reich, *The Mass Psychology of Fascism*, 3rd ed., Vincent R. Carfagno, trans. (New York: Farrar, Straus and Giroux, 1933, 1980).
2   Geert Lovink, *Dark Fiber: Tracking Critical Internet Culture* (Cambridge: MIT Press, 2002).
3   Jean Baudrillard, *In the Shadow of the Silent Majorities, or, The End of the Social*, John Johnston, Paul Patton, and Stuart Kendall, trans. (Cambridge: Semiotext(e), 1978, 2007).
4   Ibid., 48.
5   Ibid., 48.
6   Quoted in Ronald Butt, "Economics are the Method; The Object is to Change the Soul," *Sunday Times*, May 3, 1981. Available online: http://www.margaretthatcher.org/document/104475.
7   Quoted in Douglas Keay, "Interview," *Woman's Own*, September 23, 1987. Available online: http://www.margaretthatcher.org/document/106689.

THE
GLOBAL
SOUTH

ENGENDERING REVOLT IN THE ANGLOPHONE CARIBBEAN

ORGANIZING THE OPPRESSED FOR SELF-EMANCIPATION

Ajamu Nangwaya

REVOLUTIONARY OR RADICAL RESISTANCE, PARTICULARLY ONE WITH A PARTICI-patory democratic character, will not take place in the Anglophone Caribbean context in the absence of preparing the working class to become receptive to oppositional political ideas. Revolutionary resistance in this article is not about capturing and exercising state power as a means to empower the people. We may easily reference the political outcomes of that approach since the French, Haitian, Russian, Cuban, Nicaraguan, and Grenadian revolutions, and other state-centric paths to supposedly emancipating the oppressed. Revolutions of the twenty-first century should focus on processes of social transformation that are not merely mimicking those from the existing systems of oppression. As a revolutionary who marches under the banner of anarchist communism,[1] I am in broad agreement with political scientist and Pan-Africanist intellectual Horace Campbell that the revolution should reflect specific humanistic and transformative sensibilities:

> My proposition is that we are not reflecting on revolution in the traditional sense of simply seizing state power; we are talking about a fundamental transformation. These are transformations at the level of consciousness, transformations at the level of material organisations, transformations in the matter of political organisation, transformations at the level of gender relations, new conceptions of leadership and transformations at the level of our relations with the planet Earth and the Universe.[2]

The people of the Caribbean have a long and rich history of insurrections, revolts, and revolutions, and may call on this tradition to inspire their imagination of the political possibilities for social transformation. It is fundamentally necessary for organizers to carry out organizing work among the people in order to facilitate their entry into radical or revolutionary organizations. Being oppressed does not necessarily lead to an instinctive will to revolt, as can be seen from the imposition of capitalist austerity programs in the region since the 1970s. There are necessary conditions that must be present to enable Caribbean people to rise up against economic and social hardship.

The following factors are vital to facilitate revolt against the exploited in the Anglophone Caribbean: heightened class consciousness by developing people's understanding and awareness of their distinct class interests, execution of systematic organizing as opposed to mobilizing within the ranks of the oppressed, undermine the perception of capitalism as the only option through mass political education and ideological development, facilitate political engagement of the revolutionary petit bourgeoisie, and organizing around the needs of the people. The petit bourgeoisie and the most politically developed members of the laboring classes are strategically placed to serve as the catalyst to enable the poor to rise up against capitalist, patriarchal, and racist oppression. This essay offers a path toward a politics of awakening the revolutionary potentiality of the Caribbean working class or laboring classes.

The article "Why Don't the Poor Rise Up?" that is written by Thomas D. Edsall and published in the *New York Times*[3] raises a pertinent question that should be on the minds of those of us who are committed to encouraging revolutions and preparing to exploit revolutionary conditions whenever and wherever they appear. In spite of the devastating economic and social impact of the Great Recession on the laboring classes in the global South and North,[4] the sufferers are not storming the barricade and creating a Hobbesian nightmare for the ruling-class. Edsall's question betrays a popular misconception that people tend to revolt when the economic and social conditions in society become unbearable. There must be the coming together of a range of factors to make insurrections or uprisings possible. While liberal bourgeois or progressive forces might speculate about the reasons behind the failure of the people to rise up in the face of the current onslaught of capitalist austerity, the future incident that might spark spontaneous insurrections may arrive like the proverbial thief in the night.

The desire to see the people "rise up" is not a maximalist expectation. I have the distinct impression that the framing of the people in motion as a "rise up" is simply desirous of a revolt of the poor. But the revolutionary dub poet Mutabaruka of Jamaica kindly reminds us that "A revolt aint a revolution,"[5] so we ought to move beyond merely rising up and sitting down after the system has violently repressed the political resistance of the oppressed, or smothered it with a package of reformist measures that does not address the substantive structural problems in society. On the other hand, the "concept of revolution has been intimately tied to the view that [humanity] could change society, that this change was in the direction of progressive steps toward the improvement of [humanity's] condition, and that this progression was in the direction of greater equality."[6] It is revolution that we must dedicate ourselves to fomenting, revolutions across the world because capitalism and its alliance with other systems of exploitation call for a dramatic, transformative, and forceful economic, social, and political rapture.

A revolution calls for a struggle that will most likely be a protracted one, convinces a critical mass of the oppressed classes that fundamental change is necessary, possible, and worth the sacrifices, and requires a revolutionary theory that articulates the values, political sensibilities, and expectations of the laboring classes or oppressed groups in terms that they can understand and share with their neighbors. Given our experience of post-revolutionary societies wherein the men (and a few women) with effective control over the means of coercion normally substitute themselves for the people, revolutionary struggles must be self-organized or participatory democratic, even when there is an armed struggle component to the process of revolution. The preceding assertion is not as easy as it might seem in stating or reading. Wars engender strong centralizing tendencies, and enemy forces that are the epitome of authoritarianism, centralism, and bureaucratic control will likely confront the revolution. It is likely that the revolutionary forces will emulate the centralist command and control ways of the enemy in pursuit of effectiveness and efficiency on the armed struggle terrain. The will toward centralization and secrecy will likely carry over into the post-revolutionary society in which it will effectively be the counterrevolution—throwing the people off the stage of history, or offering them the peripheral roles of extras and props.

Revolutionaries, of necessity and political obligation, must be interested in the question "Why don't the people rise up?" They must devote the time and resources in studying why and under what conditions revolutions take place. Once that question has been sufficiently answered, the forces of revolution should go about the task of making revolution irresistible to the people without whom it is impossible.

Contextualizing the Poor and Revolt/Rise Up

We need to engage with the query that animates this book before moving on to the barriers against the laboring classes, in the English-speaking Caribbean, to rising up and creating the path to the emancipated society. The reference to "the poor" is taken here as a euphemism or stand-in reference to the laboring classes or the working class, which implicitly implicates capitalism as the problem. In the centers of capitalism, there is a noticeable reluctance to address the class struggle or the existence of opposing classes as a fact of life. It is for that reason that the ruling class and its agents in academia and the media promote the idea of North America and Europe as being predominantly middle-class.[7] The preceding state of affairs informed the Occupy Movement's popular slogan, "We are the 99%." If we use the measurement of income or wealth, the slogan includes major chief executive officers, presidents and prime ministers, ministers of government, judges in the supreme courts, and other decision-making agents of the ruling class.[8]

The poor are seen as a small group that has somehow escaped the generalized prosperity or opportunities that are present in these centers of imperialism. The poor becomes a sociological category that is not implicated in the irreconcilable clash of interests between classes. In other words, the ruling class and even social reformers are peddling the language of "the poor," "the underprivileged" or "the underclass" as a way not to engage, or to mask issues related to the class struggle, class interests, or class warfare, with respect to the conflict between the working-class majority and the parasitic minority, the bourgeoisie (the real minority). In the United States, the poor is much larger than what the state and capital have conceded. Salvatore Babones argues that the decision of the state's policymakers to not measure poverty by what is now seen as a decent or reasonable standard of living has artificially reduced the ranks of the poor:

> The official poverty line for a family of four is $22,350. Updating that figure for growth in U.S. national income per capita since 1969 would yield a 2011 poverty line of $46,651.

By that standard, about 28 percent of American families of four are now living in poverty, almost twice the official poverty rate. If that sounds high, it's only because we are much more stingy today than our grandparents were in 1969.[9]

Relative poverty is the measurement used within a country to indicate the level of income that is below that which is needed to afford an individual or family the average standard of living. Based on this definition, Buchheit states that 18% of Americans are living in poverty and 32% of them are in the low-income category, which is twice the level of the official poverty line.[10]

Capitalist societies might play politics with whom to statistically include within the ranks of the poor, but it cannot objectively exclude them from the laboring classes. When radicals or revolutionaries engage the category "the poor," they are ideologically or politically obligated to embrace the people in this social grouping as members of the working class or the laboring classes. This positioning allows radical and revolutionary organizers to be programmatically preoccupied with the oppressive condition of the people in the working class who are women, racialized, people with disabilities, queers or LGBTQ (lesbians, gays, bisexual, transgendered, queers), young people, or the elderly. The class struggle and its proponents should not look to members of the laboring classes as if they live compartmentalized lives. They experience exploitation beyond their role within capitalism. The uprising of the poor or the laboring classes must give primary importance to ending racism, patriarchy or sexism, homophobia, colonialism, ableism, ageism, and all other forms of oppression. We should approach the laboring classes in this manner in both the global North and South.

What exactly do we have in mind when the poor of the Caribbean are called on to rise up or revolt against oppression or class inequality? Is rising up or revolting against oppression exclusively an issue of the enactment of insurrections, rebellions, uprisings, mass demonstrations and/or other public protest actions? The act or process of rising up or revolting against the neoliberal capitalist regimes across the Anglophone Caribbean must take on an overt, public, oppositional, and mass character that engages a critical cross section of the people. Demonstrations, rallies, occupations, marches, press conferences, and vigils are useful instruments in expressing the people's objection to inequities in society. It is generally a good thing when the people are in motion.

However, if the laboring classes and radical and revolutionary elements of the petit bourgeoisie are *only* reliant on demonstrations, rallies, occupations, marches, press conferences, and vigils as the tools of revolt or rising up for a just and equitable society, they would simply be engaged in the mobilizing of the people. Mobilizing actions tend to be episodic or take place infrequently, and the people serve as props or extras in the scripted, ritualized, and predictable drama of public protests. The oppressive system is carrying out acts of injustice every second of the day. But the apostles of the mobilizing approach to resistance are unwittingly telling the people that resistance to exploitation is not a 24/7 engagement.

Mobilizing endeavors impose minimal commitment on the oppressed or activists; while equipping them with the comforting illusion that they are involved in important or substantive acts of resistance to domination. An example might concretely illustrate the case being made against the mobilization approach. In most cases of alleged unlawful or extrajudicial killing of people from Jamaica's working-class communities by police, the residents tend to block roads or engage in public marches and hold public space for a few or several hours.[11] However, the politicians and the police know that the people will surely stand down after venting their anger at routinized police violence and their deadly use of force against members of the working class. Momentary acts of rebellion are insufficient to the task of building a counterforce to the existing neocolonial regimes across the Caribbean. It takes more than instinctive lashing out in anger or frustration to enable the people to rise up.

When the people rise up, the expectation is that they are seeking a qualitative change in the operation of society, or the destruction of the existing one. If a critical mass of the people has risen up for policies and programs that are not substantively different from those of the status quo, the people in motion are not really rising up. They simply want to join what is the societal norm with some adjustments. The act of truly rising up by the oppressed is fundamentally progressive or emancipatory in goals and demands. Nothing less than revolution or the process of making the revolution should serve as the people's festival of resistance!

Context of the English-speaking Caribbean

The Anglophone Caribbean includes the islands of the Caribbean Sea and the Atlantic Ocean as well as territories on the mainland (Belize and Guyana). This sub-region is often invisible or excluded in economic and political discussion of Latin America. In a recent conversation with a comrade, he told me that some Canadian-based activists from Latin America do not view the English-speaking Caribbean as a part of that region. These South American and Central American mainlanders argued that these Anglophone countries did not wage wars of independence but had their independence "given" to them by British colonialism. It is on the preceding basis that, unlike Cuba,

Haiti, and the Dominican Republic, the Anglophone Caribbean has been willed out of Latin America. It is not clear to keen observers how the legacies of wars of independence have positively mediated the neocolonial status of the Spanish-speaking and Portuguese-speaking territories and the exploited economic, social, and political condition of their laboring classes. These politicos are infatuated with a political game that is a futile exercise in the valorizing of a distinction without a difference.

The Anglophone Caribbean is very much a part of Latin America. It shares in that larger region's experience of genocide, enslavement, patriarchal domination of women, European and American imperialism, colonialism, neocolonialism, and ecological destruction. The countries that constitute the English-speaking Caribbean occupy islands in the West Indies and territories in Central America and South America. These territories encompass politically independent states as well as those that are colonies or "overseas territories" of British colonialism and are as follows: Anguilla, Antiqua and Barbuda, Bahamas, Barbados, Belize, British Virgin Islands, Cayman Islands, Dominica, Grenada, Guyana, Jamaica, St. Kitts and Nevis, St. Lucia, St. Vincent and the Grenadines and The Turks and Caicos Islands and Trinidad and Tobago.[12] These territories have adopted the Westminster political system to the Caribbean environment and have engaged in the constitutional transfer of power through periodic elections to the victorious parties. D'Agostino cautions us not to be fooled by appearances because "Such systems boast formal democratic institutions and processes, yet in practice they tend to operate on the basis of personalism, patron-client relationships, and the exclusion of the popular classes."[13] The Anglophone Caribbean's adaptation of the Westminster tradition made the region an anomaly in the 1960s, 1970s, and 1980s when other regions in the global South were largely dominated by one-party regimes or military governments.

D'Agostino acknowledges the authoritarian political tradition of British colonialism that has been practiced in the region for centuries,[14] but he (un)wittingly implies that the Westminster political system of governance in Britain is a paragon of democratic virtues over which the British popular classes rule supreme. It is a different type of authoritarian system of governance that is effectively controlled by the middle class or the bourgeoisie. Mars appears to fall for the same argument when he refers to the Anglophone Caribbean's "institutionalization of a rather truncated form of Westminster democracy with its inherent tendency to foster autocratic types of rule."[15] At best, we might assert that the political elites in the English-speaking Caribbean adopted a vulgar form of an already established authoritarian political system.

These countries also embraced the capitalist economic model since the British ensured that its own political system served as a way to tutor and groom the local elite to accept liberal capitalist democracy and its accompanying economic model. When the Marxist People's Progressive Party won the 1953 elections in British Guiana under the internal self-government regime, the American and British fear of communism led Britain's Prime Minister Winston Churchill to declare that "We ought surely to get American support in doing all that we can to break the communist teeth in British Guiana."[16] Britain eventually suspended British Guiana's constitution, dismissed the government, and arrested Premier Cheddi Jagan and his wife, Janet Jagan. British colonialism made it clear that they would not tolerate a government that might follow the path of socialism. American imperialism then demonstrated to people in the Caribbean that even a regime committed to a reformist social democratic economic, social, and political program would not be tolerated. The United States, through its Central Intelligence Agency (CIA), allegedly sponsored and armed lumpen criminal elements that destabilized the regime of Prime Minister Michael Manley in the 1970s.[17]

The government of the United States and international capital engaged in political and economic warfare against Jamaica's democratic socialist regime that included measures such as "production cutbacks and transfers, lawsuits, and a media campaign designed to undermine the tourist industry."[18] The International Monetary Fund (IMF) played a major part in the economic destabilization of Jamaica by way of its punishing structural adjustment program (capitalist austerity measures) that weakened the reformist capacity of the government. Perry Mars documents Western imperialism's hostility and active undermining of "socialist oriented" regimes in this sub-region from the 1950s to the 1980s.[19] American imperialism had no desire to see another Cuba established in its sphere of influence, notwithstanding the desire of the people for just and equitable societies.

Besides the present dependent capitalist character of the Anglophone Caribbean, these countries also share critical features on the economic front. They experienced plantation slavery that depended on the labor power of enslaved Afrikans who were kidnapped and sold into the European slave trade that resulted in millions of them being transported to the Americas. Enslaved Africans were used to facilitate capitalist development and prosperity in Europe and for the economic exploitation of the Caribbean and the rest of the Americas. In the Caribbean, the economic patterns imposed on the region gave rise to what the late Caribbean economist George Beckford calls the plantation society, with their tendency toward dependence on one major agricultural staple (for example, sugarcane in the case of the Anglophone Caribbean, or cotton in the Southern United States) and an economy that is highly dependent and vulnerable to political and economic events in imperialist or metropolitan centers. The proponents of the plantation economy school argue that the legacy of this non-dynamic economic arrangement is still bedeviling the Caribbean's development prospects and informing the services, manufacturing, and mineral extractive sectors of this region.[20]

Caribbean economies are reliant on natural resources as the primary source of their export earnings.[21] This state of affairs places the region in the unenviable position of contracting economic pneumonia when the economies in North America and Europe catch the cold. The economies in the Anglophone Caribbean were designed from the early days of colonialism and plantation slavery to export raw materials and semi-processed goods to Europe. As a part of the mercantile capitalist outlook of the imperial centers, the colonies were discouraged from engaging in the manufacturing or processing of raw materials, because this higher valued-added process and accompanying industrial and financial sector development were reserved for the metropolitan economies. This pattern of economic development is still a feature of the Caribbean, despite the prevailing free trade ideology of economic imperialism. The dependence on the export of natural resources and the vagaries of the international commodity markets have made the Caribbean susceptible to the economic and political machinations of imperialism.

The region's defenseless economic status can be seen in its elite's politically suicidal adoption of neoliberal capitalist orthodoxy from the 1970s to today under the guidance of the IMF, the World Bank, and U.S. imperialism. In order for these Caribbean territories to receive access to loans from private international financial institutions at relatively reasonable rates, they must get the seal of approval from the IMF. With a steady diet of IMF structural adjustment programs that demand the disinvestment in health care, education, and other social programs, the political elite are eroding the patron-clientele character of its version of the Westminster political system and undermining the very basis of their power:

> The adoption of neoliberal economic policies has limited the ability of Caribbean governments to fund social welfare programs and thereby maintain the statist bargain. This has had a deleterious impact on the quality of life for millions across the region, a problematic trend given the heightened expectations held by increasingly mobilized populations. The failure to fulfill such expectations, drastically exacerbated by global economic crisis in the first decade of the twenty-first century, has undermined the public's faith in political parties, popularly elected leaders and democratic politics in general.[22]

In the face of this attack on the laboring classes through the implementation of structural adjustment programs, one regime in the region was almost thrown into the cesspool of history by way of a coup. The people of Trinidad experienced a reduction of over 50% in the per capita Gross National Product between 1982 and 1987, and the state's structural adjustment program in the period 1982–1990 threw an additional 66,000 workers into the ranks of the unemployed, which led to an estimated rate of joblessness of 22% to 25%.[23] The government of the day was widely unpopular, and many of the civil society groups that supported it had abandoned the regime.[24] It was in this atmosphere that the Jamaat al Muslimeen formation carried out an attempt to overthrow the A.N.R. Robinson-led government. The Jamaat al Muslimeen had a property-related dispute that served as a triggering cause for the insurrection, but its leader Abu Bakr clothed the uprising in language that suggested a non-sectarian, universal basis: "The people don't know how to use a gun. All free men have guns and land. There must be a vanguard. Somebody must take the lead."[25] This religious organization directly linked its coup attempt with the people's resultant suffering from the state's capitalist austerity program.[26] The people did not rally to the side of the insurrectionists, but sections of the poor took the opportunity to liberate goods from stores as a payback for the years of economic warfare against it.[27]

Why Don't the Poor Rise Up in the Anglophone Caribbean?

There is a constellation of factors implicated in the failure of the people to rise up against the punishing blows of the longstanding capitalist austerity program in the Anglophone Caribbean and the fallout from the Great Recession. If the working-class in Europe and North America are reeling from the social and economic hardship that came about as a result of the Great Recession of 2008, the laboring classes in the open, dependent, and export-led economies of the Caribbean should be suffering much more than their counterparts in the global North. After all, the Caribbean does not possess the highly developed social welfare programs of the global North, which can absorb some of the blows of severe economic downturns in the capitalist business cycle. Some of the crucial factors that have worked against the people rising up against capitalist austerity are the legitimacy of the regimes, self-employment in the informal sector, massive inflow of overseas remittances, absence of a permissive external environment, and political irrelevance of the radical petit bourgeoisie.

Legitimacy of the Regimes

The governments in the English-speaking Caribbean are seen as somewhat legitimate in the eyes of the people. They are the outcome of an institutionalized process that is grudgingly accepted despite the corruption, political victimization, patron-clientelism, and democratic deficit with which it is associated. The Anglophone Caribbean, since the introduction of universal adult suffrage in the 1940s, has been largely defined, politically, by their competitive elections, constitutional transfer of power, active political parties, and electoral outcomes that are generally accepted by the opposition and the people. Guyana under Forbes Burnham (with the active and tacit support of Britain and the United States) and Grenada under Eric Gairy and the People's Revolutionary Government under Maurice Bishop, are the exceptions that confirm this general tendency. According to Jorge Domínguez, "The Caribbean achievement is far superior to that of Latin America and also to that of countries of Africa and Asia that acquired their formal independence from European powers after the Second World War."[28] However, the political acceptance of liberal capitalist democracy by the laboring classes is a reflection of the ideological hegemony of the ruling-class over the former's worldview and this is, in part, a continuation of a process that started during the enslavement period.[29] The acceptance of the liberal capitalist democracy and its procedures is not unlike the situation in the capitalist democracies in the centers of imperialism, North America and Europe.

D'Agostino identifies the forces at work that have made the Anglophone Caribbean the most successful and stable global South region under liberal capitalist democracy:

> With respect to the former British colonies, many observers point to nature and duration of colonial rule as key to the region's success. The introduction of the Westminster-style parliamentary system provided the necessary framework within which Caribbean democracy could flourish, and the liberal political culture that would sustain this system became deeply rooted in West Indian societies. The long, gradual process of decolonization in the Anglo-Caribbean differed markedly from the experiences of British colonies in Africa and Asia, providing opportunity for institutional development, nation building, and "tutelage" in the way of democratic governance.[30]

British colonialism did not independently figure out the best way to provide "tutelage" to its colonized "Afro-Saxons." It was forced to decolonize and offer internal self-government by the mass labor rebellions of the 1930s in the Anglophone Caribbean, which gave birth to modern mass-based political parties and trade unions. These parties and trade unions emerged as organs through which the laboring classes felt that their economic and political aspirations could be represented in society.

D'Agostino points to how liberal capitalist democracy became institutionalized in these Caribbean societies and why its outcomes would still be legitimate, even when the masses are not satisfied with its actual performance:

> Among the pillars upon which Caribbean democracy has rested is a well-established institutional infrastructure. The emergence of strong political party systems, regular competitive elections, and vibrant civil societies (including labour unions, professional associations, and the like) has done much to bolster the cause of democracy in the Caribbean.[31]

The cause of democracy, bolstered by the African petit bourgeois political elite that emerged from the labor rebellions of the 1930s, was acceptable to British colonialism and Western imperialism after independence because they accepted the "basic philosophy of free market capitalist development."[32] It is the hegemony of the economic and political elite that is evident in the working class's embrace of liberal capitalist democracy and its use of elections to change political parties when they are not performing to expectation. Despite the legitimacy of these regimes, the laboring classes are still experiencing democratic deficit and the lack of political efficacy. In Jamaica's general and local government elections in 2016, only 47.7% and 30% of eligible voters went to the polls, respectively. Just like in the United States and Canada, the political elite governs with a very narrow base of support. If the people were presented with a one-party system, they would have likely linked their economic marginalization as being the result of not electing the government of the day.

Politically Stabilizing Effect of the Informal Economy

The deterioration of the economy in the Caribbean is due to the bitter medicine of the IMF's structural adjustment programs that prescribe attacks on state ownership of productive assets, withdrawal of subsidies on basic needs, goods, and services, and the slashing of social program spending in education, health care, social housing, and social services. The onslaught of imperialism's economic globalization policies force these import-dependent, open, vulnerable, and weak economies of the Anglophone Caribbean to one-sidedly expose their societies to the full competition of imported goods, lower taxes to attract foreign investments, overly generous investment packages offered to international capital, and removal of trade measures that once encouraged international businesses to produce inside national borders in order to access domestic markets. The sum total of these neoliberal policies are high unemployment and underemployment and people's entry into the informal economy as micro-enterprise and small- and medium-sized business entrepreneurs.

But entering the informal sector in order to survive provides hope for a better tomorrow, which limits the possibility of rising up or giving the time of day to political forces that are advocating revolution or radical social change. The Caribbean states such as Jamaica and Guyana have experienced unimpressive economic performance over the last three decades, and that state of affairs drove many people into the informal sector. The late George Girvan, a progressive intellectual and economist, suggested that the informal sector reinforces certain conservative inclinations with respect to capitalism:

> We also need to consider the impact of the flourishing of self-employment and informal sector activities, which has been a major survival mechanism of the people in response to the crisis of the 1980s. Judging from casual observation in countries like Jamaica and Guyana, this development has strongly reinforced the tendencies towards economic individualism which, it may be argued, has been a prominent feature of Caribbean culture ever since Emancipation.[33]

Capitalist entrepreneurship is associated with economic independence and control, which suggests that members of the laboring classes will develop a stake in society when they have investments in the economy. They are unlikely, then, to find rising up against the established economic order very appealing, and might actually serve as stout defenders of the status quo.

C.Y. Thomas was dismissive of the scope of the informal sector by stating that it reflects "a small minority ... (who have) been able to 'capture' supplies for themselves and to monopolise the scarcity values these commodities generate in the market place."[34] Thomas could not be further from the truth in characterizing the informal sector as the preoccupation of "a small minority." In 2001, the Inter-American Development Bank (IADB) reported that informal economic activities were the equivalent of 43% of Jamaica's official Gross Domestic Product (GDP).[35] The estimated size of the informal sector in Trinidad and Tobago, Barbados and Guyana is 25%, 36%, and 55% of the official GDP figures, respectively.[36] Jamaica's informal economy has absorbed many workers, and an investigation of this phenomenon in the 1990s estimated that it provided jobs to between 24% and 39% of employees in the non-agricultural workforce.[37] The massive 62% reduction in poverty between 1991 and 2001, and the fall in inequality could have been partly the result of activities in the informal sector.[38]

It is not the reduction in relative deprivation that makes the informal sector a factor in the people not rising up. The informal sector provides the entrepreneurs and workers with the opportunity to put bread on their table for another day, and it is the source of hope that better days are ahead of them. The entrepreneurs in the informal sector might be able to see a way out that is better than their prior condition as workers in the formal sector. In the IADB's study about 33% of the business owners in the informal economy had a university education, which was higher than that of workers in the formal sector.[39] Some of these petit bourgeois entrepreneurs might have been catalysts for social change, if they had not found self-employment in the informal sector. Neville Graham, a *Jamaica Gleaner* reporter, captures the politically stabilizing effects of the informal economy when he writes, "He [Ralston Hyman of Jamaica's Economic Programme Oversight Committee] says that the fact that so many of our economic statistics are adverse and the county is not falling apart is directly attributable to the informal economy, simply because people can get by using informal activity."[40]

Massive Inflow of Remittances

The massive inflow of remittances to the English-speaking Caribbean has tempered the economic and social grievances that might have been expressed through attraction to radical or revolutionary ideologies or mass protest actions. Migration has historically functioned as a safety valve for potential social disruption from high unemployment and limited social and economic opportunities in the region. This migration has served as the conduit for the injection of hard currency into these economies. In 2012, the Caribbean Community (CARICOM) states received US$4.5 billion dollars in remittances, and three of these states (St. Kitts and Nevis, Jamaica, and Guyana) were among the ten highest per capita recipients of remittances across the globe in that year.[41] Jamaica received over US$1.13 billion in remittances in 2002[42] and is a member of the "Billion Dollar Remittances Club." In 2014, Jamaica received US$1.92 billion in net remittances (gross remittances were US$2.15 billion), which comes in second to tourism that normally nets over US$2 billion annually.[43] Remittances are significant to the Anglophone Caribbean, and they exceed the total value of official aid and direct foreign investment (FDI). In the case of Jamaica, FDI came in at US$595 million in 2015, while gross remittances to the island were US$2.16 billion, which was three-and-half times the inflow of the former.[44] According to the World Bank's report on migration and remittances, for the first eight months of 2016, Jamaica, Guyana, Trinidad and Tobago, and Barbados generated US$2.4 billion, US$296 million, US$128 million and US$106 million in remittances, respectively.[45]

Based on my personal experience with sending remittances, and my knowledge of others who do, most of the funds are used for consumption purposes. Lim and Simmons's study of the use of remittances in thirteen CARICOM countries reveals that "remittance inflows into the Caribbean are mostly to finance consumption needs rather than investing in growth-enhancing projects which may accumulate the capital stock in the economies."[46] Remittances enable some working-class recipients to escape relative poverty, and governments may opportunistically trumpet poverty reduction statistics as if their policies are the primary source of poverty alleviation. Remittances weaken the resolve to engage in collective political action or confrontation with the state over the provision of public goods or advancing programs to facilitate economic equity. People are able to access the consumption of goods and services courtesy of relatives and friends who are overseas.

Absence of a Permissive External Environment

The Anglophone Caribbean represents plantation societies whose political economy is unavoidably impacted by economic and ideological currents that emanate from imperialist North America and Europe. In other words, this region does not operate in an environment of its own making. This situation has been the status quo since Europe colonized the region and integrated the Caribbean into the economy of that metropolitan region. In the 1960s and 1970s, imperialism was on the defensive with the political struggles and national liberation processes across the Third World. At this same time, the former Soviet Union was a source of political, economic, ideological, and military support for states or guerrilla movements in Africa, Asia, and Latin America that were seeking a path of liberation away from Western capitalism and imperialism. In North America and Europe, they were also experiencing internal political challenges and rebellions from women, racialized groups, and students, the elderly, sexual minorities, and national minorities who were actively fighting oppressive conditions. The preceding enabling factors created a permissive external environment for progressive nationalist, anti-imperialist, or state socialist developments in the Caribbean and Latin America, Africa and Asia.[47] John Foran refers to the permissive external environment as a "world-systemic opening (a let-up of external controls)"[48] by the major powers.

The Cuban, Nicaraguan, and Grenadian revolutions, and the socialist orientation of the Michael Manley regime, were possible because the external geopolitical environment was a politically enabling one (in addition to internal factors that were germane to these societies).[49] In the current geo-political environment of the Caribbean, American imperialism has strongly indicated that it will aggressively undermine any radical social transformation, as exemplified by its behavior toward the Bolivarian Revolution in Venezuela.[50] The United States financed and carried out a low intensity war against the revolution in Nicaragua, and it invaded Grenada and put an end to its revolution after a violent split in the leadership.[51] America is the sole global superpower that is violently opposed to socialist-oriented or explicitly revolutionary socialist governments in the global South. In the current period, there is no countervailing power from which material assistance may be procured for the pursuit of a non-capitalist or revolutionary socialist development path. The United States stands ready to use the full weight of its economic, political, diplomatic, and military might to thwart or frustrate such a development in the Anglophone Caribbean.

In the context of such a hostile environment, it is understandable if the people view capitalism as the only permissible game in town. The global financial institutions such as the IMF, World Bank, and IADB that are controlled by global North states are only positive toward regimes that are on the capitalist development path. Furthermore, in the context of the English-speaking Caribbean, many radicals and even mass publics were deeply disturbed by the violent implosion of the Grenadian revolution. The way that the revolution ended probably created deep reservation among the Anglophone Caribbean people about violent, revolutionary experimentation. However, the attitude of the United States toward anti-capitalist political and economic events in the Caribbean is much more of a deterring factor than memories of the Grenadian Revolution.

Political Irrelevance of the Radical Petite Bourgeoisie

The radical petit bourgeoisie in the English-speaking Caribbean have virtually abandoned organized political resistance and have retreated into various pursuits that are not necessarily committed to destroying the existing hegemonic capitalist and state forces. It is reasonable to assert that the English-speaking

Caribbean Left experienced an ideological crisis of faith with the collapse of the Grenadian Revolution. According to Caribbean academic David Hinds, "The demise of the Grenadian Revolution left the Caribbean Left in disarray. The revolution had become the hope for fundamental transformation in the Anglophone Caribbean. It was a popular revolution whose effects went far beyond the shores of Grenada."[52] In 1998, Mars outlined a number of paths that the embattled Caribbean Left might take, and it has definitely embraced "a process of self-liquidation by acknowledging defeat and the impossibility of realizing egalitarian socialism in the teeth of a more powerful capitalist system."[53] The year 1983 marks the start of the slow decline and extinction of radical and revolutionary left parties in the region, with the vibrant and seemingly strong Workers Party of Jamaica becoming defunct in 1992.

In spite of the blanket anti-petite bourgeois prejudices among many people who are politically aware, a sustained revolutionary resistance will not likely take place under current conditions, without the catalytic or triggering role of the radical or revolutionary petit bourgeoisie or middle-class. Since 1789, how many national liberation struggles or social revolutions have not been led or initiated by the radical or revolutionary petit bourgeoisie? The Haitian Revolution and the Mexican Revolution are probably the only two cases that were not led by petit bourgeois forces that committed Amilcar Cabral's "class suicide" and joined the ranks of the laboring classes as agents of the social revolution.[54] The radical or revolutionary petit bourgeois has acquired knowledge, skills, and attitudes in the universities and other post-secondary institutions that are essential to the people rising up for justice and equity. It is for this reason that Frantz Fanon called on this class to put these critical resources at the disposal of the people.[55]

In the late 1960s, the radical and revolutionary petit bourgeois elements (both students and lecturers) at the University of the West Indies (UWI) embraced the political trajectory advocated by Frantz Fanon[56] and the revolutionary Marxist historian Walter Rodney.[57] However, the students and lecturers are currently absent from overt and oppositional organizing for socialism or revolutionary political projects. The UWI is the premier English-language university in the Caribbean and is the principal manifestation of regional cooperation. According to Brian Meeks, a former member of the communist Workers Party of Jamaica and current university-based intellectual:

> At the UWI, the pendulum has swung dramatically from a point at which a critical mass of students and academics were concerned with issues of transformation to one in which the vast majority of students seem obsessed with certification and

career, while the academics have retreated from the public sphere and focus on consultancies and salary increments.[58]

The neoliberal capitalist turn, with its glorification of the ethical "me-myself-and-I" stance, has infected the ideological sensibilities and political behaviors of many academic workers and students. This development has effectively neutered any inclination toward the revolution. If the lecturers, as a group, have abandoned revolutionary agitation and organizing, it is unlikely that corrupting the minds of the learners and turning them against the gods of social conformity will be the animating thrust of their activities as academic workers.

In addition to the above reality, the political tendency at the UWI seems to have been impacted by the "'cultural' turn within the social sciences"[59] and the humanities. Identity politics has superseded the focus on the interaction between the political and economic structures in maintaining capitalist hegemony in the Anglophone Caribbean. In the introduction to a 1997 double issue of *Caribbean Quarterly*, Barry Chevannes celebrates the establishment of culture as the ascendant force in Caribbean scholarship. He claims that the plenary speeches in that double issue of the *Caribbean Quarterly* "represented a powerful symbol of culture coming (back) in from the cold where it had been thrown out by a social science that had lost its bearing and wandered far afield in realms of vanguardism and name-calling."[60] The leftist intellectuals who came out of the social sciences in the 1970s and 1980s at UWI, Mona, did more than just condemn capitalism and imperialism. The Jamaican Marxist revolutionary intelligentsia engaged in organizing around women's liberation, expanded trade union terrain, and organized junior medical doctors. These leftists also gave critical support to the Michael Manley administration and engaged in public education around the need for socialism, the class struggle, and the development of working-class consciousness.

While Meeks is critical of the failure of Caribbean Marxism to adapt itself to the specific conditions of the Caribbean, he acknowledges an endearing feature, which "was its orientation toward activism and a healthy notion of *praxis*."[61] To what extent is the cultural turn among intellectuals in the Anglophone Caribbean fostering an enabling environment for the people to rise up? They are not engaged in the organizing work that the revolutionary intelligentsia of the 1970s and 1980s was actively involved in, whether the 1970 February Revolution in Trinidad, resistance to the Burnham regime in Guyana, or seminal roles played in the Grenadian Revolution, as in the case of Maurice Bishop, Phyllis Coard, and Bernard Coard. Close to two decades after Chevannes publicly gave his blessings to the "centrality of culture now replacing the centrality of politics,"[62] I would conclude that the cultural preoccupations among most intellectuals in the English-speaking Caribbean is a sort of "counterrevolution," when compared with the anti-capitalist or socialist political activism of the petit bourgeois actors who were shaped by the social sciences and its radical political imperatives. The forces of capitalism, racism, patriarchy, and imperialism are not fazed if the proponents of the cultural turn engage in the researching, documenting, and celebrating of the Caribbean's creative arts, birthing rituals, musical genres, African-Caribbean religions, Rastafari as culture bearers, and numerous other cultural phenomena. Instead, they would have a problem if the cultural-privileging petit bourgeois forces engage with questions of political economy from a socialist perspective and attempt to organize the people behind revolutionary political programs by way of social movement organizations. The issue is not a problem of focusing on the culture of the people; it is a matter of being divorced from organizing with the people to bring an end to class exploitation and other forms of oppression.

Engendering Revolt by *Di Suffrahs* and Allies

It is always easier to articulate the reasons why social, economic, and political conditions are the way they are, than to engage in solutions to eliminate the undesirable conditions. In the section below, an attempt will be made to address this shortcoming (insufficient attention to the practical matter of social transformation) that affects many activists or organizers. This section addresses several activities that might facilitate the people becoming self-consciously and actively opposed to their oppressive conditions by incorporating the following into their resistance strategies: fostering memories of resistance; developing "political cultures of opposition and resistance"; encouraging political education and fostering class consciousness; and organizing around the needs of the people.

Instilling Memories of
the Tradition of Revolt and Revolution

The African working-class and other oppressed peoples in the Caribbean, who are the creators of the national cultures of the respective Caribbean territories and the popular culture of the Caribbean, are peoples of memories. It is fundamentally necessary to bring the tradition of revolt and revolution to the center of the organizing and political education work that is carried out among the people. After all, it is their history, and it is important for them to institutionalize the appropriateness of using any means necessary to remove oppressive conditions into their worldview. Mutabaruka's poem "Revolt Ain't a Revolution" informs the people that "we have to remember what happened in slavery / so as not to repeat that history."[63] He makes it explicitly clear to the African-Caribbean people that "we have to seek shaka [and] hannibal / in these times of aggression /and understand what was their mission."[64] Shaka Zulu of South Africa and Hannibal of Carthage are as seen as military and historical figures that are worthy of emulation in the present. Mutabaruka calls on the Caribbean revolutionary tradition when he asserts that:

> If some thing is not worth dyin for
> it is not worth livin for
> but if it takes war to free us
> then it is just WAR….[65]

Mutabaruka is showing us the gold mine that is the collective memory of the people of the Caribbean people. He and his fellow cultural workers and organic intellectuals are instructing the people on the value of the past in the present and the realizing of the future.

When the Trinidadian calypsonian The Mighty Sparrow recounts his experience of being purchased in Africa, journeying through the brutality of the Middle Passage, toiling hard under the watchful eyes of the slave masters, and then living through the farce of Emancipation in the song *Slave*,[66] he is demonstrating the role of memory as a tool of resistance and documentation. When the former I-Three (back-up singer of Bob Marley and the Wailers) Judy Mowatt recalls the suffering, exploitation, and abuse of African women during the Holocaust of Enslavement in her popular song *Black Woman*,[67] she is calling forth memories in her testimony on the trials and tribulations of this group. When the reggae cultural worker Burning Spear asks us, "Do you remember the days of slavery?" in the song *Slavery Days*,68 he is testing our memories of the horrors of chattel slavery. When Bob Marley states in the song *Crazy Baldhead* that "I and I build the cabin / I and I plant the corn / Didn't my people before me slave for this country? / Now you look me with scorn,"[69] he is invoking memories of the economic exploitation of slavery and capitalism and linking it to the continuing racist and capitalist oppression in contemporary Caribbean society. When Marley asserts that "We're gonna chase those crazy baldheads out of town," he is relying on memories of revolts in fighting chattel slavery. The non-scribal, folk philosophers, and cultural workers of the Caribbean are the major forces who articulate and remind the people of the pain of the past and its relevance to their present and future. The Akan's adinkra symbol of the Sankofa bird looking backward while projecting a forward movement, while also holding an egg (symbol of the potentiality of a new life) in its beak, is a popular symbol among African-centered Diaspora Africans. It is an appropriate symbol to invoke and center for the Caribbean revolutionary or radical organizers who want *di suffrahs* to become conversant with the tradition of revolt and revolution in the region. There are two contrasting historical memories that confront the oppressed in the Caribbean. Campbell states that there is the memory of the fight against genocide, slavery, and indentureship, and it provides the potentiality for liberation.[70] The other memory pertains to the experience of slavery, colonialism, capitalist economic exploitation, imperialist wars, and cultural imperialism, which serves as the social reaction in the path of revolutionary possibilities and counterhegemonic developments.[71] The organizers in the Caribbean should not shy away from an open discussion of revolutionary organizing as an option in seeking a substantive transformation of society. These organizers must consistently commemorate anniversaries of revolts, uprisings, revolutions, and the exemplary contribution of individuals and groups that reflect a revolutionary or oppositional legacy. These commemorative moments should strive to make credible and relevant links to the social, economic, and political issues that are germane to the lives of the Caribbean laboring classes.

Develop "political cultures of opposition and resistance"

In the social struggle in the Anglophone Caribbean, it will be necessary to develop the cultural revolution in order to give birth to the political revolution. When the intellectuals or petit bourgeois forces in the Caribbean talk or write about the centrality of culture, they are on to something. But if their cultural thrust is divorced from political organizing and a revolutionary program, culture becomes celebratory in their hands and useless to the emancipation of the people. Fanon alerts readers to the problem of the colonized intellectuals and organizers who are estranged from actual political organizing:

> When the colonized intellectual writing for his [or her] people uses the past he [or she] must do so with the intention of opening up the future, of spurring them into action and fostering hope. But in order to secure hope, in order to give it substance, he [or she] must take part in the action and commit himself [or herself] body and soul to the national struggle. You can talk about anything you like, but when it comes to talking about that one thing in a man's [or woman's] life that involves opening up new horizons, enlightening your country and standing tall alongside your people, then muscle power is required.[72]

It cannot be overemphasized that "One cannot divorce the combat for culture from the people's struggle for liberation."[73] A critical source of ideas for the development of the "political cultures of opposition and resistance" is the culture of the people.

A theorist of revolution, John Foran developed the notion of *political cultures of opposition and resistance*, which is a critical component of his model of the coalescing of factors that are necessary in affecting successful revolutions. Foran describes political cultures of opposition and resistance as the "process by which both ordinary citizens and revolutionary leaderships came to perceive the economic and political realities of their societies, and to fashion a set of understandings that simultaneously made sense of those conditions, gave voice to their grievances, and found a discourse capable of enjoining others to act with them in the attempt to remake their societies."[74] Given the religious, ethnic, racial, and political diversity present in contemporary societies, especially in the global South, this reservoir of oppositional, anti-regime ideas is presented as a multi-source one. The political culture of opposition and resistance might emerge from religious sources such as Rastafari[75] and Native Baptist religious expression that informed the 1831 Emancipation Rebellion and the 1865 Morant Bay Rebellion in Jamaica, as well as from the idioms of the people such as the numerous proverbs across the Caribbean that speak to justice, fairness, and retribution. Historical memories of experiences, conflicts, or revolts[76] may be used to generate ideas of political resistance. In the foregoing case, chattel slavery and the numerous uprisings against it, and the success of the Jamaican Maroons in winning their freedom from slavery, might serve as examples of the possibility of victory through militant organizing.

In the English-speaking Caribbean, the reggae and calypso musical genres are bountiful resources for the extraction of ideas for the construction of an "independent culture of resistance" that is essential to countering the ideological hegemony of the ruling class.[77] In Jamaica, organizers who are working with reggae and dancehall artists must find ways to introduce them to revolutionary social theories, as well as encourage these working-class cultural workers to read political ideas. The level of their political analysis as reflected in the insufficient ideational sophistication of their currents songs would be greatly expanded. The current reggae artists who are seen as a part of the "Reggae Revival"[78] movement represent a political maturity or edginess in their lyrical construction and social commentary on oppressive conditions and liberation. This youth-led, Rastafarian roots reggae renewal movement makes explicit critiques of capitalism, racism, imperialism, and life in general in *Babylon*.[79] Cultural workers such as Chronixx, Jesse Royal, Proteje, Jah9, and Kabaka Pyramid are members of this reggae renewal movement. This development is welcome, given the domination of the socially backward ideological themes in many of the dancehall songs over the last thirty years.

Political Education and Fostering Class Consciousness

In preparing the laboring classes to self-organize or self-emancipate and rise up against their oppressive situation, the revolutionary organizers will have to engage in mass political education and ideological development in all available spaces in society. It is an open secret that the members of the working class have a low level of class-consciousness, or awareness, of themselves as a distinct class with interests that are irreconcilable with those of the bourgeoisie or capitalist class. The Anglophone Caribbean's working class is politically divided between the two bourgeois-led major parties that are normally present in the region's Westminster political system. It is middle-class political actors who are chief enablers of capitalism in the region. According to Mars, "it should be recalled that the real power of the Caribbean middle-classes inheres in their connections with international capital. Not only does the commercial section of the middle-classes live by this international connection, but it is through the connection of the middle classes that capitalist domination of the Caribbean is facilitated and advanced."[80] The populist orientation or patron-clientelistic nature of the political systems in the Anglophone Caribbean tend to mask the capitalist and imperialist commitments of the middle class or petit bourgeois characters who run these mass-based political parties.

The revolutionary intelligentsia at all levels of the educational system should use their position as educators to open the minds of the students to revolutionary ideas by cultivating critical thinking, strong problem-solving, and organizing knowledge and skills. Paolo Freire and Amilcar Cabral's use of the problem-posing or Socratic Method of questioning should be a central pedagogical tool in the educational process. The central purpose behind using this approach to teaching and learning is the cultivation of the people's capacity for critical inquiry and prejudicing their minds toward praxis or social action to change the world. This dialogic pedagogical approach will prove useful in the teaching and learning experiences in workshop settings or doing outreach in communities, workplaces, schools, and other spaces where a large number of people congregate. Given the commitment to struggle that is opposed to a vanguard leadership over the people, the capacity building, or community development workshop, will become the principal instrument that is used to provide the people with knowledge, skills, and attitudes that are needed to run their self-managed organizations and institutions. If we are going to eliminate dependence on petit bourgeois organizers for critical organizational skills, it is essential that the movement develop practical resources that will enable the people to be the true architects of the revolution. Education for mass critical consciousness is still necessary.

The broad Anglophone Caribbean Left has a tradition of carrying out political education programs. The radical and revolutionary organizations of the Left, and its middle-class forces, have engaged in mass political education within the population, with the goal of facilitating a heightened awareness of oppression.[81] They are in a position to initially function as public educators-cum-organic intellectuals. This relatively privileged class tends to have a higher level of access to different media spaces and are in possession of the knowledge, skills, and attitude to carry out public lectures, deliver community development or capacity-building workshops, write op-ed articles for national and local newspapers as well as internet-based publications, and fulfill the role of guest on news programs. It is essential for today's organizers to learn from the missteps of the past with respect to implementing educational programs as highlighted by Mars:

> The first is what could be termed the Procrustean bed, or vice-like, effect of Marxist-Leninist theory and socialist ideology on the overwhelmed mass public, in the sense that there is an apparent forcing theory down the throats, so to speak, of the masses. The second is what appears to be in effect intellectuals speaking only to themselves since much of the theoretical underpinnings are graspable only at their level of training and preparation. The third is the probable exclusion of the rich experiences of the masses from playing a necessary part in the educational content and curriculum.[82]

The organizers should emphasize developing the capabilities of the members of the laboring classes and other oppressed groups to competently and effectively function as public educators-cum-organic intellectuals. Furthermore, the content of the educational program ought to be relevant to the lives of the people, a critique raised earlier in this essay by Brian Meeks. The organizers must approach public education as an instrument to lead the masses to the path of self-emancipation and organizing (24/7) to rid the world of capitalism, racism, patriarchy, and imperialism.

Organizing Around the People's Needs

In fighting to create the classless, stateless, and self-organized (communist) society, twenty-first century activists and organizers in the Caribbean must prioritize organizing, and not mobilizing, the people, and should do so around their self-identified and objective needs within today's oppressive conditions. The organizing approach to building the capacity for revolution must be elevated over simply embracing the mobilizing approach to resistance, which merely brings the people out for a show of force against oppression. Under the latter approach to rising up against oppression, the organizational and movement leaders—not the rank and file—monopolize the ideational, strategic, and operational leadership roles. In an essay on organizing versus mobilizing approaches, I outlined a few of the features of organizing:

> When I raised the issue of organizing the oppressed, this project is centrally focused on building the capacity of the people to become central actors on the stage of history or in the drama of emancipation. The socially marginalized are placed in organizational situations where they are equipped with the knowledge, skills and attitude to work for their own freedom and the construction of a transformed social reality.
>
> Under the organizing model the people are the principal participants and decision-makers in the organizations and movements that are working for social change. The people are not seen as entities who are so ideologically underdeveloped that they need a revolutionary vanguard or dictatorship to lead them to the "New Jerusalem." The supreme organizer and humanist Ella Baker took the position that the masses will figure out the path to freedom in her popular assertion, "Give people light and they will find a way."[83]

The organizing approach is the preferred way to demonstrate to the Caribbean people that they will have to create the path to emancipation with their own brains, hearts, and muscles. It must be done through their autonomous, self-organized organizations because "It is impossible to fight capitalist exploitation, police violence, the oppression of women, white supremacy, homophobia, and other forms of dehumanization outside of collective action and organized structures—organizations and movements."[84]

It is through the formation of organizations that the people will be able to give concrete forms to organizing around their needs, such as education, employment, housing, financial services, collective self-defense, restorative justice, and food security. Organizations call for greater commitment of time and other resources of the people than showing up for a demonstration, march, rally, or vigil. However, membership-based organization with the needs of the people centered and guided by a transformative vision of justice, respect, dignity, and self-determination opens up the possibility for the people to create self-managed economic and social institutions and institute participatory democratic practices. In this vein, the organizers must draw on the sugar workers' cooperatives that were established during the democratic socialist administration of Michael Manley as an instructive of labor attempting to exercise control over capital. The text *A New Earth: The Jamaican Sugar Workers' Cooperatives, 1975–1985* is an excellent source on this experience of worker control and the lessons that should be drawn from it for the current phase of the struggle. It is essential that the organizers work with the people in developing the supporting structures and organizations to make economic and social cooperation and alternative institution building a material reality in the lives of the people.[86] A necessary part of rising up against oppression and preparing the oppressed in the Caribbean for rising up is the formation of self-managed alternative institutions to hold territory and serve as incubators of the values, sensibilities, and practices of the future anarchist communist society. Therefore, as the people are meeting their needs, developing a critical ideological and political understanding of oppressive conditions in society, acquiring the knowledge, skills, and attitude of self-organization, they are building the embryonic structures and enabling conditions for the just Caribbean society of the future.

Concluding Words

The revolutionary organizations and organizers in the English-speaking Caribbean are faced with the daunting task of organizing in an environment in which American imperialism is strongly opposed to the development of counterhegemonic national projects. Given this state of affairs, the revolutionary or progressive forces must continue the anti-capitalist and anti-imperialist tradition of radical thought,[87] and cultivate movements to defend the Anglophone Caribbean from the full onslaught of imperialist aggression.[88] A permissive external environment is critical for fomenting revolution in dependent capitalist societies, such as are present in the Caribbean. We need effective anti-imperialist activism inside North America and Europe to support the self-emancipation initiatives of the people of the Caribbean. We are fighting common enemies of human emancipation; resistance in the Caribbean is a contribution to the fight for freedom in Europe and North America, and vice versa. Amilcar Cabral shared the same outlook on the worldwide fight to defeat imperialism, in a meeting before a group of African Americans.[89] The people themselves must make the revolution, through self-emancipation rooted in a prefigurative politics of liberation. Oppositional economic, social, cultural, and political institutions must function as tools of resistance and laboratories of experimentation for how we will live politically transgressive lives for the anarchist communist societies of the future.

Endnotes

1   Peter Kropotkin's essays "Anarchist Communism: Its Basis and Principles" and "Anarchism: Its Philosophy and Ideals" provide a good introduction to anarchism, and they are included in his *Fugitive Writings* (Montreal: Black Rose Books, 1993).

2   Horace G. Campbell, "The Grenadian Revolution and the Challenges for Revolutionary Change in the Caribbean," *Journal of Eastern Caribbean Studies*, 35, nos. 3 and 4 (2010): 37.

3   Thomas D. Edsall, "Why Don't the Poor Rise Up?," *New York Times*, June 25, 2015. Available online: https://www.nytimes.com/2015/06/24/opinion/why-dont-the-poor-rise-up.html?_r=0.

4   United Nations, *The Global Social Crisis: Report on the World Social Situation 2011*, (New York: United Nations Publication, 2011), Available online: www.un.org/esa/socdev/rwss/docs/2011/rwss2011.pdf.

5   Mutabaruka, *Mutabaruka: The Next Poems* (Kingston: Paul Issa Publications, 2005), 20.

6   Brian Meeks, *Caribbean Revolutions and Revolutionary Theory: An Assessment of Cuba, Nicaragua and Grenada* (Kingston, Jamaica: University of the West Indies Press, 2001), 7–8.

7   Michael Lind, "Are We Still a Middle-Class Nation?" *The Atlantic*, January/February 2004. Available online: www.theatlantic.com/magazine/archive/2004/01/are-we-still-a-middle-class-nation/302870/.

8   Ajamu Nangwaya, "Why are we afraid of naming and confronting capitalism?" *Pambazuka News*, January 15, 2015. Available online: https://www.pambazuka.org/global-south/why-are-we-afraid-naming-and-confronting-capitalism.

9   Salvatore Babones, "America's Real Poverty Rate," *Inequality.org*, November 14, 2011. Available online: http://inequality.org/americas-real-poverty-rate/.

10 Paul Buchheit, "The Real Numbers: Half of America Is in Poverty -- and It's Creeping Upward It's much worse for black families," *AlterNet*, January, 20, 2015. Available online: http://www.alternet.org/economy/real-numbers-half-america-poverty-and-its-creeping-upward.

11 Jamaica Observer, "Wakefield residents protest against police killing," *Jamaica Observer*, May 11, 2016. Available online: http://www.jamaicaobserver.com/news/Wakefield-residents-protest-against-police-killing-------_60503; Paul Clarke, "Hannah Town residents block road to protest against police killing," *Jamaica Observer*, January 19, 2006. Available online: http://www.jamaicaobserver.com/news/96852_Hannah-Town-residents-block-road-to-protest-against-police-killing.

12 Thomas D. Doswell, "The Caribbean: A Geographic Preface," In *Understanding the Contemporary Caribbean*, eds. Richard S. Hillman & Thomas J. D'Agostino, 2nd ed. (Kingston, Jamaica: Ian Randle Publishers, 2009), 21–22; Perry Mars, *Ideology and Change: The Transformation of the Caribbean Left* (Kingston, Jamaica: The Press University of the West Indies, 1998), 18–19.

13 Thomas J. D'Agostino, "Caribbean Politics," In *Understanding the Contemporary Caribbean*, eds. Richard S. Hillman & Thomas J. D'Agostino, 2nd ed, 98.

14 Ibid., 98.

15 Mars, *Ideology and Change*, 19.
16 Associated Press, "MI5 files reveal details of 1953 coup that overthrew British Guiana's leaders," *Associated Press*, August 26, 2011. Available online: https://www.theguardian.com/world/2011/aug/26/mi5-files-coup-british-guiana; Agostino, "Caribbean Politics," 115.
17 Casey Gane-McCalla, "Jamaica's Shower Posse: How The CIA Created 'The Most Notorious Criminal Organization,'" *Global Research*, June 3, 2010. Available online: http://www.globalresearch.ca/jamaica-s-shower-posse-how-the-cia-created-the-most-notorious-criminal-organization/19696.
18 D'Agostino, "Caribbean Politics," 114.
19 Perry Mars, "Destabilization and Socialist Orientation in the English-Speaking Caribbean," *Latin American Perspective*, 11, no.3 (1984): 83–110.
20 Dennis A. Pantin & Marlene Attzs, "The Economies of the Caribbean," in *Understanding the Contemporary Caribbean*, eds. Richard S. Hillman & Thomas J. D'Agostino, 2nd ed., 135.
21 Ibid., 135.
22 D'Agostino, "Caribbean Politics," 127.
23 Brian Meeks, "Caribbean Insurrections," *Caribbean Quarterly*, 41, no. 2 (1995), 13.
24 Ibid.
25 Brian Meeks, *Radical Caribbean: From Black Power to Abu Bakr*, (Kingston, Jamaica: The Press The University of the West Indies, 1996), 85.
26 D'Agostino, "Caribbean Politics," 124.
27 Meeks, "Radical Caribbean," 86.
28 Jorge I. Domínguez, "The Caribbean Question: Why Has Liberal Democracy (Surprisingly) Flourished?," in *Democracy in the Caribbean: Political, Economic and Social Perspectives*, eds., Jorge I. Domínquez, Robert A. Pastor, and R. DeLisle Worrell, (Baltimore: John Hopkins Press, 1993), 3.
29 Ian Boxill, "The Two Faces of Caribbean Music," *Social and Economic Studies*, 43, no. 2 (1994): 36–37.
30 D'Agostino, "Caribbean Politics," 126.
31 Ibid.
32 Boxill, "The Two Faces of Caribbean Music," 37.
33 Norman Girvan, "C.Y. Thomas and the 'The Poor and the Powerless': The Limitations of Conventional Radicalism," *Social and Economic Studies*, 37, no. 4 (1988): 270.
34 Cited in Girvan, 270.
35 Inter-American Development Bank, *The Informal Sector in Jamaica*, Economic Sector and Study Series – RE3-06-010, December 2006. Available online: https://publications.iadb.org/handle/11319/4326.
36 Kevin Greenidge, Carlos Holder & Stuart Mayers, "Estimating the Size of the Informal Economy in Barbados," *Business, Finance & Economics in Emerging Economies*, vol. 4 no. 1 (2009): 9209–10.
37 Ibid., 7.
38 Ibid., 7.
39 Ibid., 2.
40 Neville Graham, "From the womb to the tomb via Jamaica's $800 million informal economy," *Jamaica Gleaner*, November 1, 2016. Available online: http://jamaica-gleaner.com/article/news/20161101/womb-tomb-jamaicas-800-million-informal-enonomy.
41 Sokchea Lim & Walter O. Simmons, "Do remittances promote economic development in the Caribbean Community and Common Market?," *Journal of Economics and Business*, 77 (2015): 43.
42 Alleyne Dillion, "Motivations to Remit in CARICOM: A GMM Approach," *Social and*

Economic Studies, 55, no. 3 (2006): 71.

43 Steven Jackson, "Remittance flows up by 5.6%," *Jamaica Observer*, March 27, 2015. Available online: http://www.jamaicaobserver.com/business/ Remittance-flows-up-by-5-6-_18645126.

44 Avia Collinder, "Total remittances climb to $2.23 billion in 2015," *Jamaica Observer*, April 1, 2016. Available online: http://www.jamaicaobserver.com/business/ Total-remittances-climb-to--2-23-billion-in-2015_56253.

45 News Americas, "Six Caribbean Nations See The Highest Remittances For 2016," *News Americas*, October 14, 2016. Available online: http://www.newsamericasnow.com/ six-caribbean-nations-see-the-highest-remittances-for-2016/.

46 Dillion, "Motivations to remit," 57.

47 Meeks, *Caribbean Revolutions*, 31.

48 John Foran, "The Comparative-Historical Sociology of Third World Revolutions," In *Theorizing Revolutions,* ed. John Foran (New York: Routledge, 1997), 228.

49 Meeks, *Caribbean Revolutions*, 61–63, 103–106, and 154–55.

50 Francisco Dominguez, "Is US-Funded Destabilization in Latin America Now Paying Off?," *Telesur*, April 14, 2016. Available online: http://www.telesurtv.net/english/opinion/ Is-US-Funded-Destabilization-in-Latin-America-Now-Paying-Off-20160413-0028.html.

51 Glenville Ashby, "Revisiting the Revolution," *Jamaica Gleaner,* January 17, 2016. Available online: http://jamaica-gleaner.com/article/art-leisure/20160117/revisiting-revolution.

52 David Hinds, "The Grenada Revolution and the Caribbean Left," *Journal of Eastern Caribbean Studies*, 35, nos. 3 and 4 (2010): 104.

53 Mars, *Ideology and Change,* 174.

54 Amilcar Cabral, *Revolution in Guinea: Selected Texts* (New York: Monthly Review Press, 1969), 110.

55 Frantz Fanon, *The Wretched of the Earth* (New York: Grove Press, 2004).

56 Ibid., 145. He projected that "Each generation must discover its mission, fulfil or betray it, in relative opacity."

57 Walter Rodney, *The Groundings with My Brothers* (Chicago: Research Associates School Times Publication, 1990), 31–32. Rodney posed the following question to his audience of students and lecturers at the University of the West Indies in the 1968: "Trotsky once wrote that Revolution is the carnival of the masses. When we have that carnival in the West Indies, are people like us here at the university going to join the bacchanal?"

58 Brian Meeks, *Critical Interventions in Caribbean Theory and Politics* (Jackson, University Press of Mississippi, 2014), 73.

59 John Foran, "Discourses and Social Forces: The Role of Culture and Cultural Studies in Understanding Revolutions," in *Theorizing Revolutions,* ed. John Foran (New York: Routledge, 1997), 203.

60 Barry Chevannes, "Introduction," *Caribbean Quarterly*, 43, 1 & 2 (1997): iii.

61 Brian Meeks, *Critical Interventions.*

62 Chevannes, "Introduction," iii.

63 Mutabaruka, *Mutabaruka: The Next Poems*, 20.

64 Ibid., 21.

65 Ibid., 21.

66 Mighty Sparrow, "Slave," *The Slave*, RCA, 1963.

67 Judy Mowatt, "Black Woman," *Black Woman*, Shanachie, 1980.

68 Burning Spear, "Slavery Days," *Marcus Garvey*, Island Records, 1975.

69 Omnibus Press, *Complete Lyrics of Bob Marley: Songs of Freedom* (New York: Omnibus Press, 2001), 34.

70 Campbell, "The Grenadian Revolution," 43.

71 Ibid.

72 Frantz Fanon, *The Wretched of the Earth*, 167.

73 Ibid., 168.

74 John Foran, *New Political Cultures of Opposition: What Future for Revolutions?* February 7, 2007. Available online: https://www.academia.edu/1277296/ 15_New_political_cultures_of_opposition.

75 A good source on the theological aspects of the Rastafari movement is Noel Leo Erskine, *From Garvey to Marley: Rastafari Theology* (Gainesville, Florida: University Press of Florida, 2007).

76 Foran, "Discourses and Social Forces," 208.

77 Boxill, "Two Faces," 44.

78 Abby Aguirre, "Reggae Revival: Meet the Millennial Musicians Behind Jamaica's New Movement," *Vogue*, October 28, 2015. Available online: http://www.vogue.com/ projects/13362670/reggae-revival-jamaica-chronixx-protoje-roots-music/.

79 There are multiple meanings for the Rastafari use of the term "Babylon." Velma Pollard provides a listing of the various ways that it is rendered: "police; policeman; soldier or people who are called wicked by the Rastafari; place of wickedness; oppressors; to do with an unprincipled way of life usually in reference to the white man's culture," in *Dread Talk: The Language of Rastafari* (Kingston, Jamaica: Canoe Press, University of the West Indies, 1994), 41.

80 Mars, *Ideology and Change*, 27–29.

81 Ibid., 119–20.

82 Ibid., 121.

83 Ajamu Nangwaya, "If organizing is the weapon of the oppressed, why are we stuck on mobilizing?," *Rabble*, August 21, 2014. Available online: http://rabble.ca/news/2014/08/ if-organizing-weapon-oppressed-why-are-we-stuck-on-mobilizing.

84 Ajamu Nangwaya, "On the rebellion in Ferguson, Missouri: Organizations are the lifeblood of social change," *Rabble*, August 20, 2014. Available online: http://rabble.ca/ news/2014/08/on-rebellion-ferguson-missouri-organizations-are-lifeblood-social-change.

85 Monica Frolander-Ulf and Frank Lindenfeld, *A New Earth: The Jamaican Sugar Workers' Cooperatives, 1975–1981* (New York: University Press of America, 1984).

86 Ajamu Nangwaya, "Seek ye first the worker self-management kingdom: Toward the solidarity economy in Jackson, Mississippi," *Pambazuka News*, September 18, 2013. Available online: https://www.pambazuka.org/governance/ seek-ye-first-worker-self-management-kingdom.

87 Rhoda Reddock, "Radical Caribbean social thought: Race, class identity and the postcolonial nation," *Current Sociology*, 62, 4 (2014).

88 This article on building solidarity inside imperialism for Africa provides proposals that are relevant to the Caribbean: Ajamu Nangwaya, "Afrikan Liberation Day and the Commitment to an Anti-imperialist Pan-Afrikan Solidarity" *Dissident Voice*, May 23, 2014. Available online: http://dissidentvoice.org/2014/05/afrikan-liberation-day-and-the-commitment-to-an-anti-imperialist-pan-afrikan-solidarity/. This article on solidarity with the Haitian people contains organizing ideas for the creation of an anti imperialist constituency inside North America and Europe: Ajamu Nangwaya, "Transform your Global Justice Sentiments into Action to End the Occupation of Haiti," *Dissident Voice*, October 23, 2014. Available online: http://dissidentvoice.org/2014/10/ transform-your-global-justice-sentiments-into-action-to-end-the-occupation-of-haiti/.

89 Amilcar Cabral, *Return to the Source: Selected Speeches of Amilcar Cabral* (Monthly Review Press, 1973), 76.

"THEY'VE TURNED THE GUNS ON THE PEOPLE!"

TOWARDS HEALING: CONFRONTING THE IMPACTS OF THE GRENADIAN REVOLUTION

Kimalee Phillip

Introduction

WE SAT ACROSS FROM EACH OTHER. THERE WAS KINDNESS, MYSTERY, AND AN unquestionable sadness in his eyes, seemingly stretching and shaping his posture. He was almost broken. Almost. I was about to interview the father of a friend. He served as a captain in the People's Revolutionary Army (PRA), and had been imprisoned along with others for the October 19th murders of Maurice Bishop and other political leaders. My friend knew that I was preparing to present at the Grenada Country Conference, "Perspectives on the Grenada Revolution 1979–83" hosted by the University of the West Indies Open Campus in St. George's, Grenada. He thought that it would be important for me to meet his father. Our encounter was the culmination of direct and intergenerational trauma as a result of the 1979–83 Grenada Revolution.

I had not expected for this stranger to help illuminate for me what are, and continue to be, silenced, yet revealing parts of my father's past. I knew that there had to be an explanation behind the bitterness and anger that sometimes seemed to percolate from his pores, but I had never made the connection to the socialist Revolution of 1979. I knew that my father was involved in the PRA, but he had never divulged what his participation had been; in fact, he rarely talked about his past. Like so many young people at the time, my father was largely apolitical, going through the daily motions in a "postcolonial" state still trying to grapple with what independence and freedom looked like. He was also born and raised in the New Jewel Movement (NJM) stronghold of St. Paul's; Mardi Gras, to be exact. The Revolution presented him and other youth an opportunity to play a critical role in shaping their country's political future.

In the years leading up to the 1979 coup d'etat, revolutionary fervor was progressively strengthening and was stretching to every corner of the 344-square-mile island, with a population of roughly 100,000. The Revolution provided political consciousness-raising and a sense of purpose to the majority working-class populace. The launch of the Grenadian Revolution (also known as and referred to throughout this chapter as the Grenada Revolution) challenged the messages coming from the state, family, and from within: that change was limited, that it was already defined, and that anything outside of colonial, patriarchal, and heterosexist boundaries would be punished.

> From being the descendants of slaves, from people who'd been colonised, from people who'd been tossed aside, we suddenly became the controllers of our own destiny. For 400 years, our forebears were enslaved. We suffered in order to produce Europe's wealth. After slavery we were further enslaved under colonialism. But in 1979, with our own ability, by our own efforts, we changed our course. Yes, others helped, but it was us.[1]

During our interview, my friend's father pronounced, with teary eyes: "I feel like we failed you, we failed your generation." His words were painted with such pain and profundity that I could not help but respond with emotion. I wondered how often he had thought about this. How many times had he really examined the impacts of such words and feelings on his psyche?

My friend's father's words are indicative of some of the voiced, yet variously experienced, impacts of the socialist revolution on Grenadians. These sentiments were evident at the Grenada Country Conference when participants and some panelists shared concerns over what they saw as a lack of political and social will by the state and society, to critically and seriously address past personal and collective wounds, hurt, and trauma. Little had been done to address the physical wounds, let alone the mental and emotional. Grenadians, participants in the Revolution and those not yet born, were experiencing the pains and trauma felt as a result of such significant events in the form of direct, historical and/or intergenerational trauma, the latter referring to the holding and passing down of collective trauma from one generation to the next. Collective trauma can be defined as the trauma resulting from a shared experience of violence, repression, and subjugation such as slavery, civil war, unrest, and/or genocide.

The words of Maurice Bishop, "they've turned the guns on the people!," as captured in Bruce Paddington's documentary on the revolution, help to explain why the implosion of the Grenada Revolution continues to weigh so heavily on the minds and bodies of Grenadians.[2] One of the rules of the PRA that helped guide the People's Militia was that at no point would the guns be turned on the people. That point came on Fort Rupert (now named Fort George) and represented a significant departure from the people-centered movement to one that was now unpredictable and disconnected from the very principles of the Revolution. They had turned the guns on the people. Furthermore, "October 19, 1983, was a decidedly public, highly spectacular moment of collective trauma for Grenadians,"[3] as Maurice Bishop, Jacqueline Creft, Fitzroy Bain, Unison Whiteman, Norris Bain, Evelyn Bullen, Keith Hayling, Evelyn Maitland, and Vincent Noel were gunned down at Fort George in front of thousands of Grenadians who had come to save their Prime Minister.

An important factor when examining the magnitude of the implosion and subsequent U.S. invasion in 1983 is the size of the island. With a population of 100,000, the killings and imprisonment—of each other, family, and community members—were personal. The soldier who jailed or killed your brother could be your own relative or someone whom you passed everyday on the street. This played a critical role in how people experienced the Revolution and in subsequent attempts to heal and transition.

The Truth and Reconciliation Commission of Grenada (TRC) was established in 2000 to explore and assess political events, particularly those related to the socialist revolution from 1976–1991. The TRC began gathering data on September 4, 2001, and acknowledged in their final report the role of direct and historical trauma. When referencing obstacles to healing and reconciliation, the Commission said:

> Going back to the days of Eric Matthew Gairy up to the 1979 revolution, then to the tragic events of October 19th, 1983, and the intervention of a combined U.S. and Caribbean forces on October 25th, 1983, one sees that apart from the many persons who lost their lives during those periods, many more have suffered and have been wounded and scarred (some permanently) physically, emotionally, psychologically, mentally,

and spiritually. Those wounds are responsible for a tremendous amount of bitterness among many Grenadians up to today.[4]

The report by the TRC coupled with the interview process with my friend's father helped galvanize my interest in exploring some of the ongoing traumatic impacts of the Grenadian Revolution on those who participated in one way or another, on those not yet born such as myself, future generations of Grenadians, and on those still imprisoned, mentally, physically, and/or emotionally. This paper just scratches the surface.

Thirty-three years since the implosion of the Revolution and the Reagan-led U.S. invasion, Grenadians of all generations continue to feel the impacts of those revolutionary years through their blood memory and in material ways, vis-à-vis economic policies, in the education system, and in how political possibilities are defined, stifled and, in some instances, criminalized. Using an anti-capitalist and Black feminist approach, this chapter will briefly interrogate some of the emotional, economic, social, and political impacts of the Grenadian Revolution of 1979–83 on the state and people of Grenada. I approach the question of "why don't the poor rise up?" recognizing the ways in which multigenerational trauma is passed on from generation to generation, and the material ways by which poverty and political conflict can seriously affect one's decision to engage in resistance and liberation movements.

The Socio-economic Landscape and Pushback of the Grenada Revolution

The Grenadian Revolution was the first socialist revolution in the Anglophone Caribbean, and was a response to the dictatorial leadership of the inaugural Prime Minister Eric Matthew Gairy. Grenada, trying to ground itself post-independence (February 7, 1974) and reeling from the impacts of a plantation economy and the global economic realities of the day, witnessed high unemployment rates, worsening poverty rates, and limited access to a restricted and colonized education system that reflected the class and race stratification of the society. By 1978, unemployment rates were at an astronomical high, at 49%, and the global oil crisis at the time meant skyrocketing inflation rates.[5] Criminal profiteering, decreasing value for Grenadian agricultural products, increasing police brutality, and sexual violence became mainstays for Grenadian women trying to keep their sources of income.[6] Contrary to Gairy's entrance into the political arena as a trade unionist challenging the plantation aristocracy and fighting for the everyday working Grenadian, by March 1979 Gairy had grown wealthy, "owning $25 million (EC) worth of property in Grenada alone."[7]

The 1970s saw the rise of neoliberalism as a response to the decreasing rate of profit affecting global capitalism.[8] Under new neoliberal policies we saw increasing demands for limited or no state intervention and new rules on tariffs, ushering in global free trade. Deregulation, rule of the market, privatization, and the elimination of the "public good" were the foundations of this growing neoliberal agenda, and newly independent Grenada had to fit its struggling economy within this global context.

It is particularly important to note that as the global economy was experiencing reductions in its growth rates,[9] the Grenadian economy under the rule of the People's Revolutionary Government (PRG) was witnessing increases in its GDP.[10] By November 1981, Grenada announced a reduction in unemployment from 50% to under 30%, approximately $4 million in financial assistance was provided to the poorest sectors of the population to assist with home repair, and the Ministry of Housing created the National Housing Project. In addition, through the Community Work Brigades, community centers, bath and laundry facilities, and post offices were built all over the island. By comparison, during the 1979–83 rule of the PRG the United States experienced two recessions, in 1980 and 1981.[11]

Uprisings in Jamaica and Trinidad and Tobago that were pushing for Black Power across the region helped to fuel resistance struggles in the smaller English-speaking islands of the Caribbean such as in St. Lucia, St. Vincent, Antigua, Dominica, and Grenada, and these regional and international resistance movements were critical in shaping the political fabric of this small island state.[12] The Grenadian Revolution did not just belong to Grenadians: other Caribbean progressives were not only paying attention to what was happening in Grenada, but were also physically involved and very much invested in the material outcomes of the Revolution.

By the 1970s, power and any semblance of democratic control were firmly in the hands of Gairy, with some support in the rural areas. His control was violently enforced.[13] Fueled by frustrations of corruption, repressive tactics by the government, and the excessive use of force by state sponsored military groups such as the Mongoose Gang, members of the New Jewel Movement began amplifying their organizing strategies and mobilizing the people of Grenada. In an interview with David Scott, Grenadian author Merle Collins discusses memory and trauma and her recollection of the Mongoose Gang in her book *Angel*:

> **DS:** *What do you know about the infamous Mongoose Gang? I'll tell you why I ask. It really doesn't figure at all in* Angel. *But I also ask because it is so central to the NJM story of the terror of Gairy, and of the need to*

look at possibilities of removing Gairy from office. But talking to some
people recently in Grenada, I have the sense that maybe that story has been
exaggerated, that the so-called Mongoose Gang didn't constitute the kind
of threat that it was portrayed to be.

MC: Well, I don't know. The mythology, if one might call it that, was
certainly there and strong in Grenada. So I don't think they exaggerated that feeling about the Mongoose Gang, the sense that Gairy had
a group of thugs that he could rely on. I can't say how much they
exaggerated details, but that feeling was there. And of course there
were the beatings [of NJM leadership] in Grenville. There was a sense
of siege within the population. I had a cousin whom I thought was
in the secret police; I don't know whether he was actually part of the
Mongoose Gang, but I heard rumors that he was in the secret police.
And on one occasion, when I was teaching in Sauteurs, I picked him
up in Paradise (in a little car I used to drive at the time). Someone was
sitting with me in the car and we started talking about politics; no big
set of talk about politics. But my friend said something like, "Let's go
up and we have to come back quickly, because these days you never
know who's stopping you on the road." And me joking about it said,
"Well, if they come, I'll just give them me gun I have here."

DS: *You said that!*

MC: Yes. And I was probably being a bit provocative because I had
heard things about him [the cousin]. And he [the cousin] made me
stop the car. And he said, "If you have a gun, you going have to give it
up." And I say, "I don't know what you're talking about." And he said,
"You just say you have a gun. If you have a gun, give it up. I'm making
a citizen's arrest." And I say, "You joking." I say, "You're sitting in my
car; I just gave you a lift! What you telling me 'bout a citizen's arrest?"
And he asked me again, "Do you have a gun?" So I said, "Look mister,
I have no gun. Just drop out here for me please." So there were these
kinds of tensions. And I don't think this was an incident that was just
me in my family. There were these tensions within [many] families,
because there was the sense that the secret police and Mongoose Gang
existed everywhere. And then I remember the Mongoose Gang group
jumping in St. George's around the time of a demonstration and sing-
ing, "Jewel, behave yourself, dey go jail us for murder." So you had
that kind of intimidation going on.

DS: *But were these fellows "jumping" in the street identifiable in a specific way as Mongoose Gang members? Were they, like the Tontons Macoutes in Haiti, dressed in a distinctive uniform?*

MC: No, not dressed in a particular way. You just knew. Around you, people would be saying, "Gairy Mongoose Gang in town." You kind of knew particular areas that [Gairy] recruited people from. [In that sense] they were people that you could identify; in most parts of St. George's, where Gairy's support was generally weak, people would hardly know who they were, but there was a sense that he recruited people from particular areas where his support was strong. So the Mongoose Gang thing was not just an invention. There was intimidation and there was a sense of fear of the Mongoose Gang. I saw them jumping on the street with that chant: "Jewel, behave yourself, dey go jail us for murder." And this was during that period in the early 1970s of intense organization by the NJM. I've also written about it in the poem "Nabel-String."[14]

"Bloody Sunday" and "Bloody Monday" were brutal examples of Gairy's repressive rule and help illustrate the terror and fear that Grenadians were living under leading up to the Revolutionary period. "Bloody Monday" also known as the "Battle of St. George's" refers to January 21, 1974, the day Maurice Bishop's father, Rupert Bishop, was gunned down as he stood in the doorway of Otway House, home of Grenada's Seamen's and Waterfront Workers Union. One account has it that he had stepped outside to appeal to the police to let the women and children be allowed to go home—the women and children had retaliated against the police after a soft drink bottle truck was confiscated. Rupert Bishop was then gunned down.[15] A month prior, on "Bloody Sunday"[16] (November 18, 1973) Grenadians witnessed the bloody beating of NJM leaders, including Maurice Bishop, Unison Whiteman, and Selwyn Strachan, who were severely beaten by Gairy's police (led by the infamous Inspector Innocent Belmar) in Grenville, St. Andrew's.[17] These were all public beatings, meant to be visible, violent, and leave an obvious message to anyone who challenged Gairy's rule.

When assessing the impact of the Revolution on the emotional, mental, and physical health of the Grenadian society, it is imperative that the events that led up to the formal Revolution of 1979–83 be brought into the equation. The reign of terror, which included the incidents of "Bloody Sunday" and "Bloody Monday," had fatal and long-lasting impacts on one's decision to join the resistance movement. Indicative of the intimidation tactics used by Gairy and his Mongoose Gang, Grenadians would joke that "a Grenadian... went to a dentist in Barbados, but the dentist couldn't get him to open his mouth."[18]

In response to the Black Power movements taking place across the region, the state increased its repressive actions. As a response to Trinidad and Tobago, Gairy stated:

> Our Police Force is being doubled to meet the situation. The force are aware of the diligence exercised by the Trinidad Police. Grenada's Police Force is certainly not on a lower level than the Trinidad Police Force in any respect. Today, the Grenadian Policeman knows that by his efforts in stamping out the attempts of those involved in Black Power or any other subversive movement, he can win the award of 'Policeman of the Year' and climb the ladder of promotion or receive monetary awards. The Police are geared to keep this country clean and in an atmosphere of peace and quiet at all times.[19]

Some have challenged the legitimacy of the Revolution and the March 13, 1979 coup, claiming that the NJM should have followed the rule of law and used the Westminster system of governance to win the leadership through general elections. However, as exemplified by the ruthless violence unleashed, encouraged and maintained by Gairy, and compounded by the public's loss of confidence in Gairy's willingness to follow "the law," this critique needs to be challenged. Locally and regionally, it was perceived that Gairy had stolen, and will probably always steal, the elections[20] (there were critiques of the first post-Independence elections of 1976 when an anti-Gairy political alliance lost the election by 78 votes.)[21] These served as reminders of his tight grip on power and how difficult it would be to remove him. It appeared that the only way to shift power was to forcibly take it. Furthermore, if the Revolution signified a shift toward decolonizing Grenada's political, economic, cultural, and social landscape, then what would it have meant to continue using a system of law that was created and implemented by the previous colonizer, and that furthermore relied on the unequal application of justice across race, class, and gender divides?

Coloniality of Nationalism and Independence

Defined as a bloodless coup, under the PRG Grenadians witnessed significant improvements in education, health care, the advancement of women's, children's, and youth rights, and new structures facilitated a more interpersonal and accountable way of governing and speaking with the masses. However, one of the more significant outcomes of the revolution was a resurgence of personal and political pride, authority, and a redefinition of our relationships with each other, with power, and with our environment, embodied by the Grenadian people. There was an overwhelming feeling of agency, urgency, hope, and an inalienable right to demand more than just basic rights. Grenadians were no longer going to beg: we were going to take what was ours. A renewed and potent sense of community, political, and militant action was developing on the island.

The PRG's internationalist approach played an important role in legitimizing the PRG, as Grenada linked its own struggles and gains to regional and global struggles for true independence and liberation. This internationalist approach impacted the Grenadian narrative and fostered an understanding of nationalism that acknowledged, yet also challenged, colonial borders. In his opening address to the *First International Conference in Solidarity with Grenada* held on the island from November 23–25th in 1981, Bishop stated that the

> Conference manifests our [Grenadians'] continuing strict adherence to international principles. We have always scrupulously avoided viewing our struggle, our revolutionary process, from a narrow nationalist perspective. We have long understood that the world revolutionary process, the struggle of oppressed mankind everywhere is one and indivisible. Thus, this International Solidarity Conference holds grave importance as it bears testimony to our commitment to the notable concept of internationalism.[22]

Though Bishop and other PRG freedom fighters did not use terms like Pan-Africanism and coloniality to explain why Grenadians chose to identify with global struggles, it clearly remained an important part of their analysis and political actions. There was a recognition that coloniality did not only manifest itself in the ways by which our bodies and minds were valued as labor producing machinery for the purposes of capital, the ways in which we saw ourselves and our global perspectives as well as the wars being waged by imperial powers; but that coloniality also represented our long-standing crisis of epistemological, cultural, economic, and political dependence. Coloniality is constitutive of the hegemonic mind, the white, masculinist, heterosexist, or national chauvinist.[23] Coloniality's hegemonic power and grasp over our labor, our lands, our sexualities, and governance structures took the form of the "nation-state, capitalism, the nuclear family, and eurocentrism."[24] The Grenada Revolution attempted to challenge the coloniality of our nation and, more so, of ourselves. However, if coloniality constitutes and is constitutive of the nation state, then is it possible to adhere to any nationalism, be it Grenadian, Black, or Afrikan nationalism? Is it possible to engage in liberation under the banner of nationalism? Can nationalism exist devoid of its historic and epistemological ties to white supremacy, coloniality, and capitalism, and not replicate the nation state structure and, ultimately, state-sanctioned violence?

Trauma and memory: the need for healing justice

Examining the impacts of the Revolution within the framework of direct and historical/intergenerational trauma is critical as it helps to shed light on a few things, such as being able to feel such visceral responses to the events of the Revolution, even for those who did not live through it. It helps to explain the feelings of empathy, pain, and anger, when told stories and experiences about the Revolution, and while visiting important physical sites, such as where Bishop and others were gunned down. The concept of "blood memory" within the context of intergenerational trauma is worth exploring.

As described in Native American tribal culture, "Blood memory is … our ancestral (genetic) connection to our language, songs, spirituality, and teachings. It is the good feeling that we experience when we are near these things."[25] It is one thing to witness my father's friend tear up when responding to the events that he lived through; but having been born post-Revolution, and not having been confronted with these sympathetic understandings of the Revolution in school, it's another thing to immediately and uncontrollably sob, when calling on the names of Revolutionary fighters.

The events of the Grenada Revolution are included in the Grenadian curriculum but are done so in an incomplete and revisionist way, influencing what, who, and how things are remembered. Public visuals and monuments, such as the monument near the Maurice Bishop airport dedicated to American soldiers (commissioned by Ronald Reagan, and built by the Cubans) and the covering of the bullet holes at Fort George where the leaders were killed, contribute to the erasure and revision of significant events. Yet, there are no public monuments or visuals intended to invoke sympathy for the murdered and disappeared Grenadian revolutionaries. The well-maintained graffiti near the old Coca-Cola bottling plant in Tempe that praises the U.S. invasion, contrasted with the fact that we still don't know where the remains of Bishop and the other revolutionary leaders gunned down on Fort George are, is indicative of how we value and devalue events in our shared collective memory. The families of those murdered at Fort George have had their closure and mourning impaired, as burials in Grenadian culture remain a significant part of the living bidding farewell to their loved ones. Burying those who embodied such a significant part of Grenadian history would have been critical in shaping the memories and social and political landscapes of the Grenadian people. The associated trauma faced by many Grenadians who have not been able to, or who have chosen not to, deal with these losses enables a silence that reconstitutes and covers up important memories.

Part of this trauma occurred not only when the leaders of the revolution were assassinated, but also through the kidnapping and destruction of their bodies. Was the brutal killing of these revolutionaries an attempt to stamp out hope of change and liberation? Furthermore, the memory of the movement became desecrated when those persons who symbolized and embodied the Revolution were killed and their bodies lost without a burial process, or closure.

The PRG existed under intense local, regional, and international pressure, which required hyper-vigilance in identifying counter-revolutionaries and protecting what Grenadians had taken so long to build. Though many of these fears were valid, one of the ways the Revolution failed the Grenadian people was its resistance to counter positions within the Grenadian populace. As Brian Meeks writes, "each Leninist measure which made the party capable of taking power, also increased its tendency toward hierarchical decision-making and enhanced the autonomy of the leadership both from ordinary party members and the people."[26] The PRG's clamp down on counter-revolutionary behavior[27]—such as the closure of the *Torchlight* newspaper[28] and the detention of Rastafarians[29]—almost mirrored Gairy's use of terror to stifle and, when necessary, squash dissent. The intended effect was increasingly limited dissent. In some ways, the PRG became the very state apparatus it had fought against.

Increased militarization is often accompanied by increased sexual violence. Whether the Revolution led to increased instances of state-sanctioned and interpersonal violence is unclear, and not much has been done to substantially explore these connections.[30] Unfortunately, however, it seems many of the claims by women under the PRG rule—some of whom were active Party members—of sexual harassment and violence were ignored or delegitimized based on moralizing grounds.[31]

The destabilizing of the Grenada Revolution influenced and hampered the Caribbean Left—a sentiment shared time and time again at the Grenada Country Conference. When looking at the current political and economic landscapes of the English-speaking Caribbean, one sees the proliferation of capitalist and heterosexist ideals that embody the state and trickle down to the day-to-day interactions and ideologies of the populace. Alternative economic systems outside of capitalism are not popular, and any leanings toward social-ism or communism are chided and ridiculed. The demise of the Grenadian Revolution impeded other possibilities for liberation.

The Grenadian poor rose up with excitement and conviction, and they were strategic and militant about it. They witnessed much physical, epistemic, and structural violence, which led them to take up arms and redefine their fu-tures, but they unfortunately faced ongoing violence and some mistrust from those in whom they had placed their hopes and dreams. In addition, before they were allowed the space to address the complexities, contradictions, and violence on their own terms, the U.S. came swooping in to "save them." Not only should the poor be encouraged to rise up, but their agency to engage in reconciliatory measures when things take a turn for the worse also needs to be allowed ample breathing room.

The Grenadian Revolution was a shared and collective experience; however, the post-Revolution shift in the political and economic landscape, coupled with increased individualism and consumerism, resulted in a personal process of healing and addressing the traumatic impacts of the Revolution. Many were swept to the margins, as individual healing proved inadequate in addressing collective grief.

It is also important to note how power shapes the historical narrative:

> It is important to recognize that groups and individuals have unequal means to generate accounts about the violent past: those in power can control, frame, and eventually even mask or bury the memory a group or individual holds of collective violence. Therefore, another common social response to a trau-matic past event is silence and inhibition.[32]

Those with access to power, publishing, and media resources, and the "ap-propriate vernacular" for telling the story dominate the theoretical and histor-ical narratives and analyses of the Grenadian Revolution. Bruce Paddington's important film, *Forward Ever: The Killing of a Revolution* (2013), is dominated throughout by voices and narratives that reflect a particular social and class perspective. What about the numerous Grenadians who speak politics to pow-er on the factory floor, in the rum shop, and on the streets? Their experiences are equally valid, but they are not scholars or writers, and unfortunately even if they were able to access publishing and media platforms they would probably be so discouraged by the feedback that they would recoil in silence.

Liberation must include the liberation of our bodies, minds, and spirits, in addition to control over our resources and labor. To ensure collective and inclusive organizing that takes into account people's full selves and accompanying intergenerational trauma, we must center healing justice in our work and praxis. By healing justice,[33] I am referring to the need to confront and analyze the impacts of collective and historical trauma as causing or influencing community survival practices and endemic community health issues. Healing justice also seeks to identify and create spaces and processes to lift up the experiences of those historically exploited, to achieve resilience and transformation.

The healing justice approach requires us to use the theoretical framing of coloniality to interrogate the material and multidimensional ways by which we view ourselves and others in terms of gender, race, sexuality, class, spirituality, and so on. Healing justice uses a historical context that lays the foundations for how we love, resist, and heal. By centering healing justice in post-Revolutionary attempts to remember, heal, excavate, and reconstruct, we honor the lives and experiences of the most exploited and actively work to construct systems, services, and spaces that transform the way we live. There should be an upheaval of the British colonial educational system that we have inherited, and it should be replaced by a curriculum that is inclusive of a vast and dynamic repository on the Grenadian Revolution; embedded in our health care and social programs should be holistic and therapeutic services that address direct and intergenerational trauma and how substance abuse is a coping mechanism. There should be a much more diverse representation of political views and possibilities, to help shift and move our electoral processes beyond the two-party state. Our British colonial laws that criminalize anyone who falls outside the male, heterosexist archetype should be scrapped, and opportunities for people-led and grassroots organizing across a range of equity issues that challenge the status quo should be encouraged and supported.

Today, some Grenadians have begun or continue different healing processes and are finding ways to confront "their demons," but the road is long and support services are limited. This paper has only scratched the surface, and much more in-depth research needs to be dedicated to interrogating the patterns of direct and vicarious trauma within post-Revolutionary and post-colonial Grenada. In the words of Merle Collins in her book *Angel*:

As long as you have life you could turn you han to someting

You have to make a move to help youself?

You caan siddown dey like de livin dead

Well yes, wi! You live an learn!

Man proposes; God disposes

Is not everything everything you could believe but some dream trying to tell you something!

Sometimes we have to drink vinegar an pretend we think is honey![34]

Endnotes

1   Carlos Martinez citing Dennis Bartholomew, representative of the People's Revolutionary Government at the Grenadian High Commission in London, phone conversation. Available online: http://www.invent-the-future.org/2014/03/legacy-of-the-grenadian-revolution/.

2   *Forward Ever: The Killing of a Revolution*. Directed by Bruce Paddington. Trinidad and Tobago. Thirdworld Newsreel, 2013.

3   Shalini Puri, *The Grenada Revolution in the Caribbean Present: Operation Urgent Memory* (New York: Palgrave MacMillan), 4.

4   "Report on certain political events which occurred in Grenada 1971–1991." Truth and Reconciliation Commission Grenada. The Grenada Revolution online. Vol. 1, Part 4. Accessed Aug. 20, 16. www.thegrenadarevolutiononline.com/trcreport4-1.html

5   Joseph Ewart Layne, *We Move Tonight* (CreateSpace Independent Publishing Platform, 2014), 29–30.

6   Ibid., 30

7   Ibid., 31

8   José A. Tapia, "From the Oil Crisis to the Great Recession: Five crises of the world economy." Working paper, (Institute for Social Research, University of Michigan, Ann Arbor, 2013).

9   Ibid., 6

10 Maurice Bishop, "Long live solidarity, friendship and co-operation!" Address at the opening of the First International Conference of Solidarity with the Grenada Revolution, The Dome, St. George's Nov. 23, 1981. Available online: http://www.thegrenadarevolutiononline.com/bish1stintnlconf.html.

11 José A. Tapia, "From the Oil Crisis to the Great Recession: Five crises of the world economy," 7.

12 Ibid., 5

13 Joseph Ewart Layne, *We Move Tonight* (CreateSpace Independent Publishing Platform, 2014).

14 David Scott, *The Fragility of Memory*, 103–104.

15 The Grenada Revolution Online. www.thegrenadarevolutiononline.com/bloodymonday.html.

16 Joseph Ewart Layne, *We Move Tonight*, 166.

17 Chris Searle, *Grenada: The Struggle Against Destabilization* (London: Writers and Readers, 1983).

18 Shalini Puri, *The Grenada Revolution in the Caribbean Present* (New York: Palgrave MacMillian, 2014), 32.

19 The Grenada Revolution Online. www.thegrenadarevolutiononline.com/gairya.html.
20 Ibid., 4, 33, 34.
21 Joseph Ewart Layne, *We Move Tonight*, 4.
22 People's Revolutionary Government. *Speeches by the People's Revolutionary Government at the First International Conference in Solidarity with Grenada* (Grenada: Fedon Publishers, 1981).
23 Lugones, Maria, "Heterosexualism and the colonial/modern gender system" *Hypatia*, Vol.22, No.1, 2007: 186–209; Lugones, Maria, "Toward a decolonial feminism" *Hypatia*, Vol.25, No.4, 2010: 742–758.
24 Steve Martinot, "The Coloniality of Power: Notes Toward De-Colonization." Available online: https://www.ocf.berkeley.edu/~marto/coloniality.htm.
25 Lightning Warrior, "Honoring The Ancestors: The Case For Metagenetics And Folk Consciousness." Available on-line: https://joshualightningwarrior.wordpress.com/2015/10/29/honoring-the-ancestors-the-case-for-metagenetics-and-folk-consciousness/.
26 Brian Meeks, *Caribbean Revolutions and Revolutionary Theory: An Assessment of Cuba, Nicaragua and Grenada* (London: Macmillan Caribbean, 1993), 152.
27 Shalini Puri, *The Grenada Revolution in the Caribbean Present*, 65–80.
28 Ibid.
29 Ras Nang Speaks: Interview with Prince Nna Nna, Available online: http://www.thegrenadarevolutiononline.com/nnaspeaks.html.
30 Shalini Puri, *The Grenada Revolution in the Caribbean Present*, 65–80.
31 Ibid., 69–70.
32 Ruth Kevers, Peter Rober, Ilse Derluyn, and Lucia De Haene, "Remembering collective violence: Broadening the notion of traumatic memory in post-conflict rehabilitation," *Culture, Medicine, and Psychiatry*, (2016): 1–21.
33 Bad Ass Visionary Healers, "Healing Justice Principles: Some of What We Believe." Available online: https://badassvisionaryhealers.wordpress.com/healing-justice-principles/ and "Just Healing Resources Site." Available online: https://justhealing.wordpress.com/resourcing-the-work/.
34 Merle Collins, *Angel* (Leeds: Peepal Tree Press, 2011).

RESOURCE-FULL ORGANIZED COMMUNITIES UNDERMINE SYSTEMS OF DOMINATION

HOW THE POOR RISE UP IN SAN CRISTOBAL DE LAS CASAS

Erin Araujo

OVER THE PAST YEAR THROUGHOUT CHIAPAS, THERE HAVE BEEN REGULAR road and highway blockades. Between May 10, 2016 and August 10, 2016, over 260 roadblocks have taken place in the state.[1] The disruption has been a daily part of life, making movement between cities and communities difficult. Community organizations, political parties, teachers' unions, and indigenous and campesino organizations block transportation and demand the annulment of elections, money, dialogue, the effectuation of workers' rights, an end to impunity, and general political change. These blockades stop the flow of money through and out of the state. They are targeted actions that specifically frustrate the movement of money from money-poor communities to national and transnational corporations. In fact, many of the blockades allow personal vehicles to pass while only stopping trucks transporting goods for transnational corporations. This type of response has not been unique to Chiapas; rather, many states in the country have similar processes in play. The states declared by CONEVAL (The National Advisory on the Politics of Social Development, a United Nations-funded advisory board in Mexico) as having the highest rates of "multi-dimensional poverty and extreme poverty" in Mexico (Chiapas, Guerrero, and Oaxaca) have experienced the most citizen-led blockades.

Chiapas is considered to have the highest rate of multidimensional poverty, comprising 76.2% of the population in 2014.[2] The designations and use of terms like "multi-dimensional poverty" and "extreme poverty" are development definitions that originate with the United Nations Millennium Development Goals. The program, which concluded in 2015, claimed to have met approximately 85% of its goals. However, in the state of Chiapas these organizations know that there is solidarity and strength, a vast array of abilities, and internal personal resources that support continued resistance. Courage is an important word here because the state's hired paramilitary thugs frequently kill protesters and teachers. It takes courage to value oneself and the community: courage in the face of physical and psychosocial violence and by being categorized as multi-dimensionally impoverished. By maintaining and creating value in-place, these communities challenge the notion that multi-dimensional poverty and extreme poverty are as widespread as the United Nations would suggest. Rather, the categories built into development goals clash with other definitions of richness embraced by organizations in Chiapas. What poverty is, and how it is manifest, come into question. This questioning and resistance visibilize how resource-full people rise up.

Multidimensional poverty is formally measured by looking at one's income, education lag, access to health services, access to food, housing quality and space, to basic housing services, social security, and the degree of social cohesion.[3] With the implementation of the United Nations (UN) Millennium Development Goals, these factors used to measure multidimensional poverty in effect became reality. The UN now has a formal metric to categorize people into several tiers of impoverishment. Once an individual is designated as being in a state of poverty or extreme poverty, not only do they become vulnerable to falling short of meeting their basic needs, but they also become vulnerable to having their lives interrupted by the imposition of capitalist structures.

Chiapas, known by many for its 1994 Zapatista uprising—and their continued resistance to this day—has many grassroots movements and organizations. Some negotiate with the state by doing actions such as blockades, as well as dialogue. Other organizations, similar to the Zapatistas, work to create autonomous regions with a self-organized infrastructure, government, economy, and education. This work in creating autonomy is not unique in the world; there are many movements and organizations that seek these goals and use similar tactics. From the perspective of the United Nations Development Program, many of these movements arise in regions that experience both poverty and extreme poverty. This process is nothing new; the term "development" means that a region will experience the replacement of its traditional non-capitalist methods of resource distribution with more capitalist mechanisms, whose objective is to profit from a divided and quantified economy. In this sense, we see collective work on community land being replaced with wage labor for individuals or education in non-indigenous languages that will incorporate rural and urban peoples into a capitalist economic-legal-social system. In this chapter I will reflect on what poverty means in Chiapas, as well as the non-capitalist alternatives to gaining access to resources and fomenting resistance to combat poverty.

What it Means To Be Poor

The term *poor* is integral in maintaining a capitalist economy. It implies that a lack of money in a region also indicates a lack of access to resources. According to neoliberal capitalism, resource access should only be mediated through the exchange of money. Access to healthcare, education, housing, food, safety, energy, and many other resources is supposed to be based on an individual's access to money. When one is poor, it is expected that one lacks access not only to money, but all other resources as a consequence. This is the reality for people who live in these highly capitalist societies and economies: access to money governs access to other resources. In these areas, the dominant message is, "No money? Sorry, you're out of luck." As Karl Marx famously explained, the accumulation of money is the accumulation of social power, where the term is defined as one's ability to accumulate just about any resource and oppress others with less money by controlling their access to resources.[4] Access to money is not a question of luck. That is to say, money is *not* an abundant resource that is easily accessible to most people on Earth. It is a socio-economic construction, and access to money is obfuscated by the naturalization of institutionalized manifestations of violence seated in coloniality.[5] These forms of structural violence include constructions of race, gender, class, ability, property, natural resources, epistemic and ontological validation, nationality, and the allocation of infrastructure. Structural violence refers to how economic, social, and political systems create harmful situations for different groups of people. Certain populations suffer disadvantages that have destructive repercussions for their well-being.[6] People are considered poor when they are denied access to resources through structural violence. The term "poor" is situated within a colonial context and enacted today through capitalism. Following Karl Polanyi, if a market economy requires a market society, then in areas where there is little money, there is also a diminished presence of capitalism both socially and economically.[7] While recognizing that poverty kills, having limited access to money does not mean that one is resource-poor, or that one will have a low quality of life. Rather, it means that for many people their access to basic resources comes from outside of capitalist interactions, or they choose to live in spaces beyond the reach of capitalism. In this way, they choose, are born in, or are forced into, a non-alienating economy where social relationships foment resource sharing and collectivization.

Non-monetary forms of exchange are nothing new. They are common everywhere.[8] Sharing amongst neighbors, collective work, volunteering, and gifting, are all common practices that emerge socially within communities. Over the last ten years, the rise of the solidarity economy movement has shown that many of these practices are being recognized and formalized into networks of value. In this way, social equality and mutual aid are gaining strength as practical methods of decreasing one's dependence on money while simultaneously creating communities that value care and support.

Economic resistance is something that each of us can do, starting right now. Social movements that incorporate immediate networks of non-capitalist economies often last longer and incorporate larger numbers of people. Contrary to the commonly held belief, local economies and/or decolonial economies need not be small; instead, they tend to pull people in and begin to distribute resources immediately in non-oppressive exchanges. Evidence for this can be seen in the Kurdish resistance in Rojava and Northern Syria,[9] the Zapatistas in Mexico,[10] the Landless Workers Movement in Brazil,[11] the Piqueteros in Argentina,[12] the autonomous region of El Alto, Bolivia,[13] and many other large movements throughout the world. Resistance through economic decoloniality tends to act on a shorter timeframe than more cultural approaches such as resisting the coloniality of thought, power, or gender. Decolonial economic praxis is the practice of using our non-capitalist knowledge and skills to create spaces that free us from the confines of the constant contemporary experiences of colonialism. It begins with talking with one's neighbors about how they would like economic exchanges to happen, about their needs, and their well-being. It starts when people begin to organize themselves around how they would like their neighborhood or community to be, and what kinds of resources are actually needed.

Obviously, this kind of thinking is not conducive to extending the reach of capitalism or the traditional capitalist lie of "eliminating poverty" through employment for all. The very existence of large transnational corporations, and the high-cost infrastructures they build, is naturally limited in places dominated by local collective economies that emphasize communal support over profit. Instead, the thrust of my argument is that we should challenge the classical concept of poverty, as understood to mean lacking access to money, and therefore resources. There are many kinds of poverty including a poverty of community, where people that have plenty of money and access to resources are completely alienated from others in the community around them, if that community exists at all. This type of poverty through isolation can be deadly to those in our community, our families and friends, old and young, who depend on the support of the community for their health and mobility. These poverties of care, love, nurturing, freedom, and joy will often arise from the isolation and oppression by systems of coloniality that divide people into incommensurable classes, races, genders, abilities, ethnicities, and sexualities. Being care-poor, love-poor, nurture-poor, community-poor, freedom-poor, and joy-poor are devastating poverties that lead to the destruction of the self.

Frantz Fanon wrote extensively about the internalization of coloniality. In *Black Skin, White Masks*, he explains how within coloniality Black men (and sometimes women) were acculturated into feelings of constant inadequacy because they were taught to believe that whiteness was the only (unachievable) good as Blackness was constantly portrayed as the source of all of the worst aspects of society.[14] In this way whiteness, the epistemic and ontological foundations of white coloniality, has been internalized into the experience of the colonized self. In *The Wretched of the Earth*, Fanon regularly refers to people who believe that they are white or Black.[15] Race is a powerful concept that is used to create oppression. The first step in the resistance against racist ideology and practices is changing how we situate ourselves in relation to each other, and refuse to allow others to devalue ourselves and our bodies. Coloniality enacted as "development" creates a constant process of division; between people, within us, and from the land. Nanda Shrestha has also written about the internalization of development and coloniality in Nepal, from his experience:

> *Bikas* [a name for capitalist development] could bring things instantly, and we did not have to work hard to acquire what we wanted. But we were all bewitched. Foreign aid had become our sole medium of material nirvana. Pride in self-achievement and self-reliance was conspicuously absent.
>
> *Bikas* solidified the colonial notion that we were incapable of doing things for ourselves and by ourselves. The colonial 'civilizing mission' was resurrected as the mission of development. These Western 'civilizers' first undermined our relative

self-sufficiency and self-reliance, and then categorized us as inferior and poverty-stricken. Closely inter-woven with nature and its cyclical rhythm, our way of life was certainly different, but not inferior. True, it was not prepared to bring nature under large-scale human subjugation. But our relatively harmonious coexistence with nature was interpreted as a sign of backwardness and primitiveness. Development was measured in terms of the distance between humans and nature. The greater the distance between the two, the higher the level of development. The distance between the two definitely increased – in some cases literally, as poor Nepalese village women walked further and further every year in search of fire wood and animal fodder.[16]

Shrestha elegantly exposes the divisive and purposeful destruction that is the expansion of coloniality through capitalist development. It internally robs people of their autonomy, pushing them into a psychology of poverty while impoverishing their landscape by ravaging all that it has to offer. This practice can only be called theft. The ravenous appetite of development not only seeks to strip the land of its resources, but also benefits from exploiting, and essentially enslaving, those it assimilates by upturning the relationships of people to the land and access to the resources the land provides.

In analyzing how coloniality has and continues to construct gender, Maria Lugones has written about the creation of sex-based genders and the subjugation of women, especially women who are not white skinned.[17] Coloniality has created extensive internalization of binary genders compounded with what was and is considered the impurity and aberration of sexuality of the non-white woman. Lugones writes that while white women were constructed as the pure, submissive, and non-sexual birthing counterpart to bourgeois white men, non-white women at the time were not even considered human.[18] Many women I know, a few who are very close to me here in Chiapas, were born in indigenous families and communities, and at a young age were sent to work for upper class families here in the more metropolitan San Cristobal de las Casas. At home and at school they were educated not to speak, not to let their presence ever be an interruption in the others' lives. The internalization of this structural violence does incredible harm to our communities. We lose so much of women's participation in creating our world, by this practice of silencing. For myself, I know that being a cis-gendered, white-presenting woman, my body and mind have been constant sites of attack over my entire life. I know that the violence lived by others who do not present the same is a source of deep pain and debilitation. However, I also know that we can have courage, we can grow, we can do things daily to stop being paralyzed through violence, and to walk a path toward well-being, collectively. As a group, we can lean on each other, learn from each other, and find ways to proceed. Only through de-normalizing our internal experiences of gender and race, and simultaneously creating communities that seek the elimination of these oppressions through immediate and constant response to each attack, will we change how we are valued. We have to do it ourselves; it will not come from anywhere, or anyone, else.

Poverty, as an expression of coloniality, also injures us through feelings of worthlessness. Years ago, I was working in HIV/AIDS prevention in Latino Communities on the east coast of the United States. In a workshop on changing behaviors that put us at high risk for HIV/AIDS, a participant was talking about the challenges of working in low-income communities. She said, "Risk behaviors are part of a larger feeling of vulnerability: You go home; you live in an apartment with holes in the walls and rats; your food doesn't fit into what is considered healthy; there are problems everywhere without solutions; you feel like your low worth is reflected in everything that is around you." People who are money-poor are constantly treated as worthless. This is part of the psychology of coloniality. It is a process of constantly devaluing people, the earth, and all forms of life.

Development and Poverty in Chiapas

In 2009, Chiapas became the first state in the world to adopt the Millennium Development Goals (MDG) of the United Nations in its constitution. The MDG was novel in its approach to creating poverty.[19] Instead of only focusing on income levels to identify poverty, it implemented this search and seizure process called multi-dimensional poverty. Now people could be identified as poor by their level of hunger, education, gender equality, child mortality, maternal health, environmental sustainability, and how connected the community was with transnational investors. There were suddenly many ways to make someone poor. People could be designated as poor simply because of their hunger. Instead of recognizing that capitalism requires the exploitation of workers and the maintenance of a class that desperately needs money because their access to resources has been curtailed, people were told that they as individuals and communities were hungry and in need of development. While the scope of this chapter is too short for an overview of all of the ways that capitalism creates hunger, it suffices to say that low wages, destruction of the land, the privatization of property, food deserts, displacement of peoples, war, and institutional violence deny people access to food or agricultural resources effectively making people hungry. Similar arguments could be made for each of the MDGs. For example, education is a process of indoctrinating people into the "society" in which they live.[20] If one is education-poor, one essentially has not been adequately indoctrinated; from an MDG perspective, such people need to be *developed*. This system of education will, over years, drive the person into thinking within a context of coloniality that makes the psychology and sociality of capitalism normalized. This is how people are molded for incorporation into the workforce. They are told that the kind of job they do, the way they are exploited, defines their worth as person, while other people are shamed by the work they do. This is what education in a capitalist system creates: workers.

The other MDGs, gender equality, child mortality, maternal health, and environmental sustainability have similar solutions. They propose to fight poverty by incorporating people into a system that creates poverty. The *Millennium Development Goals in Mexico: Progress Report, Executive Summary* (2013) states, "The Mexican population's wellbeing cannot be improved without effective economic changes that foster productivity, growth, investments, generate more and better formal jobs and a sustained increase in wages."[21] The MDGs fall into a circular argument where the problems created by coloniality through the system of capitalism can only be solved by the same system. People who live in poverty need quality access to health care, education, infrastructure, dignified treatment, and autonomy, but this will never be fully realized within a capitalist system. The capitalist economic system creates an exploitable working class in which people are made desperate to earn wages. Capitalism creates poverty which creates wealth for the rich. As long as people are dependent on money for access to social services that foster well-being, but are denied sufficient money to allow participation in that same system, they are forced into a system of exploitation.

On June 18, 2016, the state governor of Chiapas added the UN 2030 Sustainable Development Agenda, officially known as *Transforming our World: the 2030 Agenda for Sustainable Development*, to the state constitution as well. The Sustainable Development Agenda is more comprehensive than the MDGs because it extends capitalism to more people through more specific means. While there were only eight MDGs, the Sustainable Development Agenda has been expanded to encompass seventeen goals. Every single goal in the Agenda has a capitalist economic solution to the problem of poverty. While we have not seen the results of the new Sustainable Development Agenda, I have no doubt that the continued incorporation of more people into neoliberal capitalism will only create more exploitation and denial of access to resources for the money-poor, and wealth for the rich. For this reason, other alternative economic systems must be developed to create value and resource access in our communities, while banishing coloniality from the oppositional economic practices of the people.

El Cambalache: Creating Inter-change

El Cambalache is a small moneyless economic project located in San Cristobal de las Casas, Chiapas. It began after eight months of talking, debating, practicing, and learning. El Cambalache (The Swap) opened its doors to the world in March 2015. Inter-changes began immediately. Our six-woman generator collective works to create moneyless economic space. The focus of our work is to distribute resources across our money-poor neighborhoods by revaluing objects (that are normally considered waste) and marginalized knowledge. So many of life's activities tend to be undervalued within capitalism. We work to give them real value. Many people from different social classes come into the project and say that they want to participate but don't know what they can offer. We start by asking people to think about their abilities and knowledge, and what they would like to share. Reflecting on valuing, generator Sarai notes, "We started to think of all of the things we could offer, and before that one never thinks about all that you can give, not only materially, but from your being. All of the knowledge, everything, everything, everything." Among the skills that have been offered there are juggling acts, puppet shows, massages, construction, TsoTsil, and French classes, equinotherapy, cooking, electrical installations, horticulture classes, and talks about cosmology. The project also offers regular classes in laptop maintenance, medical consultations, and haircuts.

In El Cambalache, we work through horizontal consensus decision-making practices, where no one person's voice is valued over any other. Our desire to function without hierarchy leads us to the creation of our exchangé value, called inter-change value (*El valor de inter-cambio* in Spanish), where everything in the economy has the same value. The objects exchanged are things one no longer needs, and skills, mutual aid, and knowledge that one wishes to share. Each person who passes through our office has access to the basic rules. We explain the rules to each new person and have them written on the walls. That way, we can talk about capitalism, money, mutual aid, undervalued abilities, and valuing each other, among other things. Many people come by the Cambalache just to spend time and talk. The project strives to make an economic space that is also socially inclusive.

In inter-change value, not only does a pencil equal a sweater or a computer or someone helping paint a house, but also we seek a change from within.

Cinthia, a generator, explains inter-change value: "*Inter-cambios* are concrete anti-capitalist actions that we can do in the quotidian... without waiting for the great revolution that overthrows the capitalist system. Through *inter-cambios* we change ourselves and at the same time our individualist, consumer, competitive relationships imposed by capitalism." In little more than a year, over seven hundred people have participated in inter-changes.

We don't have much web presence. There is little time to devote to Internet communications, and many people in our networks do not have regular access to the Internet. Most people know about us by word of mouth. Through talking in person with other women, two Cambalaches have opened in San Andres Tuxtla, Veracruz and Bacalar, Quintana Roo. Each of these Cambalaches is different from ours here in San Cristobal de las Casas. The Cambalache in San Andres Tuxtla involves exchanging things once a month and having community potlucks on inter-change days. While the Cambalache in Bacalar is located in a women's spiritual healing center where women come and exchange things as part of a full moon ceremony once a month. For us, what makes a Cambalache is that it has inter-change value. Beyond that we expect that each new endeavor will meet the needs and interests that people have in their areas.

By embracing horizontal power relationships with each person who enters into the project, we are trying to practice anarchist ideals of non-domination. Instead of an anarchist economy operating out of chaos, non-hierarchical relationships require that each person who participates in the project be responsible for their participation. The responsibility of each person is to the group, and there are no negative repercussions for not participating. Rather, we expect that each member of the group, in each project, express what they can do in the context of their own daily lives. That's enough. In a non-alienating economy, the experience and struggles of each person is an important part of how exchanges occur.

El Cambalache is small. In thinking about larger social movements, there are specific mechanisms that economic resistance presents that support organizing and well-being for money-poor, resource-full communities. When one is money-poor, one is vulnerable, under constant judgment, ridicule, and mistreatment. Race, gender, ethnicity, and sexuality come to the forefront as social excuses to treat people badly. The wealthy more easily overcome obstacles of structural violence. This means that in a society where purchasing power allows us to buy security, weapons, people's labor, health care, property, sex, religion, and just about anything—except for liberation from the rigid class structure and social violence we must constantly navigate—the only way to resist and overcome that is by changing the rules of the game. This is not an easy task, but it is far from impossible. It requires looking at one another as resource-full individuals. As individuals we may not have enough, but as a community, we do. A common tendency among the left is to constantly cut away at our alliances. However, in creating mass movements, non-oppressive resistance requires solidarity, even when people disagree with each other. It requires being generous with one another, recognizing that each person has had different experiences, and we are always in a state of growth and transformation. Our conversations, and talking about feelings, are part of economic resistance.

In October of 2014, when we were trying to envision and build our economy, some of the generators did a workshop on exchange value. I arrived at our meeting ready to talk about monetary and non-monetary ways that people exchange goods and services. However, the workshop was not about either of those kinds of exchanges. Instead, we focused on how one feels valued on a personal level when exchanges, both monetary and non-monetary, occur. Disillusionment, low self-worth, failure, and incompetence were all feelings associated with not being able to make a purchase while, on the other hand, feelings of euphoria, being a good person, and making other people happy were associated with being able to make purchases. As a collective, we decided that this emotional bipolarity was not acceptable. Money was not going to decide how we felt about ourselves, and we did not want that to happen to other people. Our economic resistance would create communities of care, and care creates social change. In our practice, we have incorporated the emotional side of economic interactions into the project by making everything that can be exchanged have the same value. Anything that is offered can be exchanged for anything else, be that a class, or a service in the form of mutual aid or objects. Each person decides the worth of what they exchange. A shirt, a toy, a pair of shoes, a telephone, a radio, a box of books or one book, a bunch of vegetables, a medical consultation, a massage, therapy, a class in embroidery: all have the same value. We have a space where the objects are kept that is organized like a store. Everything that enters and leaves is registered. The abilities and mutual aid that are inter-changed are written onto an exchange board. People can freely choose what they would like to give and receive. In that way, no one is denied access to anything El Cambalache has to offer.

Economic Resistance Without the State

In anarchism, there is essentially one metric against which all other theories and practices are measured: Is this practice or theory a vehicle for creating or maintaining any form of domination? The state, colonialism, and capitalism operate as mutually interdependent processes. This means that "global" capitalism can only exist when there is a legal system that enforces the existence of private property and the mistreatment of other people through the exploitation of their labor. The state can only exist when borders are created and other territories (colonies, post-colonial territories, and strategically impoverished neighboring states) are robbed of their resources for the benefit of the most oppressive states. Race, gender, ethnicity, ability, sexuality, class, and criminality have been created through the construction of the non-human-ness of others. In that way, we return to the creation of the money-poor as an institutionalized legal system fueled by the processes of colonialism, capitalism, and the state.[22] For this reason, a truly liberatory economy cannot be capitalist, and it cannot exist within the structure of the state. The combined system is by design an oppressive organization of people and institutions. Of course, I am not the first person to call for economic resistance with or without the formation of the state. A great number of incredible thinkers such as Emma Goldman,[23] Peter Kropotkin,[24] Lucy Parsons,[25] and Mikhail Bakunin[26] have called for this kind of change. If a resistance movement does not include a non-capitalist economic process, the money-poor will be excluded from the movement. If a movement cannot meet the needs of people that have difficulty meeting them, they will not and cannot participate on a long-term basis without another economic system that meets their needs incorporated into the resistance movement. This is why the Sustainable Development Agenda has created seventeen different needs to be met and then used as a tactic for incorporating people into capitalism.

Conclusion

Non-capitalist economic resistance is essential for creating resource-full communities. In Chiapas, despite the constant work being done to create multi-dimensional poverty and extreme poverty, people keep resisting. They demand that the state incorporate their needs, desires, and ideas into the creation of the many worlds that exist here. The process is constant. Our worlds are vulnerable and under constant assault by local and international organizations that work to incorporate each one of us into capitalism and obedience to the state. We have been injured repeatedly. Healing these injuries brings people together. As Maya Angelou famously said to Tupac Shakur, "Do you know how important you are? Do you know that our people slept, laid spoon fashion, in the filthy hatches of slave ships in their own and in each other's excrement, and urine and menstrual flow so that you could live two hundred years later? Do you know that? Do you know that our people stood on auction blocks so that you could live? When is the last time anyone told you how important you are?"[27] In heeding Dr. Angelou, our collective work in El Cambalache is to remind people how important they are, that their experience is valuable, and that our inter-changes as a community bring us together. In El Cambalache, we insist that each person inter-change something because we know that everyone has something to offer. Knowing that each of us can give, that each person is rich in knowledge and abilities is a first step. For us, it's a step worth taking every day.

In eliminating poverty, social movements must provide economic systems and practices that help us meet our own and each other's needs. When social movements do not include economic systems of resistance they exclude the money-poor and maintain class divisions. We live in precarious times, and our economies must create care for each other. Otherwise, more people will fall into poverty. Development can only offer a separation from nature, our bodies, and our selves, for they are all the same. The belief that developed countries are rich is a lie. Capitalists know poverty, albeit not experientially: they create it, and they have names and faces.

In Chiapas I see people rise up every day. They are organized. They refuse to be poor.

Endnotes

1   I compiled this data through reviewing social media sites alertachiapas.com and ret.io.

2   Anahi Rama and Anna Yukhananov, "Mexican government says poverty rate rose to 46.2 percent in 2014," *Reuters*, July 23, 2015. Available online: http://www.reuters.com/article/us-mexico-poverty-idUSKCN0PX2B320150723.

3   CONEVAL, *The Millennium Development Goals in Mexico: Progress Report 2013*, Executive Summary. (Mexico: INEGI, 2013).

4   Karl Marx, *Capital: Volume One: A Critique of Political Economy* (London: Penguin Classics, 1990), 229–230.

5   Coloniality refers to the continuity of a colonial mentality where nation states that were once governed under colonial rule continue to be controlled economically, politically, and socially as inferior to a western way of thought and being. See the work of Maria Lugones, Walter Mignolo and Anibal Quijano, for starters.

6   See http://www.structuralviolence.org/structural-violence/.

7   Karl Polanyi, *The Great Transformation: The Political and Economic Origins of Our Time* (Boston: Beacon Press, 2001).

8   I refrain here from using terms that indicate the developed/undeveloped world, first/third world, global north/south because even in the most "developed" countries we find people who are money-poor relative to their economy.

9   Strangers in a Tangled Wilderness, *A Small Key Can Open a Large Door: The Rojava Revolution* (Combustion Press, 2015).

10 Subcomandante Marcos, *YA BASTA!: Ten Years Of The Zapatista Uprising—Writings Of Subcomandante Insurgente Marcos* (Oakland: Ak Press, 2004).

11 http://www.mstbrazil.org/.

12 Moira Birss, "The Piquetero Movement: Organizing for Democracy and Social Change in Argentina's Informal Sector." Available online: http://hdl.handle.net/2027/spo.4750978.0012.206.

13 Raúl Zibechi, *Dispersing Power: Social Movements as Anti-State Forces*, Ramor Ryan, trans. (Oakland: AK Press, 2010).

14 Frantz Fanon, *Black Skin, White Masks*, Richard Philcox, trans. (New York: Grove Press, 2008).

15 Frantz Fanon, *The Wretched of the Earth*, Constance Farrington, trans. (New York: Grove Press, 1963).

16 Nanda Shrestha, "Becoming a Development Category," in *The Power of Development*, Johnathan Crush, ed. (London and New York: Routledge, 1995), 274.

17 Maria Lugones, "Toward a Decolonial Feminism," *Hypatia* 25.4 (2010): 732–759.

18 Ibid.

19 Here I refer to the MDG as creating poverty because the process of identifying who has been made poor by a capitalist market is calculated numerically, through a set of Western, development-oriented standards that envision access to resources as solely being dependent on access to capital. However, many groups of people actively choose to resist incorporation into the capitalist political-economic system, while development strives to include them into that system. From a decolonial perspective, rather than communities being designated as poor, they should be able to choose which services, goods, and protections they should have access to, instead of being obligated into denial of resources because they are now part of a monied system without having access to money.

20 Noam Chomsky, "How the young are indoctrinated to obey," *Alternet*, *April 4, 2012*. Available online: http://www.alternet.org/story/154849/chomsky%3A_how_the_young_are_indoctrinated_to_obey.

21 Instituto Nacional de Estadística y Geografía, "Millenium Development Goals in Mexico: Progress Report, Executive Summary," (INEGI, 2013).

22 Theorists/historians such as Immanuel Wallerstein, Benedict Andersen, and Karl Polanyi (among many others) have documented and explored how the creation of markets required standardization of exchange values and monetary instruments. This process was dependent on the institutionalization of capitalist market interactions to build what Polanyi calls the market society, and Andersen refers to the cultural domination of econ-omized people as the creation of imagined communities. Wallerstein refers to this process as the creation of world systems that are dependent on coloniality where capitalism is the economic system created by colonialism.

23 For more information see: http://www.lib.berkeley.edu/goldman/PrimarySources/index.html.

24 For more information see: http://dwardmac.pitzer.edu/Anarchist_Archives/kropotkin/Kropotkinarchive.html.

25 For more information see: http://dwardmac.pitzer.edu/Anarchist_Archives/bright/lparsons/lparsonsbio.html and http://www.iww.org/history/biography/LucyParsons/1.

26 For more information see: http://dwardmac.pitzer.edu/Anarchist_Archives/bakunin/BakuninCW.html.

27 See: https://www.youtube.com/watch?v=X1gZiYPmOvs.

IN DEFENSE OF THE TERRITORY OF LIFE

A LOOK INTO THE TERRITORY OF THE COMMUNITY POLICE IN GUERRERO[1]

David Gómez Vazquez
Translation by Enrique Avila Lopez

Changes in expression of the movements of the poor

FOR MOST OF THE TWENTIETH CENTURY, SOCIAL MOVEMENTS AND ORGANIZA-tions accustomed the majority of the population to massive and perceptible methods of struggle, since much of North America had the same forms of struggle: occupying public squares to hold rallies, marches, strikes, etc. In Latin America, most movements of the time had a common denominator: they were massive irruptions, often violent confrontations that directly faced the ruling regimes, and along with that, of course, was a combative, energetic, and transforming discourse within the prevailing system(s). Two strong examples are the Bogotazo in Colombia and the Cordobazo in Argentina, on April 9, 1948 and May 29 and 30, 1969, respectively—the last one, during a military dictatorship.

These events were watersheds for the movements of the region; they made the population aware of active revolutionary organizations. It should be remembered that many Latin American countries of this period were governed by military dictatorships, which exercised total censorship and repression.

The continent has been a frequent scene of struggles built by the poor with the intention of improving their existing living conditions; however, following the events already mentioned (the Bogotazo and Cordobazo), there was a shift in the logic of the movement. Beyond improving the living conditions of the population, a revolutionary sensibility also advocated for a change of the hegemonic political-economic system. In Mexico, as in all of Latin America historically, the population had to organize to meet their demands and needs; we have seen women struggle for the right to vote, railroad workers fight for wage improvements, students in the 1960s and 1970s agitate for the democratization of the country, peasants fight for land, and so on in almost all sectors of the country. For a long time, the spirit and methods of resistance continued. But, often, once organized sectors won specific demands, many resistors demobilized. There were few organizations that, after gaining a victory, were prepared for a new battle.

This pattern continued until January 1, 1994, a day that changed the perspective and the horizon of many social movements and organizations in Mexico and in Latin America. On that day, the world learned of the Zapatista Army of National Liberation (EZLN), which carried out an insurrection and took control of some municipalities in the state of Chiapas; the majority of its members were indigenous. The EZLN arose in arms to fulfill the most heartfelt demands of Mexican society: democracy, health, food, and justice. The dignified rage for a dignified life included demands that addressed the diversity of problems of people who until then had been silenced.

The EZLN, which was unknown to many at the time, with no important role at the national level, announced themselves as no other organization had in contemporary Mexican history.

Thousands of armed men and women took municipal property, declaring war on the Mexican state, without any demands of the government, but with support from the Mexican people. The EZLN seemed not to exist, since it was not visible, did not give interviews, did not send press releases, did not march or organize rallies—they were unconventional compared to other social movements on the continent. Since 1983, they experimented with a very different way of doing politics and fighting. This novel approach did not seek the seizure of power but the control of a territory in which to apply self-government, democracy, justice, self-defense, and solidarity—what the Zapatistas call autonomy. By observing and analyzing this test of autonomy in the Zapatista communities, little by little a change in the form and methods for building resistance began—a new form of resistance from the poor in the face of oppression was nurtured and assumed a territorial character in Mexico.

The Regional Coordinator of Community Authorities—Community Police (CRAC-PC) from Guerrero

The Community Police (PC) of the Regional Coordinator of Community Authorities—Community Police (CRAC-PC) in the municipality of Troncón in the state of Guerrero is where the effort to promote the training of community health builders began. Where did the PC's idea to train health workers come from? What is the role of health in the field of domination and power? Do trained health workers mean to promote popular power? How can a community health worker respond to the current conditions of marginalization and resistance in Guerrero? We'll get to those questions, but, first, some history and context.

The PC as "a carrier of indigenous insurgency of a worldview different from the Western"[2] in matters of security and justice, of which the PC group of the Troncón community is part, is an ethnic phenomenon that first emerged in 1995 in Santa Cruz del Rincón, Costa Chica, which since 1998 "imparts justice through an oral process, immediate, simple and expeditious, based on the indigenous worldview and community compensation process. It is governed by the principles of impartiality and independence."[3] Since their founding as Regional Coordinator of Indigenous Authorities (CRAI), and later as Regional Coordinator of Community Authorities-Community Police (CRAC-PC), it was a benchmark in security and justice for other communities due to the discrimination and racism of the legal class system in Mexico:

> Racism and arbitrariness in the exercise of justice is embodied in corruption. In the action of the agents of the Public Ministry, the main problem denounced by the population is the custom of demanding money in exchange for investigation and prosecution, which benefits the wealthy (merchants or landlords) and excludes from the system of law enforcement the majority of the population that lacks economic resources.[4]

Communities such as Troncón have sown distrust in the specialized institutions of the State to impart justice in an "impartial" way. Finding themselves abandoned by these security mechanisms and by the classist state in the administration of justice, they have chosen to construct and integrate alternative models of security that respond to the needs of communities where violence, insecurity, and injustice are a constant:

In Santa Cruz del Rincón, municipality of Malinaltepec, on October 15, 1995, in a Community Assembly with the participation of thirty-eight communities, the Community Police was founded. "Its fundamental objective was to restore the security that was threatened in the hands of criminals." Its members are called "community police" because they arise from the communities themselves and give them their services without receiving a salary. They do not discriminate, but promote the idea that it is a service for the life of the people.[5]

Although the PC originated in the areas of the Costa Chica and Montaña, due to increasing insecurity from 2012 to 2013, communities in the central region began to think about being part of the CRAC-PC as a means to address the problems of drug trafficking, criminal violence, kidnappings, assaults and robberies, and because legal support for the organization was available through international conventions, through initiatives such as 169 of the International Labor Organization (OIT), a pair of articles of the Mexican constitution, and the 701 Recognition Law, Rights and Culture of Indigenous Peoples and Communities of the State of Guerrero.

This is how the CRAC-PC project started four years ago in the central area of Guerrero where the community of Troncón is located. Backed by over twenty years of experience from their colleagues from the Costa Chica and Montaña, where crime decreased by up to 90% where the PC operates in the territory, members of the PC in the downtown area have remained firm in their role as bulwarks of security and justice, despite the increasing repression against them—repression in the form of murder, imprisonment, threats, and division and fragmentation among its members, fomented by state cooptation. CRAC Commander Nahum Santos Bartolo describes the struggle of the communal police:

> The work we are doing is important. It is an example for all people to join the fight. There are times we feel tired of so much struggle, when a community member approaches with a problem, difficulty, and we are tired, they know we worked all day. However, at night we have the patrols, we put on the uniform, and change our attitude. We're rejuvenated when we wear our uniforms and grab the gun. Once in the meeting, we forget all the problems we have, we focus on the work we do. It feels nice when we all get together and make plans, if peers are very disciplined...[6]

The Construction of Health in Conjunction with Security and Justice

Making progress in terms of security and justice, the PC of the downtown area looked to new horizons and sought answers to other neglected problems in the community. So they focused on health care. It is necessary, when building popular power, to identify that capitalist rule covers all aspects of life, including health. For many, "health is politics by other means"[7] and health policies are a clear window into how a society (or at least the people who implement the policies of society) conceives of life.

> Power relations have been exercised in a variety of ways in medicine, and we rely on the reflections of Michel Foucault when he analyzes biopower—the nature of power, its mode of constitution, and its type of diffusion in the articulations in society.[8]

The Mexican health system is governed by the rules of capitalism. In a capitalist society in which people are reliant on state structures, with labor on one side and consumers on the other, health care is a product that is sold to those who can buy it. Far from considering health as a fundamental right and an integral part of life, the concept of health in capitalist states, such as Mexico, is based on the idea of "soundness,"[9] that is to say, they look at health care only as a means for working people to reproduce, obey, and be submissive. Care is most often only available to insured employees.

For those who lack health insurance, there are the public services overseen by the Ministry of Health. However, according to the inhabitants of urban and rural areas in Guerrero and other states, attention to their needs is almost nonexistent, and although the government speaks of "universal" and accessible services, the patients or their families often pay for education, drugs, materials, and equipment. Among other complaints, people have told us during consultations and workshops that they are discriminated against when seeking medical care, that there are not enough staff, no drugs, that indigenous women have reported suffering forced sterilization, and so on. Access to health services is extremely difficult for much of the Mexican population, especially those doing informal work, working in the fields, or those simply unemployed.

In the municipality of Tixtla, a part of Troncón, official statistics show that in 2010 71.2% of the population lived in poverty and more than 40% of the population was without access to health services. There is also intense pressure to privatize government institutions. There is not enough focus on disease prevention and no holistic health care, in which the spiritual, emotional, and mental aspects of well being are considered. Clearly, the health care system in

Mexico provides the minimum necessary to ensure the survival of the working population in order to facilitate the smooth functioning of capitalism. Through the health care structures in Mexico we see that the vast majority of people are considered disposable bodies. In the case of indigenous communities, colonization increasingly separates people from their identity, their traditional knowledge and practices, and so on.

The community health care network in Guerrero knows that capitalism generates relations of dominators and dominated, exploiters and exploited. We reflect together on how the field of health is dominated by capitalist oppression and the contemporary colonial/imperial and patriarchal system; and so we theorize how this community project can function differently.

In January of 2015 with these reflections and questions in mind we started the Community Health Brigade 43, which was the first training workshop for women and men interested in becoming community health workers. The goal with this project is to build and maintain the health field that the neoliberal government has neglected in the community, and to avoid reproducing the capitalist model of health with its profit motive and dehumanizing features.

The goal of community health care is to make people aware of the work of security, justice, and community health, which involves the construction of popular power in communities and laying the foundation for the collective empowerment of men and women initially in these three fields. We have noticed that among the major problems that the rural communities regularly face are forms of security, education, health, and work. Building popular power weakens the ability of the government to exercise control over the community:

> It involves understanding that power is not a set of institutions to take, but a complex web of social relations that we need to radically change, hence the need to build a counter power of the subaltern classes, a popular power. This is a more difficult and expensive way, much more complex in terms of the factors involved.[10]

Developing the community health project strengthens the community police center, a relationship that is not coincidental given the current conditions of life in Guerrero and Mexico in general. Insecurity, killings, and forced disappearances have become an everyday reality, causing profound effects on both the physical security of the inhabitants and their mental and emotional health. This, coupled with decades of economic and social marginalization, is part of the reason Guerrero is one of the "poorest" states.

Guerrero, Scene of Decades of Repression, Impunity, and Resistance

In Guerrero, crimes against humanity and terror sown by the State and criminal groups is not new, neither is the daily resistance and social organization of the marginalized, nor the repression brought about by the collusion of the government, the army, and the drug gangs. In September 2014, the world was shocked by the mass disappearance of the 43 normalistas (students) from the Ayotzinapa Rural Teacher's College in Iguala, Guerrero. In Guerrero, the Dirty War of the 60s and 70s is still present in the minds and hearts of its inhabitants:

> Declassified official documents reveal that 227 military commanders with their troops ransacked houses of popular colonies and of towns in search of their enemies, for which they also established checkpoints on roads, dirt roads, and in the entrances of cities and towns of the center regions, Costa Grande and Costa Chica de Guerrero. Military commanders detained, without warrants, between 500 and 1,500 students, teachers, activists, peasants, indigenous people, women, infants, and the elderly. In their official reports, they were named "packages for review." They transferred the "packages" in helicopters and trucks to military installations to torture them, and the vast majority were disappeared... That is to say: the Army is the main institution responsible for 512 cases of enforced disappearances documented by Comverdad [Guerrero Truth Commission]. The figure rises to 1,500 cases of enforced disappearances only at the military base of Pie de la Cuesta, Acapulco, according to the testimony cited by one of the perpetrators, former military police Gustavo Tarin, who says that the victims were thrown from airplanes to the sea.[11]

Physical evidence and testimony also make it clear that the Dirty War crimes were carried out through a coordinated effort between government institutions and criminal groups.

> Another contribution of the report disclosed for the first time how the Army and Governor Rubén Figueroa Figueroa used former soldiers, policemen, and criminals to crush half a dozen guerrillas and the political opposition that appeared in Guerrero at the time. One of these paramilitary groups, known as Blood Group, was in charge by Captain Francisco Javier Barquín.[12]

Human rights violations and attempts to break the organizations of the poor were not limited to the Dirty War. Guerrero, even in the 80s and 90s, continued to suffer massacres, directed particularly against social organizations. One of the most notable was the Aguas Blancas in 1995 in which en route to a protest, seventeen farmers of the Campesino Organization of the Southern Sierra (OCSS) were killed and another twenty one injured in a planned attack carried out by police forces under the command of the governor. Another was the community of El Charco in 1998 in the area of the Costa Chica, where, at dawn, hundreds of military troops besieged farmers, students, and members of the Revolutionary Army guerrilla group, the Insurgent People (ERPI), who had gathered in the community school to discuss social and economic problems in the area. The attack left eleven dead (several of them killed by coup de grace), five injured, and twenty two arrested.

All these historical antecedents are still present in the minds of many poor people in Guerrero and elsewhere—in the hearts of the children of the disappeared, in the footsteps of tortured former political prisoners, in communities that have been and continue to be hotbeds of army raids because they are concentrated areas of popular movements, etc. Partly for the same reasons, the clear and direct involvement of the police forces and the army in the murder and forced disappearance of normalistas of Ayotzinapa has not been a surprise for the people of Guerrero; but the people also harbor indignation and distrust of the state, and seek justice.

While long periods of strenuous repression have never been able to completely prevent mobilizing by the marginalized in Guerrero, they have had an effect on the focus of the popular organization and its methods. Organizers had to adapt to the specific conditions of the terrain. In recent years, moreover, another factor has been added to the difficult social and political realm: that of organized crime.

Neoliberalism, between the dispossession of territory and structural violence

In the state of Guerrero, at least eighteen organized crime groups are currently operating, but the violence has been concentrated in Iguala, Acapulco, Chilpancingo, and Chilapa.[13] Guerrero is the largest producer of the poppy plant in the country, which has led Mexico to become the third largest producer of heroin in the world, most of which is sent to the United States, representing a market of hundreds of millions of dollars annually.[14] The economic importance of the production of narcotics has increased despite the devastating consequences the so-called "war on drugs" has brought to the population of Guerrero. Between 2005 and 2011, homicides increased by 310% in Guerrero.[15] In March 2016, a note from *La Jornada* Guerrero states that Guerrero "has practically the highest malicious homicide rate in the country with 9.09 cases per 100,0000 inhabitants."[16] And that, says the journalist, despite a contribution of more than 200 million pesos annually since 2012 by the Fund for Public Security Contributions to fight crime. While there are no exact figures, it is believed that 50,000 people or more have been displaced by violence.[17]

While these statistics appear as cold numbers in an essay, in real life they translate into horrifying images of mutilated bodies in newspapers, casualties discovered with regular frequency in the countryside and urban neighborhoods, and relatives who have armed brigades searching for their missing loved ones due to the lack of response by the judicial institutions in the most "egregious" cases (such as the forced disappearance of 43 students). These events disintegrate the social fabric in the state, allowing fear to penetrate all spheres of life. As Dr. Carlos Beristain, an expert at the Inter-American Court of Human Rights and member of the Interdisciplinary Group of Independent Experts, which investigated the attacks against the normalistas of Ayotzinapa, said:

> There are impacts on collective behavior, impacts on the remaining victims of marginalization, on the children who have problems with the management of rage, hatred, fear. There is also a dehumanization that becomes insensitive to violence, and the capacity for empathy is lost.[18]

In her paper entitled "Social Violence in Mexico: Its Impact on Citizen Security," Professor Aída Imelda Valero Chávez stresses that:

> The perception of insecurity and fear leads people to seek safe spaces by taking refuge in their own homes, isolating themselves, locking themselves in individualism and distrust, in anger, in resentment, and in the desire for revenge. A vicious circle is established: violence ends communal life, and when this happens violence is encouraged. Violence is intimately linked to the vulnerability of the population. As community life deteriorates because of the climate of insecurity that causes fear, isolation, and discouragement to participate in public life, the social fabric that provides security to members of the community weakens.[19]

Of course, the extreme level of violence is an essential tool of capitalism. Guerrero, although considered a poor state, is one of the richest in natural resources including gold, titanium, and uranium. Therefore, the state is covered in mega projects—most mines are owned by Canadian companies such as Goldcorp, Newstrike Capital, Alamos Gold, and Torex Gold Resources.[20] According to journalist Dawn Paley, who has extensively researched the relationship between neoliberal projects, the drug war and repression in Latin America,

> In Guerrero these crime groups operate in a highly militarized environment and each one will often have various kinds of relations with state forces.... Over and over again, the same forces that are supposedly protecting these transnational corporations have also been found to be working closely with these criminal groups.[21]

Other research supports Paley's observations. In an article in *El Financiero* in December 2015, the author recounts how "masked gunmen often come to the mountainous enclave near the Los Filos mine to assassinate and kidnap, while demanding a fee from the royalties generated from the mine in exchange for the captives' lives."[22] The Los Filos mine, owned by Goldcorp, is one of the country's most important gold mines.

According to journalist Francisco Cruz, one of the authors of the book *La guerra que nos ocultan* (The War that We Hide), in which the role of the Mexican government and military in the killings and forced disappearance of normalistas of Ayotzinapa is evidenced,

> We find that in this country there is a process of historical decomposition, and Guerrero is the clearest example ... Guerrero, the poorest state and one of the richest states, is littered with gold... The investigation found that organized crime works with mining, serves to evict the people ... the narcos control part of the mining business, such as transport...[23]

Territorial construction of life: a new expression of the movements of the poor

Amid the historical decomposition process referred to by Francisco Cruz, the health care workers make up what we can call "social self-defense." That is, with security and community justice, an anti-capitalist orientation is helping to achieve the strengthening of communities that is crucial in the territorial struggle between neoliberal forces, on one side, and the popular power of the people, on the other. Creating territories free of crime, kidnapping, murder, disappearance, dispossession, environmental devastation, and other crimes, from a community perspective that incorporates indigenous worldviews, goes hand-in-hand with bolstering community health, which enhances the full life of the people against a background of so much death and terror.

Health is more than the treatment of disease or injury, it's also the construction of new ways of relating to each other, in a healing environment, strengthening horizontal links, sharing knowledge, rescuing traditional forms of healing, etc. This holistic approach is used in the training and tasks of health workers, who study anatomy and physiology along with the importance of listening, traditional knowledge, care for the environment, the importance of history, mental health and healing, and about the power and the importance of acting for the benefit of the community.

The PC health workers are a resource for those marginalized due to the social, economic, and political conditions that exist in the Guerrero, and particularly where this new phase of capitalism has reduced human life itself to a new kind of commodity—evidenced in the increasing practice of human trafficking, disappearances, turning young people into disposable drug dealers, and extreme violence. In return, the work of both the PC and its health workers supports the principle that the integrity of each individual life is necessary for the integrity of the community, and vice versa. In this way, the health initiative is a strategic "project" that allows for organization and therefore autonomy. The process of organization and strengthening of the community members and their relations are fundamental pillars in achieving and maintaining emotional, mental, and physical health, resulting in collective forms of recovery. We recover what Zibechi has called "the healing power of the community,"[24] a front of struggle for the poor, which is extremely important in this era of territorial struggle.

While these actions do not represent a systemic challenge to capitalism, they are micropowers to crack the hegemonic power of the state in affected communities. You have to understand the "power reflected between dominance and resistance as a dialectic of contradictions between power to power, including the power of the people and the bourgeois power, which is the history of class struggle in our America."[25] The peasants and indigenous people show that they are collective actors integral to social transformation. In Tixtla and in their communities, farmers with rifles in hand are assuming these responsibilities and organizational tasks of social transformation. The peasants and indigenous peoples are becoming more visible, and responding to current conditions with resistance. The communities remain firm in the conviction of continuing the struggle and safeguarding security in their territories for a complete defense of the right to a safe and healthy life for all of us.

Endnotes

1   The editors would like to thank Mandeep Dhillon, for her collaboration on this chapter.

2   Raúl Zibechi, *Autonomías y emancipaciones, América Latina en movimiento* (Lima, Perú, Fondo Editorial de la Facultad de Ciencias Sociales, 2007), 21.

3   Centro de Derechos Humanos Tlachinollan, "La justicia del pueblo y para el pueblo: un año turbulento," en Matías Alonso Marcos, Aréstegui Ruiz Rafael, Vázquez Villanueva Aurelio (compiladores) *La rebelión ciudadana y la justicia comunitaria en Guerrero*, Instituto de Estudios Parlamentarios "Eduardo Neri" del Congreso del Estado de Guerrero. (México, D.F., FECHA), 35.

4   Centro de Derechos Humanos de la Montaña Tlachinollan, Digna Rebeldía, "Guerrero, el epicentro de las luchas de resistencia," *Informe* XIX, Junio 2012–Mayo 2013, (Tlapa de Comonfort, Guerrero, México), 16.

5   De la Torre Rangel Jesús Antonio, Justicia comunitaria: resistencia y contribución "una visión desde el sistema comunitario dela Montaña y Costa Chica de Guerrero en Sistema de Seguridad e Impartición de Justicia Comunitaria: Costa-Montaña de Guerrero, Coordinadores Medardo Reyes Salinas, Homero Castro Guzmán, Edit. Plaza y Valdés, 2008, 102.

6   Santos Bartolo, Nahum. Entrevistado por Polco Gatica, Daniel. Entrevista personal. El Troncón, 16 de enero, 2016.

7   Alondra Nelson, *Body and Soul: The Black Panther Party and the Fight against Medical Discrimination* (Minneapolis: University of Minnesota Press, 2011), ix.

8   Valls Llobet Carme, *Mujeres, Salud y poder* (España: Universidad de Valencia, Instituto de la Mujer, 2009), 29.

9   Sharla M. Fett, *Working Cures: Healing, Health, and Power on Southern Slave Plantations* (Chapel Hill: The University of North Carolina Press, 2002), 15–35.

10 Luciano Fabbri, *Apuntes sobre feminismo y construcción del poder popular*, Edit. Puño y letra (Rosario, Argentina, 2013), 58.

11 Castellanos, Laura, "'Guerra Sucia'. Ejército la ordenó" *El universal*, January 26, 2015. Available online: archivo.eluniversal.com.mx/nacion-mexico/2015/impreso/-8216guerra-sucia-8217-ejercito-la-ordeno-222551.html.

12 Ibid.

13 *El Sur*, July 10, 2015, "Año veintitrés, quinta época," Número 6359, p 5, Acapulco Gro. Consultado el día 14 de Julio del 2015.

14 Laura Woldenberg, "La guerra perdida: México es ya el tercer productor de heroína en el mundo y primer proveedor de EU." *Vice News*, May 3, 2016. Available online: http://www.sinembargo.mx/03-05-2016/1655896.

15 INEGI. Boletín de Prensa Núm. 310/12.20 August 2012. Available online: http//www.inegi.org.mx/inegi/contenidos/ español/prensa/ Boletines/boletín /Comunicados/ Especiales/2012/comunicado 29.pdf.

16 Fabiola Martínez, "Guerrero, número uno en homicidios, pese a recibir más recursos para abatir crimen." *La Jornada* Guerrero, March 26, 2016. Available online: http://www.jornada .unam.mx/2016/03/26/politica/006n1pol.

17 Woldenberg, Laura, "La guerra perdida: México es ya el tercer productor de heroína en el mundo y primer proveedor de EU."

18 Aída Imelda Valero Chávez, "Violencia Social en México: su impacto en la seguridad ciudadana." Available online: http://www.umdcipe.org/conferences/DecliningMiddleClassesSpain/Papers/Valero.pdf.

19 Ibid.

20 Joseph Czikk, "Canadian Mining Companies are Destroying Latin America." *Vice News*, Feb. 12, 2015. Available online: http://www.vice.com/en_ca/read/canadian-mining-companies-are-destroying-latin-america-924.

21 Ibid.

22 Editores, "Oro y narco aumentan violencia en Guerrero." *El Financiero*. Available online: http://www.elfinanciero.com.mx/nacional/oro-y-narco-aumentan-violencia-en-guerrero.html.

23 Maribel Gutiérrez, "En el caso Ayotzinapa hay un manejo institucional para encubrir al Ejército, señalan periodistas." *El Sur* de Acapulco. Availalable online: http://suracapulco.mx/2/en-el-caso-ayotzinapa-hay-un-manejo-institucional-para-encubrir-al-ejercito-senalan-periodistas/.

24 Zibechi, 39.

25 Fabbri, 29.

ON FIRE AND THE "MULTIPLICATIONS" OF THE POOR IN MATHARE, NAIROBI

Wangui Kimari

"Hiti ndīrīaga mwana, na mūī ūrīa īrī ngoroku"
[Even] The hyena does not eat its baby, and you know how insatiable it is.
—Gikuyu Proverb

"I am not ashamed of poverty; there is nothing shameful in it, but slavery…"
—Ayi Kwei Armah, *The Beautyful Ones Are Not Yet Born* (1968)

NAIROBI IS THE KIND OF A CITY THAT, USING KOJO LAING'S EXPRESSION, "holds the neck of the crow" when it is crowing in the morning.[1] It is vibrant, creative, and industrious, but it is not an easy city for everyone, and especially not for the poor majority (70% of the population) who live on only 6% of its land.[2] In view of the violence that this statistic symbolizes, how can we understand people's lives as a productive assemblage,[3] a convening of many plotlines, of survival but also determined struggles against their enslavement—a rising up? In trying to do this, I relay stories from three people in Mathare, Nairobi. Mathare is a poor urban settlement in the east of the city that, for over nine decades, has been denied basic services by the government. Yet, even in its historical stigmatization—in both the colonial and postcolonial period—as a place of prostitution, crime, and illegally produced alcohol, its residents survive and contest structural dehumanization in a variety of imperfect ways. The short stories that follow offer portraits of these grave struggles in which they engage, and also highlight the dangers that exist when one chooses to organize against a martial state. Nonetheless, subsequent to these glimpses into three lives on the margins of Nairobi, I briefly discuss the tenacity of residents in the face of oppression. In this urban settlement where, both in the colonial and postcolonial period, occupants have taken oaths against the government; in this space where protests for water and against land-grabbing happen frequently; where mothers work multiple jobs with little return to keep families alive, we cannot ignore the small doors that are opened each day when the poor rise.

Minor stories

Nti[4] told me about the second time he went to jail. It was not for the usual misadventures that saw generations of poor youth like him carted off to the city's overcrowded prisons. This initial episode of incarceration was for a charge of "robbery with violence." And so, at the tender age of seventeen—a minor—he was sentenced to serve ten years in the country's most notorious jail. It was a female judge who made the decision to incarcerate him, and he still remembers her name twenty-five years later, like it was yesterday. Nti, whose father was killed by Daniel Arap Moi's regime for what was rumored to be his role in the unsuccessful 1982 coup, spent ten years in Kamiti Maximum Prison.[5] It is in this same place, the principal borstal of the colonial period in Kenya, that Dedan Kimathi, a senior Mau Mau leader, was executed and his body hidden in 1956. We still do not know where his body was concealed. It is somewhere in this colonial architecture, amidst these prison walls that have boxed in all our best freedom fighters and "worst criminals." In the hearts of the poor, like in Mathare, such titles are interchangeable, because whatever the initial crime of many of these prisoners—political or otherwise—imprisonment is the singular fate of being born in the country's ghettos.

The second time that Nti went to prison was for seeking justice for a woman who had been killed by the "stray" bullet of a policeman who had allegedly been in pursuit of a thief in the area. As usual, the police came guns blazing. If there was adequate housing in the area the bullet may have merely ricocheted off a solid wall or even gotten stuck in metal scaffolding. But this was Mathare where there is no water or basic infrastructure, and most houses are put together by a determined patchwork of old corrugated iron sheets and other recycled materials—cardboard, plastic, wood—that are easily penetrable and prone to fire. And so here, the bullet was stopped by a young woman's body.

When this happened, Nti and others reacted immediately; they chased the policeman through the narrow warrens of Mathare. They wanted to act and felt justice should not be out of reach. For now, this man who came in blazing fire was now running from it. He was almost caught but made a lucky escape by ducking into a small compound that had been fenced. There is a Swahili saying that states "dawa ya moto ni moto" [the medicine for fire is fire], which was taken literally by the baying crowd. They had managed to surround the policeman and decided on the spot that he would be burned inside the compound where he had hidden. And kerosene stove oil—a staple for these households without electricity and who cannot afford a gas burner—was lit in an episode of what is colloquially known as "mob justice."

As the fire began to spread, a mother, who they did not know was in the compound, jumped from the third floor to save her life. The policeman also emerged from his burning hiding place and found himself face to face with the infuriated crowd. They did not kill him, but they did make sure that he would spend three weeks in a hospital bed. And after he had nursed his injuries and was sent back home, the policeman knew exactly who he was looking for. This is how Nti went to jail for the second time.

***

And yet another stray bullet from a police revolver passed through the metal sheets of a home where a young mother was breastfeeding her two-month-old daughter; it punctured the mother's forehead. Even with this bullet lodged firmly in place, she gathered enough strength to stand up, lift her baby, place her gently on the table and shout to her neighbor that she had just been shot before collapsing in a heap on the uneven mud floor.

***

I had taught Gichuru when he was nine, although he had the body of a six-year-old child. His small stature reflected the malnutrition that has become standard for over 25% of children under five in Kenya.[6] These were uncertain times for me in Mathare; I was in my early twenties and was unsure about whether the books, porridge, and remedial mathematics and English classes were impactful, and not just the palliatives of middle-class charity and guilt. We came to offer solidarity through education, since we knew that the government schools in this area did not have enough teachers or books, and that many of these children could not afford to go to school because they had to work to support their families or themselves. Together with other older community members I wanted to instill in these young Africans that they were loved and mattered, even if the government and society at large had long since deemed them the progeny and future accessories of urban decay. These were our minor counter-hegemonic efforts,[7] our genuine but equally inarticulate attempts to usurp the institutionalized "realities" that structured our lives. And even in these hesitant but sincere ventures, over fifty children would show up every Saturday to attend our "homework club." The older ones, between the ages of eleven and thirteen, would take turns lighting the charcoal stoves used for the preparation of the millet porridge, and would then apportion the food to make sure all who showed up would eat—even a stranger who might pop in unexpectedly.

For me, Gichuru glowed even in his shyness. I do not remember at what point he joined our convenings, but I do remember his small brown face and huge smile. He could not write the English required of him by formal institutions, even after three years in primary school, but his math skills surpassed most of the group who, unlike him, attended school. One day, when we were not saving the 10 shillings ($0.01) to take our club swimming, we all chipped in to purchase the required school, and other, clothes for Gichuru. His mother had died, and he was living with his recently married sister in a small 10' x 10' house. She already had her own family and could barely cope with the additional responsibility of her young brother.

One morning, ten years after he joined our "homework club," the police executed Gichuru as he was on the way to a goat slaughterhouse to give his brother, who worked in this abattoir, the house keys, and to get some breakfast.[8] In front of residents conducting their everyday morning activities, they shot him twice in the head and chest, planted a knife and cellphones in his pocket, and then walked away. His body was left on the road for hours before a police van was sent to pick it up. This is the fate of many of the young people who are labeled "suspected gangsters" by the police and the press.

On the day of his funeral, we spent the whole morning working to secure the release of three members of his family from the local police station. The same police who killed Gichuru had gone to the family's home the night before, taken the money that had been raised for the funeral, threatened to shoot one of his aunts, and assaulted and detained his brother and two of his uncles. A mother who saw us at the station said bitterly: "They are killing us like chickens, and if they think we are chickens they should just tell us." We did not get to bury Gichuru that day.

***

Yet, even as a system, far worse than a hyena, keeps killings its own children, people keep on rising in the morning to care for each other, to walk the streets looking for small margins, to remember victims of "stray" bullets. As we can see from these three stories, in this part of Nairobi the costs of demanding an end to stray bullets, breastfeeding a child, or getting breakfast can be life or death. These deeply layered portraits of life illustrate the complexities of poor urban life and of "rising-up." At the same time, even in these simple bids to "make this despair bearable,"[9] there is also a self-destructive undoing—popularized ethnic tensions that render suspicion, mob justice that is rarely justice, young people coopted by transactional political processes to evict or harm each other, and the continuous re-election of a gerontocratic male elite who use every opportunity to criminalize dissent. These contradictions create grave inequalities that frame how people claim justice; they compel a frustrated reach for kerosene oil because residents know they will never get their rights in a court of law immersed in a neo-imperial political economy that increasingly impoverishes, surveils, and disposes, and in this way restricts, even the smallest chances of escape.

Still, Nti is back in Mathare and, while no longer chasing policemen through alleyways, is a remarkable community organizer. Increased documentation of extra-judicial killings by various community groups is posing a large challenge to police executions in Nairobi and beyond. Gichuru's peers are engaged in multiple groups working for water provision, self-esteem, cultural memory, and all types of practices required for community survival. Everywhere one turns, new groups are forming and multiplying and in their own ways questioning the violence they live every day. In these practices, they always "return to the source,"[10] who are the people, and in these struggles—full of imperfect fires, misfires, multiplications, and stumbles—work to create something greater than the present moment. Unquestionably, without these minor barefoot multiplications, life would be much harder. So, even if resistance is only visible in fleeting moments, we must recognize that it territorializes the rage and resistance of a people who will never fully submit to the crossfires that govern their lives. Poverty is nothing shameful, but slavery….

And even if these actions constitute small "triumph[s]" in which "tragedy has always been implicit,"[11] in this city that holds the neck of the crow every morning, we must always remember that the crow will always rise.

Endnotes

1 Kojo Laing, *Search Sweet Country* (San Francisco: McSweeney's Books, 2011), 151.
2 Christopher Swope, "Nairobi Governor Evans Kidero: devolution is 'bringing services closer to the people,'" *Citiscope*, October 29, 2015. Available online: http://citiscope.org/story/2015/nairobi-governor-evans-kidero-devolution-bringing-services-closer-people.

3   Gilles Deleuze and Félix Guattari, *A Thousand Plateaus: Capitalism and Schizophrenia* (Minneapolis: University of Minnesota Press, 1987).

4   This is a pseudonym.

5   On August 1, 1982, there was a failed coup by Kenya Air Force Soldiers to remove the president, Daniel Arap Moi. Hundreds of civilians and soldiers were killed during this coup attempt that lasted less than twelve hours. While it was quelled the same day it was launched, the coup became the perfect excuse for the president to enact an even more extreme dictatorship over the following two decades of his rule.

6   Kenya National Bureau of Statistics and Republic of Kenya, *Kenya Demographic and Health Survey* (Nairobi: KNBS, 2014), 157.

7   Antonio Gramsci, *Selections from The Prison Notebooks* (New York: International Publishers, 1971).

8   Read more on Steven Gichuru's murder on the official Mathare Social Justice Centre website (MSJC): http://matharesocialjustice.org/stephen-gichuru-age-17-one-of-the-latest-victims-of-extrajudicial-killings-in-mathare-constituency/.

9   Ayi Kwei Armah, *The Beautiful Ones Are Not Yet Born* (Oxford: Heinemann, 1968), 83.

10 Amilcar Cabral, *Return to the Source: Selected Speeches of Amilcar Cabral* (New York: Monthly Review Press, 1974).

11 James Baldwin, "An Open Letter to My Sister, Miss Angela Davis," *The New York Review of Books*, November 19, 1970. Available online: http://www.nybooks.com/articles/1971/01/07/an-open-letter-to-my-sister-miss-angela-davis/.

CRITICAL CONSCIOUSNESS AS AN ACT OF CULTURE

AN ILLUSTRATION FROM SUDAN

Gussai H. Sheikheldin

"We see therefore that, if imperialist domination has the vital need to practice cultural oppression, national liberation is necessarily an act of culture."
—Amilcar Cabral, "National Liberation and Culture," 1970

Introduction

IF YOU AND I MEET SOMEWHERE IN A "NO MAN'S LAND," AWAY FROM THE JURIS-dictions of legal authorities, and we both are going to remain there for years on our own, we will have only two options: either we openly compete and fight for resources, or we openly cooperate as equals.

There is little room for tricking one another into thinking what is not true about the other person's long-term intentions. If we both understand that we will improve our chances of survival through cooperation, we will do it; and we will understand that we could only maintain that cooperation effectively if we treat each other as equals. If we fail to see the point in cooperation, and we both need to survive by competing for the same resources, we will likely become adversaries. Either way we will know clearly where we stand in relation to each other.

That clarity is lost in long-standing social aggregates—in states and markets. When human groups are larger, more complicated rules come into play. States and markets normalize the exploitation and oppression of many in society through the pretext of order and justice. We often do not know where we stand in relation to each other because the privileged groups claim (and some believe) that we cannot forego order and justice, while marginalized groups are divided about whether such claims are true or false.

The marginalized folk—the poor, the oppressed, the underprivileged, the disenfranchised, and the exploited—are often confused because clarity is distorted by complex social hierarchies, bureaucracies, and the division of labor, as well as by being entangled in a very large web of human relations, ceremonies, and protocols. Additionally, sentimental notions such as patriotism, religious group loyalty, ethnic cohesion, etc., play a part—unintentionally or intentionally—in making it more difficult for the marginalized to see where the lines are drawn. Privileged and marginalized groups in the same society share many of these kinships, relations of production, traditions, and ethos. Therefore, it is not easy to dissect where the privileged are the adversary, and where they are simply on the same team. It is confusing to the point that many marginalized people are admiring fans of some of the famous members of privileged group(s);[1] venerating them as role models and leading lights. It is confusing to the point that some members of the privileged group(s) themselves are not acutely aware of their privileges in society, and how those privileges are maintained by mechanisms that systemically undermine the well-being and legitimate aspirations of majorities in society.[2]

Indeed, some members of the privileged group(s) sincerely think that what is taking place is natural and circumstantial, and not a consequence of structural biases in society. We are all familiar with the rhetoric of economic elites in most societies, whereby rich folks claim to be so because they are hard-working and entrepreneurial, and poor folks are so because they are not hard-working or entrepreneurial enough.[3] At the macro and global levels, there exists an intellectual tradition that venerates capitalism, and claims that it naturally and objectively rewards innovation, industry, good planning, and fair competition.[4]

As Paulo Freire, the renowned adult educator, explained, critical consciousness is about becoming aware of the structural sources of oppression in society.[5] Freire described the process by which individuals develop critical consciousness as "conscientization." It is a process that is self-reflective and allows for the person to learn from events, activities, and experiences in the surrounding environment (including people) in a critical manner. In other words, conscientization is a form of critical education grounded in social reality.[6] If large social aggregates can reduce clarity in relations of marginalization among members of that society (whether in a country, region, or the global community), conscientization is the process by which this obscurity is unveiled and demystified. When the sources of oppressive relations are obscure, those who are their chronic victims will not do much to change them, because they are neither critically conscious of them nor do they have a clue about how to change them. They may frequently complain, to each other and beyond, about their difficult conditions and the injustice they regularly endure, but will not often connect all these experiences together in a coherent critique of the social system itself. Moreover, those persons of goodwill and empathy who benefit from the status quo will not do much if they too do not acquire critical consciousness. This process, of developing consciousness and choosing to side with a just cause beyond narrow class interests, is what Cabral calls "class suicide"—a strategic, long-term commitment to sustainable progress and the right side of history. At its core it's a moral commitment.[7]

One could interject, however, that becoming aware of a phenomenon does not automatically imply that one will care to transform it, so understanding structural sources of oppression in society does not necessarily mean that one will seek to combat them. That is objectively true, but we should also be mindful that any genuine care is unlikely to happen *without* that understanding. Then there's the difference between understanding on the one hand, and "consciousness" (understanding plus caring), on the other. An intelligent member of the privileged classes may understand that the status quo is maintained by marginalizing a majority of the population, but that person may not have any material or moral stake in changing that status quo. While some members of the privileged classes may be persuaded morally to take a stand against a system that privileges them, members of the marginalized classes are reasonably expected to care about changing the status quo when they understand the structural nature of their marginalization. Attaining consciousness, in that case, means allowing one's acquired understanding to change their perspective and priorities (i.e. to care).

Conscientization and Culture

While it is difficult to find a comprehensive, agreed-upon, definition of culture, Amilcar Cabral defines it well as the fruit of a people's history that is simultaneously the determinant of that history. It is shaped by their cumulative history, hence a fruit of it, but it also determines it "through the positive or negative influences it exerts on the evolution of the interaction" between humans and their surroundings (including between themselves) as individuals or groups.[8] This instrumental definition could be complemented, as well, by Steve Biko's definition: "A culture is essentially the society's composite answer to the varied problems of life. We are experiencing new problems every day, and whatever we do adds to the richness of our cultural heritage."[9]

Culture is inherently dynamic. Every time the conditions of life change, culture changes in response. When a people are under conditions of dispossession, exploitation, and poverty, their culture carries a signature informed and shaped by these conditions, yet it also carries the keys to innovating and navigating beyond them. One of these keys is resistance. Hence, Cabral asserts that the process of liberation from external domination—or oppression or exploitation—is an act of culture. While Cabral focused on exploring resistance by a colonized people against foreign domination, we can see that the formula he proposed can extend to the relations of domination and marginalization within the various strata of the same society.

Building on the above, I argue that conscientization itself can be viewed as an act of culture, a radical act. Since conscientization is mainly concerned with combating and transforming structures of oppression within a society, culture is the vehicle by which it often expresses itself in both building critical consciousness and using it to practice change (praxis).

And just as it takes place among the marginalized, conscientization can sometimes take place during dialogue with privileged individuals and groups. The human ability of empathy allows us, through our imagination, to get a glimpse of other lives, personalities, and experiences. The dictionary definition of empathy is "the intellectual identification with or vicarious experiencing of the feelings, thoughts, or attitudes of another."[10] Through empathy, we can identify with humanity in a "humane" way. We can appreciate the thoughts and feelings of those who differ from us; we can try to understand their responses. The phrase "to put oneself in someone else's shoes" captures the essence of empathy. According to Freire, the purpose of human dialogue is transformative; It, however, needs to be practiced in certain ways to be humane and positive for the people: "Human existence cannot be silent, nor can it be nourished by false words, but only by true words, with which man transforms the world. To exist, humanly, is to name the world, to change it."[11] For some informed individuals from privileged groups in society, empathy assists in developing critical consciousness from dialogue, which leads them to the realization of what Nyerere once articulated:

> We can try to cut ourselves from our fellows on the basis of [the privileges] we have had; we can try to carve out for ourselves an unfair share of the wealth of society. But the cost to us, as well as to our fellow citizens, will be very high. It will be high not only in terms of satisfactions forgone, but also in terms of our own security and well-being.[12]

While it is an established historical truth that rights are not voluntarily offered by the powers-that-be, but are taken by serious and persistent demands and resistance, it is also a historical truth that those who have a just cause eventually find allies of good conscience (and critical consciousness) from the other camp. Empathy plays a critical role in this process. Yet, empathy is facilitated by culture: the common cultural experiences (other than economic and political) that the privileged[13] and the marginalized share make it possible for them to relate to one another. Since culture has facets other than the socioeconomic and politics (such as arts, ceremonies, folk history, food, architecture, humor, symbols, values, and beliefs), it tends to provide a broad area of psychological overlap between the privileged and marginalized in a society, and through that area empathy can be facilitated. Granted, it is not usually that simplistic in reality, but the general theoretical strokes are valid.

Therefore, we can say that by facilitating empathy, culture is reinforced as an important vehicle for conscientization. It is not only a vehicle for conscientization among the poor, but also a vehicle for forging alliances between the marginalized and the conscientized privileged ones. It should however be kept in mind that critical consciousness is not inclusive of, or a substitute for, organized collective action. In desirable cases of social transformation, the two will overlap, integrate, and inform each other. Nonetheless, they are not the same thing; this essay addresses only one of them.

Case study: CUSH Manifesto and marginalization in Sudan

As iterated earlier, it is not uncommon that privileged groups are isolated from the grim realities of marginalized groups. In Sudan, it is true with regards to urban and rural areas, but it is more accurate to use the terms "center" and "margins." The center is not simply a geographic location. It is more a description of a socio-political, and somewhat cultural, social stratum. The center is not necessarily distinguished by ethnic affiliation (although ethnicity plays a large role) or clear geopolitical affiliation. It cannot be called a coherent socioeconomic class, either. However, it tends to sustain its power over the other social groups, and reproduce itself, through ideology and privilege. The ideology may carry a religious veil, or some other "sacred" veil. The privilege is that of social status—of perceived and politically imposed superiority. Economic privileges usually accompany the political ones, but may not be equally distributed across the center stratum. The margins, on the other hand, are basically all the other groups within the country, with different degrees of marginalization.

Marginalization is a complex process, not easy to define comprehensively. It often expresses itself overtly in a cultural context, but its direct material existence is in the distribution of power and wealth. If culture, after all, is a historical expression of a collective identity of a group of people with shared experiences and, sometimes, shared language and ancestry, then by itself it does not marginalize. It does not necessarily determine the rules of engagement with others (that is, other cultures or sub-cultures within the main/common culture). Marginalization only starts to manifest in systemic denials of fair access to power and wealth in a given geopolitical context. Such is the case in contemporary Sudan. Certain aspects of culture are utilized as a basis for marginalizing other groups. This is why combating marginalization is essentially an act of culture. The complex aspects of marginalization in post-colonial Sudan were first conceptualized by the late Ali Mazrui, and were later expounded on by others.[14]

One of the strongest treatises of political analysis in Sudan is the CUSH Manifesto. The strength of the manifesto derives from its approach to political analysis through understanding culture and marginalization, and then how it illuminates the structures of oppression with a conscientization approach. CUSH is an acronym for the Congress of United Sudan Homeland (a name that evokes the Sudanic, Meroetic, and ancient civilization of Cush that emerged and flourished in the land of present-day Sudan). In the mid-1990s a group of Sudanese intellectuals in Khartoum representing almost all marginalized areas began to formulate, under dangerous political conditions, a manifesto that ccould serve as a political platform for a broad alliance of marginalized Sudanese groups. It was initially drafted by a young man from the Nuba Mountains and then went through successive revisions in consultation with representatives of multiple marginalized groups. The Manifesto was widely circulated after reaching a sufficient level of coherence and consensus among the representatives.

The document marks the first time that a diverse group of Sudanese citizens who represent various marginalized groups decided to bring their collective voice together for the human right of self-determination. The significance of this initiative, however, is the authentic approach to sociopolitical analysis that came to light through it. "CUSH views the conflict in the Sudan as to be cultural in essence, with political, economic, and social manifestations," says the manifesto.[15] Before this statement, rarely had anyone spoken in Sudan about the political role of culture. Few and isolated voices spoke of this angle before the CUSH Manifesto (such as Mazrui, Mahmoud M. Taha, and others[16]), but still not in the same unique way. The main thesis presented in the manifesto is based on three concepts: the center, the margins, and marginalization. Each one of these three is clearly defined and articulated in the CUSH manifesto:[17]

> *The centre*: refers to the social stratum that is in control of the state's central authority, and with it acquires an unfair share of power and wealth in the nation. The centre's social stratum legitimizes its existence, and reproduces itself, through claiming to represent certain cultural symbols; namely Islam and Arabism. By doing so, the centre does not really perform the job of the 'noble custodian' and 'protector' of Islam and Arabism in Sudan, but rather empties and exploits these two symbols – which are otherwise genuine members of Sudan's cultural mosaic, among other members – as vehicles of legitimizing its unfair distribution of power and wealth, and its repressive measures taken to keep the status quo. The centre, therefore, creates an oppressive "Islamo-Arab ideology," very different from the genuine cultural expressions of both Islam and Arabism in general Sudanese society. Thus, agents of the centre do not necessarily have to belong to certain ethnic groups in Sudan, pertaining to Islam and Arabism, but they have to be consistently portraying themselves as custodians of these two.
>
> *The margins*: refer to the social strata that do not subscribe to the cultural 'Frankenstein' created by the centre [i.e. other cultural identities and expressions that belong to the Sudanese cultural mosaic but are neither Islamic nor Arab-influenced]. They either do not subscribe to it by conscious choice or by being ethnically associated with cultural symbols different from Islam and Arabism.
>
> *Marginalization:* refers to the process of activating and maintaining the monopoly over power and wealth by the centre and denying the rightful demands of the margins (i.e. fair distribution of power and wealth). Marginalization materializes in two forms: developmental and cultural. Power facilitates both. Developmental marginalization is embodied in allocating more economic resources to improve the standards of living of the centre social stratum and those who are complicit with it (for one reason or another). Cultural marginalization is added on top of developmental marginalization, and those who suffer this double marginalization are the most oppressed – the ones who do not associate, by their ethnic identities, to either Islam

or Arabism (or both). Cultural marginalization deems those targeted as almost invisible. They don't deserve development or deserve to have access to expressing themselves as equal contributors to the Sudanese cultural mosaic (which is portrayed as a mono-culture by the centre).

While developmental marginalization is easily quantified through economic, educational, and health indicators, cultural marginalization is less quantifiable and more insulting.[18] It kills the marginalized slowly, but not always, as sometimes-direct violent measures are taken to keep them quiet, such as what we have witnessed during the vicious military attacks and war crimes by the Sudanese central government against civilians of marginalized communities in Darfur and South Kordofan in recent years.[19] It is also cultural marginalization that depletes the viable resources of resistance through continuously suffocating and eliminating diverse spaces for non-conforming cultural expressions. Marginalization ultimately begins with culture and ends with culture, according to the manifesto.

Therefore, the manifesto concludes that culture itself should be the main weapon of countering marginalization:

> [T]his situation should be changed through cultural democracy. Hereby, we, in the movement of CUSH, proclaim the reign of the outburst of Sudanese creativity in all its cultural and linguistic spectra. The reign of centricity eradication has come: no 'national' broadcast, no 'national' TV, no 'national' newspapers! It is high time we call things with their real names; these media have never been national, but central all the time. We proclaim the reign of real national creativity in its cultural pluralistic nature which begin by dismantling the cultural taboos enveloped with silence so as to expose them.[20]

Other proposals included in the manifesto relate to political and economic reform, broadly based on acknowledging historical injustices and working to redress them through strategic development plans and programs and political restructuring schemes (for example, land reform, a political federation, reorienting development priorities).

The manifesto then ends with clarifying remarks about the difference between the Islamo-Arab ideology of the center, as a tool of oppression, on the one hand, and the Islamic and Arabic (and Arabophone) elements of the culture of many Sudanese groups, on the other hand:

> We are not against the Islamic and Arab Middle of the Sudan;
> it belongs to us and we belong to it. We are against the Centre
> and its Islamo-Arab ideology of hegemony and persecution...
> It is the right of any group of Sudanese people to identify with
> the Islamic and Arabic culture as far as it finds itself in that;
> likewise, it is the right of any group of the Sudanese people
> to identify with its pre-Arab and pre-Islamic African culture,
> without this being an excuse for breaching its fundamental
> rights. In this, the institution of the State should not take sides
> in favour of a certain culture at the expense of other cultures.[21]

As a Sudanese who belongs to cultural strata that largely identify with Islam and Arabophone expression (albeit often in syncretic forms with native Nubian and other influences) and generally belongs to a privileged class of urban natives who had access to higher education in post-colonial settings, I observe my country with critical eyes. It seems that groups of the center in Sudan are not only unable to understand the suffering of the peoples of the margins, but can't grasp their own inability to understand. Although most of the population of the center groups have been living under conditions of relative poverty and political repression by tyrannical regimes, in most of Sudan's post-colonial years, there is plenty of historic evidence that marginalized groups have been consistently worse off under the same regimes, in addition to enduring more forms of cultural and state violence.[22] The July 2011 secession of South Sudan, and the creation of the youngest state in the world, is but one result of that history of marginalization.[23] When I read the CUSH Manifesto, it helped me see the structures of oppression stacked up against the marginalized groups of Sudan more clearly, and inspired me to be an ally of their struggle.

Logically, the manifesto concludes by proposing channels of organized sociopolitical action informed by the expressed principles and goals. It also proposes various ways of reorienting Sudan toward broad pan-African interests and identities. The original signatories to the manifesto comprised small groups from the margins as well as independent intellectuals and some political figures. It was foreseen that the Congress would grow into a larger alliance and become a new collective movement. Yet, although it received serious acclaim from heavyweight representatives of the Sudanese left, it has yet to gain appreciable momentum to more greatly influence the Sudanese scene.[24] Nonetheless, the perspective of the manifesto itself has already percolated into the Sudanese sociopolitical discourse, analyses, and progressive aspirations. For example, the terminologies of the margin, the center, and marginalization, are already widely used in the Sudanese left in cultural, political, and socioeconomic discussions (albeit with some deviations from the original definitions of the manifesto). Clearly there is more potential, however. For others and myself, the manifesto strongly speaks to the current affairs of Sudan. A future harmonious, egalitarian, and prosperous Sudanese nation requires a greater incorporation of the manifesto.

Endnotes

1 This state of affairs is the longstanding reason for low levels of, or non-existent, critical consciousness among the poor. They often do not see themselves as members of a marginalized class with oppositional socioeconomic and political interests to those of the privileged classes.

2 In spite of some members of the privileged classes not being self-conscious of the mechanisms that maintain their socially and economically elevated status, they do display a much higher degree of class consciousness than the marginalized. Members of the privileged classes invariably advocate for policies and programs that advance their (short- and/or long-term) economic interests and class standings in society.

3 Jana Kasperkevic, "Do the rich just work harder? Some CEOs certainly think so." *The Guardian*, September 26, 2014. Available online: https://www.theguardian.com/money/us-money-blog/2014/sep/26/rich-work-harder-ceos-jack-ma.

4 Niall Ferguson, *Civilization: The West and the Rest* (London: Penguin Press, 2011).

5 Gerald Doré, "Case study: Conscientization as a Specific Form of Community Practice and Training in Quebec," in *Community Development Around the World: Practice, Theory, Research, Training,* ed. Hubert Campfens (Toronto: University of Toronto Press, 1997), 93–100.

6 Margaret Ledwith, *Community Development: a critical approach* (Bristol: The Policy Press, 2005).

7 Amilcar Cabral, "The Weapon of Theory," Address delivered to the first Tricontinental Conference of the Peoples of Asia, Africa and Latin America held in Havana in January, 1966.

8 Amilcar Cabral, "National liberation and culture." *Transition*, 45 (1974), 13 (paper originally delivered on 20 February 1970 as a contribution to the Eduardo Mondlane Memorial Lecture Series at Syracuse University).

9 Stephen Biko, *I Write What I Like: Selected Writings* (Chicago: University of Chicago Press, 2002), 96.

10 "Empathy." Dictionary.com. Available online: http://www.dictionary.com/browse/empathy.

11 Paulo Freire, *Pedagogy of the Oppressed,* translated by Bergman Ramos (New York: Continuum, 1984), 77.

12 Julius Kambarage Nyerere, *Freedom and Development (Uhuru na Maendeleo): A Selection from Writings and Speeches, 1968–1973* (New York: Oxford University Press, 1974).

13 It is usually a minority of the privileged members of society that supports the cause of the marginalized, but the support is usually critical in cases of reformist or revolutionary struggles.

14 Ali A. Mazrui, "The Multiple Marginality of the Sudan" in *Sudan in Africa: Studies presented to the First International Conference sponsored by the Sudan Research Unit, 7–11 February 1968,* ed. Y. Fadl Hassan (Khartoum: University of Khartoum Press, 1971), 240–255.

15 Congress of United Sudan Homeland (CUSH), *The CUSH Manifesto* (Khartoum, April 1996). This document was published as a political pamphlet.

16 Mahmoud M. Taha, *Ath-thawra' Ath-Thaqafiyya (the Cultural Revolution)* (Arbaji, Sudan, 1972).

17 CUSH, *The CUSH Manifesto,* (mostly verbatim).

18 Muna A. Abdalla, "Poverty and inequality in urban Sudan: Policies, institutions and governance" (PhD diss. Universiteit Leiden, 2008). For data on development inequality in Sudan: African Studies Centre, *African Studies Collection*, vol. 13, available online: https://openaccess.leidenuniv.nl/bitstream/handle/1887/13106/ASC-075287668-1015-01.pdf?sequence=2.

19 Raluca Besliu, "South Kordofan: Sudan's Hidden Ethnic Cleansing" *Global Politics,* June 6, 2015, available online: http://global-politics.co.uk/wp/2015/06/06/south-kordofan-an-ethnic-cleansing-rooted-in-the-1960s/.

20 Congress of United Sudan Homeland (CUSH), *The CUSH Manifesto.*

21 Ibid.

22 Mansour Khalid, *War and Peace in Sudan: A Tale of Two Countries* (London: Kegan Paul International, 2003).

23 Sara Suliman and Gussai Sheikheldin, "Sudan's Secession Referendum: A Historical Punctuation Mark in the Making," *Science for Peace: The Bulletin*, April 2011. Available online: http://scienceforpeace.ca/files/bulletin-201104.pdf.

24 It was widely alleged that the late Dr. John Garang DeMebior, renowned national figure and leader of the Sudan People's Liberation Movement/Army (SPLM/A), after reading the CUSH manifesto, described it as "the most comprehensive treatise of its kind."

POWERS OF THE UNCIVIL

NOTES FROM SOUTH AFRICA

Aragorn Eloff and **Anna Selmeczi**

Dear Anna,

It's great to be collaborating with you on this chapter, which I hope will evolve, as our conversation unfolds, into an honest and reflexive engagement with the infinitely complex terrain we find ourselves in here in South Africa in 2016.

There are so many directions this could take—so much of import to discuss—and I'm worried about losing focus. Then again, trying to describe this messy assemblage of grassroots movements, service delivery protests, radical groupings, political parties, and myriad forms of everyday resistance that is South African politics as a single coherent whole with a determinable trajectory is not only futile but probably also deeply dishonest. Perhaps I should simply begin by sharing some questions that I've been dwelling on recently.

The first is one that I'm sure many of us ask ourselves: *what would be sufficient?* If we're serious about ending hierarchy and domination in the world in favor of a society of free equals, what do we need in order to get there? Although this question can, I suspect, only be adequately answered retrospectively, there are strong incentives to console ourselves with easy answers in the present. When things are going our way and anything feels possible—during what the Free Association[1] call "moments of excess" and CrimethInc call "crests"[2]—it feels as though it's almost enough to shout "just a little more of this and we'll be there!" As though a few more road blockades, one more spontaneous protest, a couple more marches will be sufficient. When, on the other hand, we sit licking our wounds during the ebbs that inevitably follow these peaks, it seems that can be too quick to judge our politics as fundamentally limited, as needing more organization, more structure and, while these are of course necessary to some extent, it can lead to the kind of burn out that leads us away from anarchism and toward either authoritarian communism—the kinds of Marxist-Leninist politics advocated by people like Jodi Dean or Mark Fisher[3]—in the direction of party politics and the Economic Freedom Fighters (EFF),[4] or in the direction of reformism, recuperation, and liberal democracy.

This dynamic of ebb and flow is easy to see stretched back over the past twenty two years of politics in South Africa. Coupled with this dynamic is a complex relationship between representation and participation, between discourses of legitimacy and rites of legitimation. While not always neatly divided, it is too often the case that there is a separation between those who participate directly in mobilizations, movements, etc., and those who analyze them and speak on their behalf. To use an example you are deeply familiar with, Abahlali baseMjondolo (AbM) is, sometimes, seen as a grassroots movement that is the poster child for a whole series of local and international academics—some sincere, some romantic, some cynical—wishing to locate a real-world example to superimpose their political analyses onto.[5] And, while some academics and activists, such as yourself, have resisted this approach and walked and worked together with groups like AbM, sharing in their struggles and applying a great amount of self-reflection in how you choose to represent these struggles to the world, there is truth in your observations that these groups are often rendered structurally voiceless—and thus purportedly in need of interlocution—or uncivil, and thus in need of some sort of political "reason" dispensed from a position of exteriority.

Already, there are too many questions here: *What would be sufficient? How do we build collective and individual resilience across longer-term struggles that have periods of ebb and flow? What is our relationship to the struggles we are part of or find ourselves in solidarity with?* These questions, in turn, lead us to the question that is the basis of this book: *Why don't the poor rise up,* and, when posing all these questions together, we're then forced to ask *who the poor are,* i.e. who are the subjects of politics, and *what constitutes rising up,* i.e. what is politics?

There is a lot more I'd like to say. I want to talk about Fallism and the different ways that it too has encountered these same dynamics, as well as the relationship it has to broader struggle.[6] I'd like to explore the established Left in South Africa and the ways in which it has influenced grassroots movements in various ways with its own quick, often anachronistic answers to the questions I've been asking. And then there's the role of the "public"—of the spaces of dominant public discourses and the sentiment of those who have hegemony over these spaces. But this is enough. Let's begin.

In friendship,
Aragorn

Dear Aragorn,

Thank you for initiating the conversation. I think the question that you pose—*What would be sufficient?*—is both topical and crucial. To respond with another question by jumping ahead to the link you make with the query that prompts this book and our exchange as part of it, is it only "uprising" and, more exactly, the uprising of "the poor" that would be sufficient to tangibly and meaningfully disrupt the manifold relations of oppression people in South Africa and elsewhere find themselves entangled in? What does it mean to assume so? Again, your questions offer apt entry points for unpacking the complex and weighty implications of such assumptions.

Almost randomly picking up one of the potential threads, let me begin with the problem of "the poor" as the political subject. What does it do when we conceive of the ultimate symptom of our failing global order as the apathy of "the poor"? Without, of course, downplaying the outrageous reality of extreme socioeconomic inequality, it seems to me that positing "the poor" as the group whose current condition and political potentiality most loudly calls for rebellion, in the South African context at least, doesn't offer a full picture and thus falls short of drawing up the promise of emancipatory politics. Even if we must admit that both sides of the famous race-class debate of the 1970s and 1980s have been reductionist and problematic,[7] it has to be noted that the same antagonism is alive and well—just think of some of the political commentary around the Rhodes Must Fall movement, for instance, the elitist dismissal of the students' foregrounding of Black pain, in the name of pinning down what "really" is the most serious source of injustice.[8] Poverty and multiple other forms of exclusion in this country are inextricably bound up with constructions of racial difference, and I doubt that we are moving closer to the desired political moment of dismantling the order of oppression if we gloss over that fact by analytically favoring one, albeit in itself overwhelming, aspect of the crisis.

On what is perhaps a more abstract level too, I feel uneasy about naming the political subject in advance. As Jacques Rancière has argued, the name of the collective political subject emerges at the moment of politics, that is, through the demonstrative event of disrupting the order of assigned societal positions and capacities.[9] It is by appearing where and how they were not supposed to be seen and heard that people effect a sensible reconfiguration of what "the public" is—to touch upon another point you raise. And this reconfiguration happens because, by making an appearance, a collective proves that it can in fact do what it wasn't supposed to and, therefore, it exceeds pregiven categories of the social order and political imaginaries. As such, and in demonstrating that misfit *in* public and, crucially, by embodying the public, it makes evident that an existing social category or a class, with corresponding assumptions about what supposed members' interests and desires are, is not identical with the collective political subject.[10]

Which is, surely, not to say that "the poor" cannot become a/the political subject. Indeed, "the poor" has been one of the names that Abahlali appropriated for their political practice in the second half of the 2000s when asserting their equality in the face of the violence of urban marginalization and infrastructural decay and, just as importantly, the dehumanizing attitude of public officials and the media toward the shack-dwellers.[11] Just like "shack-dwellers," which is the English equivalent of isiZulu Abahlali baseMjondolo, when occupying the generic name of the "the poor" and, crucially, "the people" or "the public," Abahlali articulate themselves as equal to all of those who are more unproblematically assumed to belong to the collective subject of the post-apartheid political order, thus at the same time proving that the self-image of this subject is mistaken.

Among all the potential conclusions that are relevant to our current conversation, one that seems to scream at us at this juncture is that the poor do rise up! Whether or not they can be read as disruptive in terms of the idea of politics I sketched above, well beyond Abahlali and their decade-long and less than linear life span, struggles around inhumane living and working conditions, corruption, and political machinations, to mention but a few, emerge every single day in contemporary South Africa. How do we account for that fact in the context of your question about what would be sufficient? To return the question to you with the genuine hope that you have an answer: *Why is that not sufficient?*

Just like you, I have so many more questions and concerns to pose, not least about the idea of the "romantic" that you mention or the kind of work the notion of "Fallism" does to thinking about the recent wave of mobilization. Most importantly at this point, however, I want to take a step back and raise the issue of what it means that we, as in you and I, are performing this conversation. On the one hand, I know that it gives shape to a part of our attempts at forging solidarities across struggles, as you allude in one of your questions—an attempt that we must not give up on. On the other hand, nevertheless, even with all our hesitation and genuine moves to destabilize hegemonic frames of thinking about politics and its actors, are we not reinstalling these frames when we—both white, educated, middle class, and me even a "foreigner"!—take on the task of speaking about the politics of "the poor"? Would you agree that we have to attend to that risk?

Dear Anna,

You raise several crucial points in your generous response and, important-ly, complicate some of the overly simplistic categories we're used to applying within our political praxis. Perhaps most saliently, you remind us of the con-stant need for reflexivity and an awareness of our own positionality, as well as the many pitfalls and injustices involved in speaking for others. As you make clear, we will not progress very far if we do not remain both cognizant of these complexities and willing to work through them with temerity and humility.

However, I worry that we often ask the question of positionality in an unnecessarily constrained and, even in the case of intersectionality, relatively binary way, and that this suggests something about the distribution of power and agency in contemporary society that we would do well to pay more at-tention to. Let me unpack this a little (and I hope you will forgive my slightly scattershot approach). My sense is that, at least some of the time, when we ask about how we relate to others across the uneven terrain of power, we tend to conceive of one side of the relation in wholly positive terms (captured by terms like "privileged") and the other in negative terms (e.g. "marginalized"). This in turn leads to a politics centered on the confessional, on guilt, tithing, and so forth, which, I feel, does not fully recognize the agency of those on either side of a too-quickly dichotomized relation (nor does it tend to lead to *politics* in Rancière's sense).

If, on the other hand, we use a more descriptive register that does not es-sentialize qualities but instead thinks of the myriad flows that intersect to form each of our positions in terms of quantity or degree, then perhaps we move closer to a different practice, one that respects the heterogeneity of each en-counter across the aforementioned terrain, and poses questions like *what can we do together? What are our collective capacities? What is the subject that emerges from our coming together as singular beings?* Highly speculative, I know, but I'm wary of the dead ends of a largely recuperated and reformist identity politics that, to some extent anyway, has become simply a new layer of the existing partitioning of the sensible.[12] I also do not think this speculation is entirely ungrounded; after all, once we do start looking at ourselves as subjects also marginalized in important ways within late capitalism, terms like *precarious labor* and *the erasure of the middle class* begin to seem apposite, and these are precisely those things about our position that we have a strong psychological motivation to disavow. Said otherwise, it's hard to deal with the existential anxiety that comes along with countenancing our real position within society, one that is more often than not far more tenuous than we take for granted. In still other words, we're almost all a paycheck or two from the streets and yet we avoid dwelling on this for obvious reasons.

Another motivating factor in our framing of "the poor" emerges from, I think, a shared sense that the odds are insurmountable—that the train is hurtling full speed toward the end of the tracks, and we're just a handful of people standing, arms outstretched, in its path. It's true: the odds are not stacked in our favor and this, along with the diffusion of capital into every facet of our lives, encourages a retreat into apathy and depression, the affective opposite of what psychologists term "flow states," which are those moments where we feel creatively empowered to change our individual lot, energized and full of optimism. From this unenviable position (bolstered also by the erosion of a sense of community, class solidarity, and so forth, subjects tackled elsewhere in this book) it is understandable that when we hear about road blockades, strikes, property destruction, expropriation, street battles, and so forth, we want to live vicariously through them in order both to change our affective state and to displace our precarity onto the lives of others. And so we idealize and imagine "the poor," imposing this homogeneous, othering grid on the complex, intersecting realities of struggles against oppression and ending up with a fetish that obscures the lives of those involved, sublimating our political impulses instead of allowing us to come closer to each other in order to ally and struggle together.

None of this, of course, really fully answers the difficult question of what exactly it means to struggle together across such uneven terrain or, rather, *how can we rise up together?* To me this is a dual task: on the one hand, we need to develop sufficiently resilient, powerful networks of collective resistance in order to make any meaningful dent in systems of domination. At the same time, if we neglect the manifestations or residue of those same systems in our interactions with each other then we're just reproducing them at what Deleuze and Guattari term the micropolitical level.[13] So, focusing too much on any one side of this task has obvious attendant risks. If we lose sight of internal struggles of composition, then we end up simply not getting rid of hierarchy at all. If, however, we lose sight of the project of working to eradicate hierarchy as it materially exists in the form of the state, capitalism, and so forth, our micropolitical struggles may well be recuperated and used against us. More than this, to be truly successful we'd probably have to reach the point where we recognize that these are in fact the exact same struggle, and that each of our collective and individual actions unfolds on both fronts.

What I'm saying also suggests that we need to start thinking about identity in slightly different ways and, in turn, that we need to rethink intersectionality, positionality, and so forth. Don't get me wrong—the idea that there are a small number of key axes of oppression (race, class, gender, sexuality, ability, species, etc.), all of which intersect in unique ways in any one person, place, situation, and so forth, is appealing and has its merits as a cursory analytic tool. If, however, we don't move beyond reifying these "abstractions with material effects," then we risk reducing the very real struggles around structural inequalities to an interpersonal and performative grappling for power between alienated neoliberal subjects that is not, to reiterate an earlier point, very likely to lead to an event that ruptures the partitioning, i.e. to the emergence of a new political subject. There's far too much to say here, but very briefly, perhaps we could start thinking of identity in terms of process instead of final product and of intersectionality as much more complex than a simple checklist of fixed and closed categories. What if power and identity are defined by leakage and flow? What if we all already overlap with each other in ever-shifting ways? When the edges blur and we become, in some ways anyway, indistinct, what internally heterogeneous collective subject emerges?

One last point. You remind us of what I'd term the issue of political imagination, the concern that if we determine the limit of the emancipatory political terrain in advance we risk not allowing the new to unfold. I am in complete agreement here and would simply like to reiterate Bookchin's wonderful observation that "the assumption that what currently exists must necessarily exist is the acid that corrodes all visionary thinking."[14] It troubles me how often one encounters this fetishizing of the present/past, this impoverishment of utopian thought because of a lack of ability to deal with the new and uncertain without bringing it under the interpretive grid of past struggles... This is sadly, of course, as I mentioned earlier, the situation with a fair amount of the left and even anarchist milieus. Our relationship to the new within the context of struggle (and perhaps this is similar to what Badiou terms *fidelity to the event*), how we adapt and respond to novel situations that call for new theorization and practice, new ontologies even, is perhaps one of the most staggeringly underdeveloped aspects of our political practice.

And, as a side-note, I'll admit to being totally stuck on the question of sufficiency. All I can do is pose the question over and over again. However, do you think it's the case that we will ever feel that anything has been sufficient? Will there be one massive "rising up" or revolutionary rupture after which we can say "that was enough," or is it instead more likely that there are an infinite series of struggles to be lost or won, and that we can only really recognize our victories retrospectively? Our heuristic for measuring success then becomes different: a matter of discerning thresholds or critical junctures past that qualitative changes in the composition of our shared terrain are initiated. I fear, however, that this is going to lead me to even more speculation, so I'll leave it there for now.

Dear Aragorn,

Thank you for engaging with my questions. I empathize with your concerns about the pitfalls of overspun cycles of self-reflexivity and the limits of operating within a matrix of essentialized qualities. From the perspective of my politico-theoretical commitments, I would articulate my approach in very similar terms. Yet, given the experience of the past several years in Cape Town and encounters within the broadly conceived activist realm—encounters that sometimes admittedly failed—I have come to think that those commitments should not always be predominant in defining my practice. There are some situations where I feel like even if I am aware that I'm being read in a way that might be unjustified—due to, for instance, the rigid frames of the privileged/marginalized binary that you mention—I accept the consequences of that reading on the potential interaction, for it is rooted in centuries of injuries and sustained by persistent structures of inequality. In the face of these, it seems to me that there is a process of grappling with and overcoming identity politics that needs to take place, a process that I cannot, or must not, actively urge in a drive to abide by my politico-theoretical commitments. Does this necessarily lead to the dead end of guilt and the navel-gazing mode of the confessional? I would hope not, or not always. While many encounters will, for now, stumble upon the solid blocks of binaries, with sustained and careful acts of solidarity, others will take off and invite alliances that move way beyond those obstacles. (This is all very tentative and perhaps not at all helpful, but now it's here on the screen and I'm really interested to hear what you make of it in light of your many more years of activist practice.)

I'm very grateful that you mention flow states as the cathartic moments of optimism, as opposed to the (more) common effect of battling with what appear to be insurmountable odds. As rare as they might be, they are probably more able to destabilize the building blocks of identity politics that I touched upon just now. At the same time, they allow me to return to the notion of the "romantic" that I failed to address in my previous response. When I think back to the experience of the removal of the statue of Cecil John Rhodes from the Upper Campus of UCT a little more than a year ago, it seems like that was precisely one of those states or moments of flow when, in the company of all those hundreds who gathered to watch the figure of the arch-colonialist lifted off his pedestal, I felt a sense of community that complemented, if not exceeded, the cerebral acknowledgment of the historical significance of the moment. It was one of those embodied (because both rationally and physically experienced) celebrations of politics as the common action of people that, to me, is romantic through and through. Or how else to describe phenomena that make you shiver and smile, and wanting it to last forever so that you can always feel like there is nothing more powerful than enacting freedom?

It does not last forever, of course—not with the same ground-shaking effect. Soon after the moment of political disruption, the logic of supposed reason prevails, and the embodied celebration is dismissed as, exactly, romantic and thus immature. In the aftermath of the overflowing event, struggles and formations are squeezed back into preexisting categories of proper and improper politics. As we saw in the wake of the Rhodes Must Fall and Fees Must Fall waves of protests, the media and political commentators in South Africa feel an uncontrollable urge to educate activists and the people at large about the right kind of political demands to articulate and the correct ways to go about them.[15] In this discourse, beyond the routine dismissal of "violence," appeals to the affective aspects of oppression are deemed narcissistic and irrational, as less than political. Similarly, the sense of urgency that emanates from claims that mobilize the notion of pain is regarded impatient, limited, and self-indulgent.[16] Surely, reflecting on Black pain in itself does not exhaust the political possibilities of the Rhodes Must Fall moment, but commentaries that worry about the constrained and improperly political nature of the student movements actually perform more of the limiting than the movements themselves. Indeed, this limiting effect is the same one that is at work in the ubiquitous media parlance of "service delivery protests." Not only does this label reflect an utter unwillingness to try and find out why people are protesting, it also relegates these instances of mobilization into the realm of the "politics of needs," of bodily urges and thus, that of immediacy as in unreflective, thoughtless.[17] Like the "interpretive grid of past struggles," as you beautifully put it, the stubborn banishment of struggles for a dignified life from an idealized sphere of politics severely limits our political imagination and thus the possibilities of working out a political practice that would operate across and undo social, spatial, and (thereby) racial divides, a practice that would, perhaps, carve out the conditions for *rising up together*.

And so, here we are once again at the question of sufficiency. What role does the fetish of *reason*able politics have in disabling the emergence of solidarities across boundaries? And how does this problem relate to your reiterated question as to what will be sufficient? Is there a way for an emancipatory practice of solidarity to attend to the very real urgency of, say, struggles for affordable higher education or dignified life in South African cities (both of which are irreducible to some sort of a "politics of the belly")[18] without revolutionary disruption? I'm just as hesitant when posing this question as you are, so let me instead conclude with another one: what would it take to conjure up praxes of solidarity that would materialize in an infinite series of political ruptures and bring success to these struggles of "the poor"?

Dear Anna,

First, thank you for reminding me about the removal of the statue. Although it was just a marker for a much broader movement, it was a deeply powerful political event, perhaps one of the most powerful in recent years. I hope that what we all felt on that day, in those moments of hushed silence as the ghost of Cecil John Rhodes was hoisted off his pedestal and into the air, continues to remind us of some of the reasons why we struggle; of what is at stake and of how powerful we are together (and against more than just monuments to old colonialists!).

Perhaps the removal of the statue—as synecdoche for the recent wave of struggles against structural racism, university neoliberalism, patriarchy, heteronormativity, and so much more—also underscores the dangers in being too quick to see our actions as failures or successes. After all, has the student movement succeeded? Absolutely. In many ways. Has it failed? Undoubtedly. Several times. Political movements are so internally heterogeneous, so full of conflicting tendencies and unfolding over so many different timeframes, that instead of thinking in such conclusive terms it may be more useful to think of our participation within them as an experiment, with outcomes that are always provisional—tentative suggestions for what to try next. And, of course, we also assign failure (success too!) for many reasons: because we've reached a dead-end, and do not know how to proceed; because we are exhausted; because we feel powerless in the face of what our experiments have revealed; because we constrain ourselves to timeframes incommensurable with the scope of our ambitions...

...Or, far too often, because we have failed to understand each other. I feel this drive especially strongly in moments where, like many of us and, as you say, for good reason, I am read in a limited way due to my positionality; in a way that does not allow me to know the person reading me, or them to know me in turn. However, what if we also view this as a call to experiment—as a new political practice of building alliances across the myriad stratifications that run over the smooth, unmarked, open space beneath? Surely, we need to practice being together in a way that digs far deeper than a mere reproduction of political identities; that gets underneath the rigid lines without denying their existence and their real effects; that allows all of us to heal from our very different wounds? Félix Guattari speaks about this as an essential part of building effective political resistance, and examines the difference between *subjugated groups*, the members of whom simply reproduce the hierarchies of the dominant order in their interactions with each other and enjoy only the weakest of ties as political "comrades," and *group subjects*, where the group does not deny the importance of practices that seek out and challenge capitalism, the State, patriarchy, white supremacy, and so forth *as they emerge within that group*, resulting in a kind of radical therapy that is simultaneously individual and collective and a space where we each know all the others as "friend."[19] Said much more simply, we need to work on overcoming our alienation from each other if we want our experiments to yield more fruit. The more we get to know each other, the more newer forms of collaboration we can develop, the more different ways we can collectively arrange ourselves into resilient networks of resistance and prefiguration, the more we can really see just what we can do.

This kind of practice is highly demanding: it takes a long time, and it is probably most vital at those low points in our movements where we least want to commit, those moments just after the streets have been returned to order and the students that were not expelled or arrested have gone back to class and the circumscribing of political legitimacy has started to take place. In order to challenge this circumscription—this repartitioning of the sensible with the language of reason, civility and so forth—perhaps we will need to develop what Deleuze and Guattari call our own minor language, instead of relying on a majoritarian tongue that can only ever reproduce what there is and that doesn't contain the words we need to articulate our felt experience, our ambitions, ourselves.[20] Beyond this, we need systems of recognition, too, ways to find each other. And we need supportive communities, places where we can seek refuge, or even catch sight of some vague images of the future we could build together. Most of all, we need to help each other to resist the dull tyranny of capitalist realism, acquiescence to the reigning order as the only remaining possibility for us.

In all of this, we will be roundly dismissed by those granted the loudest voices within our current society, but the more they denounce the affective nature of our struggles and reduce the rising up of the poor as a base and visionless politics of immediate needs, the more we will hear in these voices nothing but *ressentiment*—a denial of their own shallow affect and their own base needs, both inculcated by the very system they identify with and seek to defend. They may have forgotten how to dream together, but we have not.

We keep asking each other what it would take, what would be sufficient. I do not think there is an answer. Instead, there are only questions. Through a cautious but joyful practice of collective and individual experimentation, as group subjects speaking and fighting and imagining together in our million minor tongues, we can pose these questions again and again, in better and better ways every time. Perhaps that is already sufficient. Perhaps that is our politics.

With love and hope,
Aragorn

Endnotes

1 The Free Association, "Moments of Excess," Freely Associating, October 2004, http://freelyassociating.org/moments-of-excess/.

2 CrimethInc. Ex-Workers' Collective, "After the Crest: The Life Cycle of Movements," *CrimethInc. Far East Blog*, September 9, 2013, http://www.crimethinc.com/blog/2013/09/09/after-the-crest-the-life-cycle-of-movements/.

3 Both Dean and Fisher endorse a return to the party form as a way of addressing what they perceive as the pitfalls of "leaderless" or "spontaneist" movements. See Jodi Dean, *The Communist Horizon* (London: Verso Books, 2012); Mark Fisher and Jeremy Gilbert, "Capitalist Realism and Neoliberal Hegemony: Jeremy Gilbert A Dialogue," *New Formations*, no. 80–81 (Winter 2013): 89–101.

4 The Economic Freedom Fighters (EFF), a relatively new South African political party (founded in 2013) that cites Chávez, the Zapatistas, and the Black Consciousness Movement as influences and is, if its rhetoric is to be believed, Leftist and revolutionary. See http://effighters.org.za/about-us/.

5 The Abahlali baseMjondolo ("shack-dwellers") movement is a South African grassroots movement of the poor that was formed in Durban in 2005 and organizes mostly outside of party politics. You can read a short history of AbM at: http://abahlali .org/a-short-history-of-abahlali-basemjondolo-the-durban-shack-dwellers-movement/.

6 A term used by members of #RhodesMustFall, #FeesMustFall, and related contemporary South African student movements to describe their political philosophy—a mix of Black consciousness, Pan-Africanism, and radical feminism. The mobilizations referred to as #RhodesMustFall (RMF) erupted in March 2015. What started as a controversy around the statue of Cecil John Rhodes on the campus of the University of Cape Town, grew into a countrywide movement calling for the decolonization of universities. See https://en.wikipedia.org/wiki/Rhodes_Must_Fall. Later that year, in October, another wave of student protests emerged in the country, when the government announced an average 10 percent increase in tuition fees. Giving shape to the #FeesMustFall movement, they eventually defied the planned increases for 2016. See https://en.wikipedia.org/wiki/FeesMustFall. Both waves of mobilization involved (occasionally successful) student initiatives for ending rape culture and the unfair outsourcing of support staff at universities, and thus can be said to have made connections with broader struggles against patriarchy and neoliberal precarity among others.

7 For a thorough account of the debate, see *South African History Online*, "Theoretical Debates and Methodological Controversies," South African History Online, February 8, 2012, http://www.sahistory.org.za/archive/

theoretical-debates-and-methodological-controversies.

8 Jeremy Seekings and Nicoli Nattrass, "Rhodes and the Politics of Pain," *GroundUp*, March 31, 2015, http://www.groundup.org.za/article/rhodes-and-politics-pain_2796/; Xolela Mangcu, "Race Transcends Class in This Country: A Response to Seekings and Nattrass," *GroundUp*, April 2, 2015, http://www.groundup.org.za/article/race-transcends-class-country-response-seekings-and-nattrass_2806/. See also Jared Sacks, "The Politics of Those Who Inflict Pain: A Response to Seekings and Nattrass," *Daily Maverick*, April 7, 2015, http://www.dailymaverick.co.za/opinionista/2015-04-07-the-politics-of-those-who-inflict-pain-a-response-to-seekings-and-nattrass/#.V7bQXGW8zFL.

9 Jacques Rancière, *Disagreement: Politics and Philosophy*, trans. Julie Rose (Minneapolis: University of Minnesota Press, 1999). While his conception of politics as an event of destabilizing a given order of things through calling into question the validity of social, political, economic, etc. classifications its hierarchies are grounded in, its transience makes it difficult to think about popular politics as a sustained practice. Indeed, it hardly allows for thinking about the work of organization in popular struggles. For a sympathetic discussion of this and other limitations of Rancière's theatrical notion of politics, see Peter Hallward, "Staging Equality: Rancière's Theatrocracy and the Limits of Anarchic Equality," in *Jacques Rancière: History, Politics, Aesthetics* (Durham and London: Duke University Press, 2009), 140–57.

10 This order of given categories and aspirations is what Rancière refers to as "the count," and where his conception of the political subject as "the part that has no part" comes from. See Ibid.

11 See, e.g., Abahlali baseMjondolo and Rural Network, *Living Learning* (Pietermaritzburg: Church Land Programme, 2009), 16, http://abahlali.org/node/5843; S'bu Zikode, "When the Poor Become Powerful outside of State Control," *Pambazuka News*, 2010, http://www.pambazuka.org/governance/when-poor-become-powerful-outside-state-control; Ashwin Desai, *We Are the Poors: Community Struggles in Post-Apartheid South Africa* (New York: Monthly Review Press, 2002). It must be noted that the phenomenon of dehumanization that renders the shack-dwellers' lives as socially invisible and disposable goes beyond the individual attitudes of officials and journalists; it is, in fact, a set of discourses and practices that allows for such attitudes as well as the inhumane policies of neoliberalizing post-apartheid cities.

12 Rancière uses this term to describe the circumscribed domain of possibility we experience in our daily participation in the social order that occludes anything outside of, beyond, or lacking from the current system. This partitioning is maintained and defended by an arrangement of ideological and material power he calls the police. Rancière argues that the partitioning itself is precisely what we should draw attention to: that we should point to what lies beyond through a radical enactment of dissensus—thought and action on behalf of our excluded groups and classes, or what Rancière calls the part that has no part—that breaks through the partitions and the police barricades in order to enact politics proper. See Rancière, *Disagreement*.

13 Which is, very roughly and not entirely accurately, the affective level of everyday interaction. See Gilles Deleuze and Félix Guattari, *A Thousand Plateaus: Capitalism and Schizophrenia*, trans. Brian Massumi (Minneapolis: University of Minnesota Press, 1987).

14 Murray Bookchin, "The Meaning of Confederalism," *Green Perspectives* 20 (November 1989), http://dwardmac.pitzer.edu/Anarchist_Archives/bookchin/gp/perspectives20.html.

15 Chris Barron, "So Many Questions: #RhodesMustFall and UCT Vandalism," *Sunday Times*, February 21, 2016, http://www.timeslive.co.za/sundaytimes/opinion/2016/02/21/So-Many-Questions-RhodesMustFall-and-UCT-vandalism; Rebecca Hodes, "Op-Ed: How Rhodes Must Fall Squandered Public Sympathy," *Daily Maverick*, August 20,

2015, http://www.dailymaverick.co.za/article/2015-08-20-op-ed-how-rhodes-must-fall-squandered-public-sympathy/#.V7bPEGW8zFL; Rhoda Kadalie, "Binging on Whingeing," Politics Web, September 30, 2015, http://www.politicsweb.co.za/opinion/binging-on-whingeing; Achille Mbembe, "Achille Mbembe on The State of South African Political Life," *Africa Is a Country*, September 19, 2015, http://africasacountry.com/2015/09/achille-mbembe-on-the-state-of-south-african-politics/. See also Jonis Ghedi Alasow, "Policing Student Politics: Is There a 'right' Way to Protest?," *Daily Maverick*, September 8, 2015, http://www.dailymaverick.co.za/opinionista/2015-09-08-policing-student-politics-is-there-a-right-way-to-protest/#.V7bRUWW8zFK.

16 Mbembe, "Achille Mbembe on The State of South African Political Life."

17 As one of the editors noted, Amílcar Cabral's thought offers a powerful alternative to the reductive binary of politics versus reflections on oppressive material conditions that such gestures of dismissal betray. Space here does not allow us to pursue this point unfortunately.

18 Shose Kessi, "Of Black Pain, Animal Rights and the Politics of the Belly," *Thoughtleader – Mail & Guardian*, September 25, 2015, http://thoughtleader.co.za/blackacademiccaucus/2015/09/25/of-black-pain-animal-rights-and-the-politics-of-the-belly/.

19 Félix Guattari, *Psychoanalysis and Transversality: Texts and Interviews 1955–1971*, trans. Ames Hodges (Semiotexte/Smart Art, 2015).

20 Gilles Deleuze and Félix Guattari, *Kafka: Toward a Minor Literature* (Minneapolis: U of Minnesota Press, 1986).

CONTRIBUTORS

Affiong Limene Affiong: With a background in Political Science and Law, Affiong began as a student activist at the University of Ibadan and University of Lagos where she developed as a student leader and organiser in the Student Representative Council and the National Association of Nigerian Students (NANS). She was incarcerated with other students by the military junta for mobilising mass support against the regime's attempt to ban the vibrant student movement.

Forced into exile after the student-led uprising against the IMF and World Bank structural adjustment program (SAP), she relocated to London where she organised as a frontline campaigner in the pro-democracy movement against military dictatorship in the struggle to return Nigeria and other Afrikan nations to civilian rule. She worked within the Black community as a national advocate on immigration, reparations, race relations and amnesty for unregistered migrants.

She campaigned against Western backed regimes in Afrika, SHELL's exploitation of the Niger Delta and Britain's financing of the deadly arms trade. On a Pan-Afrikan level, she mobilised to bring contemporary struggles into the public domain and political agenda in Europe as a leading organiser of the Afrikan Liberation Support Campaign (ALISC).

She was Head of the Accra based Secretariat of the Jubilee 2000 Afrika Campaign against Third World debt slavery, which exposed the role of Western financial institutions in Afrika's economic crisis and advocated for the unconditional cancellation of the so-called debt. The Campaign also called for repudiation of the odious debt and reparations for the genocide and atrocities of slavery and colonialism.

Co-founder of *Moyo wa Taifa*, a Pan-Afrikan Women's Solidarity Network, she is a revolutionary Pan-Afrikanist and Socialist whose current research is on the legacy of Kwame Nkrumah and other freedom fighters in the interrupted trajectory of Afrikan liberation politics.

Kali Akuno is a founder and co-director of Cooperation Jackson (www. CooperationJackson.org), which is an emerging network of worker cooperatives and supporting institutions. Cooperation Jackson is fighting to create economic democracy by creating a vibrant solidarity economy in Jackson, MS that will help transform Mississippi and the South. Kali is an organizer with the Malcolm X Grassroots Movement (MXGM), a revolutionary nationalist organization fighting for self-determination for New Afrikan people and fundamental human rights for people of Afrikan descent throughout the world. Kali has authored many articles and pamphlets on Black, international and working class politics, with a focus on how government counterinsurgency, state violence, the drug war, mass incarceration and neoliberalism impact Black communities.

Erin Araujo is a Ph.D. Candidate in the department of Geography at the Memorial University of Newfoundland in Canada as well as a member of the Cambalache Collective, a women-generated money-less economy for all located in San Cristobal de las Casas, Chiapas as well as other parts of Mexico. Originally from New York, she has resided in Chiapas for around nine years, is a lifelong anarchist and artist, and has participated in several resistance movements throughout the Americas.

Franco Berardi, aka "Bifo," founder of the famous "Radio Alice" in Bologna and an important figure of the Italian Autonomia Movement, is a writer, media theorist, and media activist. He currently teaches Social History of the Media at the Accademia di Brera, Milan. His books include *Heroes: Mass Murder and Suicide* (Verso, 2015), *The Uprising: On Poetry and Finance* (Semiotexte, 2012), and *Precarious Rhapsody: Semio-capitalism and the Pathologies of the Post-Alpha Generation* (Autonomedia, 2009).

Ben Brucato is a critical scholar of police, surveillance, and technology. He is a postdoctoral researcher at the Center for Humanistic Inquiry at Amherst College and holds a Ph.D. in Science & Technology Studies from Rensselaer Polytechnic Institute. Brucato's research attends to strategies of activists to document and expose injustices. In particular, recent work focuses on civilians who use cell phone cameras and social media applications to produce the new visibility of policing. His articles appear in *Theoria, Surveillance & Society, Media & Communication, Anarchist Studies, Humanity & Society,* and in several edited collections.

Ellie Adekur Carlson is a community organizer and human rights activist in Toronto focusing on issues of policing, antiblack racism and sex workers' rights. She is also a graduate student at the University of Toronto, working with the local trade union (CUPE3902) representing graduate student and postdoctoral academic workers.

Thandisizwe Chimurenga is a Los Angeles-based freelance writer. Her work has appeared on *Ebony, The Final Call, Truthout, Counterpunch* and *Daily Kos*, as well as several local publications. She has contributed to several anthologies, and is the author of *No Doubt: The Murder(s) of Oscar Grant* (2014) and *Reparations... Not Yet* (2015).

Jordy Cummings is a PhD candidate at York University, Toronto, whose work surrounds the intersection of popular culture and revolutionary social movements. He was for many years the interventions editor of *Alternate Routes: A Journal of Critical Social Research*, and has written for a variety of publications, including *CounterPunch, Rabble, the Bullet* and *Red Wedge*. He is an active member of CUPE Local 3903 and has been involved in a variety of social movements since the late 90s.

Aragorn Eloff is a long-time anarchist and Earth and animal liberation activist. He is a member of the Cape Town-based bolo'bolo anarchist collective and as an independent researcher and activist has a particular interest in the application of poststructuralist, neo-materialist and anarchist philosophy towards analysing and dismantling all forms of oppressive social and ecological relations based on inculturated practices of hierarchy, exploitation and domination.

Nathan Jun is Associate Professor of Philosophy and Coordinator of the Philosophy Program at Midwestern State University in Wichita Falls, Texas. He is the author of *Anarchism and Political Modernity* (2012) and the co-editor of *Without Borders or Limits: An Interdisciplinary Approach to Anarchist Studies* (with J. Meléndez-Badillo, 2013), *Revolutionary Hope: Essays in Honor of William L. McBride* (with S. Wahl, 2013), *Deleuze and Ethics* (with D. Smith, 2011), and *New Perspectives on Anarchism* (with S. Wahl, 2010).

Alex Khasnabish is an associate professor in the Department of Sociology & Anthropology at Mount Saint Vincent University and co-director of the Radical Imagination Project (www.radicalimagination.org). His work focuses on radical social movements, the radical imagination, globalization, and social change. He is the author of *Zapatistas: Rebellion from the Grassroots to the Global* (Zed Books) and *Zapatismo Beyond Borders* (University of Toronto Press), co-editor (with Jeffrey Juris) of *Insurgent Encounters: Transnational*

Activism, Ethnography, and the Political (Duke University Press), and co-author (with Max Haiven) of *The Radical Imagination* (2014, Zed Books).

Wangui Kimari is the participatory action research coordinator for Mathare Social Justice Centre (MSJC) a grassroots social justice organization based in Mathare, Nairobi. MSJC began as a way to document the rampant police killings and state violations that have been legitimized for decades in Nairobi's poor urban settlements, so as to have people research for people action. Her writing has appeared in a recent anthology commemorating the life and praxis of Amilcar Cabral (*Claim No Easy Victories: The Legacy of Amilcar Cabral*), and in *CounterPunch, Black Agenda Report, Pambazuka*, and *Africa Is a Country* (AIAC).

Ajamu Nangwaya, Ph.D., is a lecturer at the University of the West Indies, Mona Campus. He has over 25 years of experience in community organizing and advocacy. He is a former provincial Vice-President of the Canadian Union of Public Employees (CUPE) in Ontario, and was a member of the executive committee of CUPE Local 3907 for six years. He was an active member of the CUPE Local 3902 at the University of Toronto, and served as a Vice-President of CUPE Toronto District Council.

He was an organizer with the Toronto-based organization Network for the Elimination of Police Violence. His writings have appeared in publications such as the *Toronto Star, CounterPunch, Dissident Voice, Huffington Post, Global Research, Rabble.ca, Pride* newspaper, *Briarpatch* magazine, the *Black Agenda Report, Truthout, NOW Magazine* and *Pambazuka News*. He is a former columnist of the weekly *Share* newspaper that serves Toronto's African Canadian community.

Kimalee Phillip is an African cis-gendered woman and trade unionist, born and raised in Grenada and currently living in Toronto. Guided by West African traditional spiritual practices, she is an organizer, researcher, consultant and writer, centred in the fields of legal studies, workers' rights, Black feminist, queer thought, anti-colonial and anti-racist pedagogies and practices. She has conducted qualitative research and has created, co-created and facilitated various workshops and learning spaces across Canada, Ghana and Grenada.

Praba Pilar is a diasporic Colombian artist disrupting the overwhelmingly passive participation in the contemporary 'cult of the techno-logic.' Over the last two decades Pilar has presented counter-narrative projects integrating performance art, street theatre, electronic installations, digital works, video, websites,

and writing that have traveled widely around the world, have been supported through numerous awards, and written about in numerous publications.
Pilar has a PhD in Performance Studies from the University of California at
Davis. Her dissertation, *Latin@s Byte Back: Contestational Performance in the
TechnoSphere*, analyzed the performance projects of U.S. based Latina/o performance artists who resist, contest and oppose the masculinist, racialized and
unethical discourses and practices of contemporary techno culture. Shaped
by resistance to the colonial project throughout the Americas, Pilar is currently developing "Decolonizing Art Practices" for Aboriginal youth at Urban
Shaman Gallery in Winnipeg, Manitoba, Canada.

Anna Selmeczi is a Postdoctoral Research Fellow of the South African Research
Chair Initiative: Social Change hosted by the University of Fort Hare in East
London, South Africa. She is a member of the Cape Town-based bolo'bolo anarchist collective. She has published on technologies of abandonment in the
context of the neoliberal city and the disruptive potentials of grassroots politics in the face thereof, as well as the knowledge practices of the South African
shack-dwellers' movement, Abahlali baseMjondolo. Her current research centers
on the notion of political consciousness and the knowledge dynamics involved in
the pedagogical and artistic practices of urban social movements in Cape Town.

Gussai H. Sheikheldin conducts interdisciplinary research on the dynamics of
technology and institutions in contexts of pursuing sustainable development.
Other related areas of interest concern governance and justice. Africa-focused
and globally engaged, she is a doctoral candidate at the University of Guelph
with backgrounds in engineering, public policy and development studies.
Native of Sudanic Africa and resident of North America, writes and publishes
in English and Arabic.

Michael Truscello, Ph.D., is an Associate Professor in English and General
Education at Mount Royal University in Calgary, Alberta, Canada. His aca-
demic interests include anarchism, the politics and poetics of infrastructure,
petroculture, media studies, and technology studies. In 2013, he co-edit-
ed a special issue of *Anarchist Studies* on "anarchism and technology" with
Uri Gordon. In 2011, he produced the documentary film *Capitalism Is The
Crisis: Radical Politics in the Age of Austerity*. He is the author of *Infrastructural
Brutalism* (MIT Press, forthcoming).

David Gomez Vazquez was a first-year law student at the Universidad Nacional
Autónoma de México (UNAM). Born and raised in the city of Guadalajara,

Jalisco, he was inspired to move to Mexico City in 2010 due to his interest in the active student movement in the country's capital. In that year, he began his studies at the Colegio de Ciencias y Humanidades (CCH) Plantel Naucalpan. Since that time, he became interested in the struggle of the community police in the state of Guerrero, where he organized for the past several years.

Alex Wilson is Swampy Cree from the Opaskwayak Cree Nation. She is an Associate Professor and the Academic Director of the Aboriginal Education Research Centre at the University of Saskatchewan. Her scholarship has greatly contributed to building and sharing knowledge about two-spirit identity, history, and teachings; indigenous research methodologies; anti-oppressive education; and the prevention of violence in the lives of indigenous peoples. As a community activist and Idle No More organizer, her work also focuses on interventions that prevent the destruction of land and water.

Lesley Wood is interested in how ideas travel, how power operates, how institutions change, how conversations influence practices, how people resist, and how conflict starts, transforms and ends. She is Associate Professor of Sociology at York University in Toronto, Ontario, Canada. She has published two books, *Direct Action, Diffusion and Deliberation: Collective Action after the WTO Protests in Seattle* (2012/14), and *Crisis and Control: The Militarization of Protest Policing* (2014). She is a regional editor of the journal *Interface: A Journal for and about Social Movements*.

INDEX

Y

Z

AK Press is small, in terms of staff and resources, but we also manage to be one of the world's most productive anarchist publishing houses. We publish close to twenty books every year, and distribute thousands of other titles published by like-minded independent presses and projects from around the globe. We're entirely worker-run and democratically managed. We operate without a corporate structure—no boss, no managers, no bullshit.

The Friends of AK program is a way you can directly contribute to the continued existence of AK Press, and ensure that we're able to keep publishing books like this one! Friends pay $25 a month directly into our publishing account ($30 for Canada, $35 for international), and receive a copy of every book AK Press publishes for the duration of their membership! Friends also receive a discount on anything they order from our website or buy at a table: 50% on AK titles, and 20% on everything else. We have a Friends of AK ebook program as well: $15 a month gets you an electronic copy of every book we publish for the duration of your membership. You can even sponsor a very discounted membership for someone in prison.

Email friendsofak@akpress.org for more info, or visit the Friends of AK Press website: https://www.akpress.org/friends.html

There are always great book projects in the works—so sign up now to become a Friend of AK Press, and let the presses roll!